ANNUAL SUMMARIES
(Of A Fourth Score Of Years)

R. Garner Brasseur, MD

authorHOUSE®

AuthorHouse™
1663 Liberty Drive
Bloomington, IN 47403
www.authorhouse.com
Phone: 1-800-839-8640

Published by AuthorHouse 3/26/2012

ISBN: 978-1-4685-6168-5 (sc)
ISBN: 978-1-4685-6167-8 (e)

Contents

Journal Year 1991

In the past year I have worked a more or less full continuous year of regular employment. Most of that work was as a full-time employee of the Sate of New Mexico; at Las Vegas Medical Center, in Las Vegas, New Mexico--the state psychiatric hospital. I have worked in the capacity of a general medical officer; my main interest has been in the acute psychiatric admissions. My primary responsibilities have been the evaluation and treatment of their medical problems. However, my main personal interest is the psychiatric aspect of their illness. In this work, I am a member of the multidisciplinary team of personnel that includes the psychiatrist, the psychologist, the general medical officer, the social worker, the ward staff of nurses, LPN, psych tech, and the ancillary services available upon the campus. I have had the good fortune to have worked on the "C" team, led by psychiatrist, Glen Hirsch. He has been an excellent mentor and has been able to squeeze the utmost of concern, effort, and beneficial therapeutic effort from the team--to the therapeutic benefit of the individual patients.

Hirsch has clear concepts of diagnostic evaluation; and is able to alter his diagnostic opinions as new and changing information evolves from the patient's interaction in the diagnostic and therapeutic milieu. He has good insight into the psycho mechanics of the social-political-economic problems of the patient. He emphasizes the primary necessity of developing and maintaining relationships, as the therapeutic climate that will permit for psychiatric psychological healing. Multiple such honest and open relationships of the patient, to individual members of the team, would seem to be potentially the more useful; and in the best interests of the patient. The ideal of relationship that he strives for is one of non-judgment, understanding, accepting, and even loving or caring concern for the patient. He appears able to achieve this to a remarkable degree. And his effort and achievement inspires and encourages the members of the tam to emulate this potentially therapeutic attitude.

In my view, from my experience and observation of the psychiatric

1

wards of LVMC, the therapeutic results to patients admitted and treated by the C-team are remarkable in their success. The other two teams (with whom we alternate the flow of inpatient admission) do not have a comparable demonstrated effectiveness.

Unfortunately, the politics of state fiscal allotment, combined with the interpersonal politics between the members of the professional staff of the hospital has brought about the circumstances that have led to severing of the employment of Dr. Hirsch by LVMC. The clientele and the treatment team staff are thereby deprived of the continuing benefit of the hospital's foremost therapist.

Dr. Camero, has also been caught-up and severed from employment at LVMC; in the same maneuvers that ended here, the employment of Dr. Hirsch. Among our general medical officers, Dr C. was our best as to conscientious effort of diagnostic determination and therapeutic effort. And I often relied upon the advise of Dr. C.--because of the limitation of experience and information that are mine in lieu of practicing in a field in which I do not have may primary training. Another deficit that I must endure and rise above.

The politics of the state, and within the hospital, would seem to make my status here at LVMC somewhat uncertain. I am therefore casting about for employment opportunity with the Veterans Administration Hospitals (esp. Shreveport and Tuscaloosa); and with the Indian hospital system. Other practice opportunity may be considered too--as they arise. In general, I wish to avoid the necessity of accepting any further employment . . . except as a paid employee. For, I do not wish any further necessity to engage in any continued futile conformity to HICFA billing and payment rules and regulations. And I do not wish to invest in the expense of purchasing malpractice insurance or being involved in the business aspects of the practice of medicine.

Perhaps I might now plan (by default and pragmatic necessity) to remain here at LVMC temporarily. Besides the continued and necessary regular income and health maintenance benefit, this also avails me of continued experience in the field of psychiatry--which opens to me an additional spectrum of opportunity for further employment.

In the past year, I have finally completed my bankruptcy proceedings. I have thus been relieved of perhaps $80,000.00 of debt; and able now to begin a new economic life without the threat and pressure of chronic harassment from claimants and creditors. Thus, there is now some potential benefit to full-time employment. Or now, it makes sense to earn more than a hand-to-mouth existence. Whatsoever I can earn above the expenses of living, can now be saved and/or invested . . . toward the hope of a possible retirement. Yes, the hope that I may eventually own my own life; and without the necessity of selling that life on a daily basis, to supply my livelihood.

The past year, I have lost to death, my oldest sister, Aloha Eaton. And my mother in Coeur d'Alene seems progressively to be deteriorating in her physical health, and in her mental status. It would appear that she may soon require care in a nursing home. My brother, Vic, with whom I have had a long, rich, and fruitful relationship has just moved down here to the state of New Mexico, to begin a two-year contact of employment with the U.S. Indian Hospital at Gallup, NM. In the past year, he has made several trips down here to work at Gallup for two to three weeks at a time. This has enabled him and me to get together for several weekends of travel, adventure, and conversation. All, good times. Brother Duane has been so tied down to the farm problems, that I have had little with him by way of contact or communication . . . I, being tied to my own employment. I have seen brother Phil briefly on a couple of trips that took me through Spokane. He feels tied to that area both for employment and because he is tending to the seemingly increasing needs of mother's advance into progressive ill-health.

My genealogy work continues with a slow progressive accumulation of names, facts, and information. I have finally completed my first genealogy book--a simple compiling of family lists of the Boepple-Pepple family. I have distributed many copies; and the further accumulation of information has already (happily) made the work in need of updating. I have managed to visit both Brasseur and Boepple relatives in Canada--a trip I made alone, the past fall. And intermittent information continues to trickle in, by postal delivery. I hope to be able to make a genealogic trip to Quebec and Ontario provinces this summer; and to concentrate more upon the Brasseur genealogy this year. But in the end, the direction of my travel will be determined largely by the doors that shall be opened unto my knockings.

I am recently now launched onto a new field of interest and investigation through my interaction with brother, Victor. Along with him, I am now investigating and acquiring an interest in wines. I have also attended a few recent meetings of a group of people discussing and writing poetry. I may continue this activity, though I am quite out of my class and medium. I have long made some intermittent efforts to write a little verse--none of which seems to come out even to my own satisfaction.

In the past 10-11 months I have invested a good deal of time and thought in a platonic relationship with Dr. E.C., a bright and handsome young woman with a character disorder that brings her into a great deal of interpersonal difficulty in her professional and personal relationships. She is making efforts to gain insight into her own psychopathology, but has had great difficulty in applying this insight toward the correction of he self-defeating pattern of behavior. I have hoped and tried to stabilize her psyche with a supportive friendship. It is a confrontational friendship that requires her to deal realistically with its many ups and downs. I expect that I have learned a great deal more from all of this than she has. An education that has been stimulating and informative.

I have seen very little of my own children and grandchildren the past year. They are all more or less now in control of their own lives and destinies; with very little chance of benefit to them from anything further I might suggest. My (whatever) influence has already been previously implanted into their psyches; and may yet be influential in those lives, as they evolve. The exception to my non-intervention policy, has been the necessity to confront and obstruct Miette's plan to enroll in Bible School--a dreadful prospect to which I could not submit without a definite plan and act of opposition. Necessary, because I see this sanctimonious fundamentalist charade of piety as counterproductive to her own best interests, and to the already overly religious tone of the entire family. And necessary because I wish the record to show that one man, at least, has put forth the effort to see through this facade, in a quest for truth and historical veracity. Necessary to assure that neither the historical record nor posterity shall obscure the fact that my personal study of history and experience of psychodynamics leaves me convinced that both the Christian interpretation of history, and the philosophy of that religion are bogus constructions by vested interests, of times past and present.

RGB
1 January 1992

1991
1992

Summary 1992
by R. Garner Brasseur

The past year I have continued to work full-time at the New Mexico Psychiatric Hospital (LVMC). I am on one of the three acute psychiatric admitting teams – my main assignment, though I also do coverage on other wards. I am very content with my work; especially since it enables me to see and evaluate the many interesting acute psychiatric problems – and follow their progress . . . and take part in their psychiatric diagnosis and treatment. My friend, Dr. Don Bedingfeld, left the staff last year, to return to practice at the US Indian Hospital in Gallup, NM. Young doctor Vigil was appointed to his position as administrative chief of medical staff – not a job I wished to have. I believe that either Dr. Gibbs or Dr. Ghosh should have been given the appointment.

In early summer I drove to Montana alone to attend the Saur family reunion. Of our family, only Pierre's family did not attend. I protested a covert plan meant to impose the troublesome fundamentalist emphasis upon this gathering. At a sudden Sunday morning announcement of a religious meeting to start then immediately, I countered by suddenly inviting Betty Scott to – alternatively – take a hike with me. We had a nice walk-talk of an hour or more. Upon return to camp my radically religious spouse attempted to generate some heat account of my presumptuous behavior. It was only one of several – of a lengthy series of – precipitating events that finally set into motion the final prolonged contemplation and writing that culminated in my separation from my spouse in September of 1992. See letter to Bayloo in which I outline the years of trouble that lay behind the event. In August I took a three-week leave of absence without pay. I traveled to Virginia to investigate the history of the Brasseurs who came first to Virginia and then to Maryland in the 1650's. Brother Vic has traced out this family fairly extensively--they seem not likely to be related to our own branch of the family. I spent a couple nights at the shore in North Carolina; then drove on to research the Brasseurs and the Boepples in Ohio. I next drove to Vermont, from whence cousin Yves Brasseur and I went to visit some Brasseurs in the province of Québec. I stayed a couple of nights at the home of Yves Brasseur on a farm north of Newport. Then drove alone into Montréal and Ottawa to do some genealogy research.

In early October I took the train to Phoenix to attend the wedding of Stephanie Brasseur – daughter of my departed brother, EVHB.

Throughout the year, brother Vic and I took a number of week-end trips of exploration through the state of New Mexico. He has been working this year at the US Indian Hospital in Gallup, New Mexico.

Since November, I have developed an interesting correspondence with BLS. And having to take some of the medicine emergency and night call, I have discovered that I can get compensatory call-time to use as vacation – instead of taking pay. Therefore, I have been taking a lot of call. As of now, I have accumulated about six weeks of time. I plan to take-off the whole month of February 1993 to drive up to Oregon to see the children and the grandchildren. I will visit only briefly with each of them; the religious-philosophical strain being too excessive to permit of any comfortable and extended conversation. And instead of getting on to any interesting and meaningful ideas, we are always deadlocked on the rudimentary; so that discussion has no basis for extension into the realities of the universe. I will visit Duane, Phil, mom, and – perhaps – Ookie in Washington State. Then to Montana, to pick up BL. We will explore southward into New Mexico for 10 to 14 days.

In March I shall attend a four or five day postgraduate education course in Salt Lake City. In July I shall attend the Germans from Russia heritage convention in Fargo group, North Dakota – perhaps BL will attend it with me. And at the end of July I hope to attend a Brasseur family living about 100 miles south of Saskatoon. Perhaps I shall extend that trip further into Canada for additional research. I am hoping then to make arrangements with Phil or Vic for a trip in the fall. In all, I'll take about a total of eight weeks of combined compensatory time and vacation leave. I may, additionally, take two or three weeks leave of absence without pay

There is some possibility that I may take work elsewhere; as the job here has always a certain uncertainty – due to state in-hospital political goings-on. I am looking into an opening about 200 miles North of Guam Island. I am also looking at possibilities of work in Maryland, Virginia, and

North Carolina. I would even be interested in working in North Dakota, if I could find work with the state psychiatric hospital there.

Again this past year, the genealogy hobby has occupied a large part of my spare time. The Brasseur genealogy manuscript now runs to 145 pages. The Peppley-Boepple Work Paper is now at just over 160 pages. I continue to get a fair amount of genealogy correspondence – but information accumulates only slowly. There's always the occasional new and surprising information from on expected sources. The genealogy work has detracted from the reading projects that I would like to extend. I hope to get more reading time this year. I would also like to do more writing – have done very little this year. I have, however, written 10 or 12 poems past year; few of them seem reasonably satisfactory to me. I sent one to the North American Open Poetry Contest last week.

My dental problems have slowly progressed in the past 10 years, due to lack of regular care and follow-up. This year (now that I have dental insurance) I was able to get full restoration – better than I had anticipated to be possible. The cost was over $2000; of which the insurance is paying only about half. All in all, I am quite pleased to now own fairly good dental health at this time.

I continue to jog 1.45 miles around the perimeter of the hospital campus three times weekly to stay in shape. It takes me 15½ to 16 min. I continue to do 25 push-ups and 40 sit-ups twice weekly. I have dropped my weight back to about 172 pounds; it had gotten to about 185 in the summer.

The year before last I began the sampling of wines as a hobby, but I socialize so little, that there is only rare occasion to open a bottle of wine – so that my experience is to meager to be useful to the learning of wines. But I do like schnapps and have gotten the habit of taking two-ounces of it before my nap, and 2 ounces before I retire.

I'll soon be age 60 and feel to be in pretty good health. Though I have hypertension, I have medicated to control this in the past 10 years. I am currently taking Propranolol 80 mg per day and Prazosin 1.0 mg twice daily. Prior to treating, I had many years of elevated diastolic pressure to 94 or 96. I should have begun treating it years ago. I have a touch of arthritis, and for 25 or 30 years have regularly used eight ASA tablets daily. I am wont to suppose that I have thereby spared myself a modicum of arthritic aches, pains, and disability. Two years ago I had limited motion in the right shoulder in consequence of a capsular tear sustained while playing volleyball years ago. However, regular progressive range of motion exercise over 6 to 8 months of time and regular use of aspirin have gradually restored the shoulder to near full-motion and usefulness.

As a result of the arthritic tendency, I am also predisposed to neck and upper back discomfort and spasms. Therefore, I use a Fiorinal tablet before I nap, and at the hour of sleep – on a regular basis – to ease those aches and spasms. Rarely do I have to take any thing as strong as Darvon to control the problem.

I have considerable problem with nasal sinus allergy congestion; and occasional sinusitis. For 20 to 25 years I have regularly used Actifed, a half tablet four or five times daily to give me breathing-room through my nasal passages. When I have a head-cold, I sometimes have to use Beconase nasal spray twice daily. Since I began to regularly keep my forehead covered with a headband eight or 10 years ago, I only rarely have those previously frequent frontal sinus headaches. When they do come, a short course of antibiotics for two or three days seems to quickly resolve them. I wear the headband both day and night – except for the hours of work.

Until the past year, I regularly used Benadryl 25 mg or 50 mg at night to aid my sleep and help control my allergies. However, about eight years ago, I began to have some difficulties in urination – trouble getting it started, incomplete emptying, etc. – so I have given up use of Benadryl. Still, much of that problem lingered. So I began to use Prazosin 1.0 mg by mouth twice daily (a antihypertensive medication with alpha adrenergic blocking properties) and the problem seemed to resolve. I therefore have given up the use of Propranolol (since I used the Prazosin).

All things considered then, one might say I enjoy good health; but this would not certainly be possible at my age, except for the wonders of fine medical and surgical benefits.

---

31 March 1993: A call from Tina Brasseur in Medford, Oregon about 9:00 PM. Real was out at a Bible study group and she called me on the QT to discuss the financial problems which are currently besetting them. Economic reality--pressing its message of truth upon them. They are making no progress on the pay-off of their student loans; and today, a call from the federal collectors indicating that they are withholding this year's federal income tax repayment – money they were counting on to pay some urgent bills. Implied also, is that the plan is to proceed with garnishment payments to be withheld from his paycheck. I gather(and presumed) that

all of this was weighing upon Real – and that he was having to reconsider the possibility of reorganizing the economic aspects of his life; and how to make a better living. They visited Pierre and Jauhn this past weekend. Jauhn being situated on a piece of land seems to have stirred in Real some innate longings for the rural life; and being situated upon the land. As though there were no economic realities in that! I inquired of her, "does Real want to go into farming? If so, I suspect we might work something out for him with Duane, my brother, who is wanting to get off of the farm. But, Real has never been involved with the long hours of hard work such as in farming; and I don't think it likely he would care much for that. As to the idea of picking up a farm through the Resolution Trust Corporation, I don't believe that is in any way likely, for they are already in financial trouble, and it is highly improbable that any bank would ever consider the possibility of financing. For they have no savings, no assets, no spendable income, no decent job; nor even any job security or benefits nor financial amenities of occupation. The essential problem is that Real has chosen to earn his living under such restricted conditions. In fact, he is well able and equipped to resume a better occupation at any time he wishes. Or, if he wishes, he can go back to school anytime he wishes, to prepare himself for another occupation. Certainly his options are far better than most others in his similar situation, for his father is able and willing to assist him economically (on the side). So, he has only, first to make up his mind to better his situation. Then decide what he wants to do; and then pursue the steps and paperwork that are necessary to accomplish that. He has a good solid educational background. I would be glad to assist should he decide to go into medicine, psychology, law, Unitarian ministry, etc.

Tina says Real is reluctant to ask me for any help; though he would not be reluctant to ask her father, if that man were able to help him. I am quite aware of the nearly life-long contest of will between Real and I. That his inability to do anything with the education and training he already owns, may be due--in part--to his intense ambiguity towards me. Not to say that he doesn't like me; for I rather suppose that he does. It is just that we are so widely separated and antagonistic concerning our views on the philosophy and realities of life. And there is an element of intensity(!) in the relationships (among our people) that tends to always weigh upon those relationships.

I further point out that most families in this land have two incomes; nor are their families so large. And I point to the example of Idris White, who went to college to begin her teaching career in her middle years; and that now, in consequence, the Whites are well situated for a potentially full and comfortable retirement. That she to (Tina) might see some value in a similar challenge of accomplishment; with some hope of avoiding social-economic chaos in their late middle years. And that, for example, Real's mother, might even be willing and pleased to be of some use towards such an accomplished.

I told Tina I would call Real in a few days to probe his thoughts on these matters; and Pro-offer some help and suggestions – and not to let out a word, that Tina and I have discussed this.

End 1992
RGB

Summary of year 1993
By R. Garner Brasseur

And now I stand at the crossroads of another year's end and beginning. In early February I shall have completed three years of employment with the State of New Mexico; at the state psychiatric hospital in Las Vegas. Employed as a physician – servicing primarily the acute psychiatric illness ward. This, at my own preference – account of my long and abiding interest in psychodynamics and the intriguing problems which these psychiatric patients manifest. And because I specifically disliked the merely custodial management and care of the elderly demented patients who occupy long-term-care nursing facility benefits . . . where there is hardly any of what we may term, psychodynamic. There are constant changes in the structuring and staffing at the hospital. The three admitting teams and wards had been diminished to two teams at midyear; then, at the end of December, into one unit comprising 44 beds. I remain in charge of that unit's medical care.

The role of the hospital in the continuation of services to the mentally-ill of New Mexico is continuously changed and challenged in response to legislative fiats and special interest groups in the counties and communities of the state. Groups who have designs for getting their fingers upon the monies allocated to mental health care. And state bureaucracies and officials are ever ready to support and encourage such notions – in the hope that they might encourage competition and a competitive bidding that that will make them appear as great champions of 'free enterprise'; and at the same time play their old game of 'favorites', 'intrigue', and personal-power management. In theory, there is the possibility of savings to the state by bringing about the disenfranchisement of state employees, from retirement and medical care benefits etc. This, the same game that big business corporations have been playing for some ten or fifteen years.

It has been nearly 16 months since I have separated from Vi. I expect it would have been better if I had done that a few years earlier, but I was preoccupied with the changes of my profession such as to enable me to continue earning my income. For many years she has become progressively detrimental to all the significant influences I would prefer to have weighed in upon the children; and has made herself a continuous obstacle to my relationship with them – an ongoing problem. She continues to portray herself as the great martyr to the (Santa Fe) sacred the faith. Says her "head is bloody but unbowed", with the implication that I (RGB) am the cruel offender. Both she and several of the Saur relatives have actually stated that I (RGB) am "killing her". In point of fact I had endured the marriage long enough to ensure the raising and education of the children, with no support from her on any significant issue. In fact, my powers are limited; to either "save them", or to "kill her". The final benefit that she may yet learn from the dissolution of this marriage, is that all of her subversive behavior and influence in this man's family must inevitably produce an unsettling consequence. A consequence that I cannot hold in abeyance forever. Our lives must eventually make their personal statements if they once ever find inspiration, strength, and courage to break free from the intimidation of ancient error and august dogmatic pronouncements.

Bayloo Scott and I have exchanged a half dozen letters subsequent to the adversity she experienced in consequence of an innocent one hour walk that we shared at the Saur family reunion in July of 1992. She flew down here to New Mexico to visit me in February of 1993. By then we were already interested in one another, in consequence of our exchanged letters – and decidedly subsequent to both the intent and the act of the separation of Vi and me. The relationship between Baylou and me has been discussed openly and honestly as to its philosophical and pragmatic basis. On the basis of that discussion we are agreed, and we are – apparently – agreeable to one another in behavior and practice. Neither of us pretends to know that disenchantment is not a possibility between us. Should such disenchantment become chronic – between us – we are content to acknowledge that, and go our separate ways: that being possible since there are no dependent children or financial connections between us.

Bayloo has thus lived with me, here in Las Vegas since the end of June 1993. She will be looking for employment here. I continue with my regular job the past three years. We usually partake of one meal daily in the apartment. Bayloo is an excellent cook. Once weekly we dine out at Teresa's Restaurant – I usually have the cheese enchilada plate. We usually watch the Rush Limbaugh and Star Trek TV programs which we pre-record during the day. On weekends we usually watch a couple of VCR movies. On Sundays, we commonly drive to the Unitarian gathering in Santa Fe, then buy fresh bagels and shop briefly at a mall, before returning to Las Vegas. I continue to jog 1.45 miles – usually on Saturdays and Sundays. During the week, I am daily exercised with quite a bit of walking – upon the campus. I generally do 40 setups and 25 push-ups on week-end days.

About three or four years ago, I began to have intermittent episodes of esophageal reflux at nap or at night. The acid materials would reflux into the windpipe, causing spasm of the vocal cords so that I wheeze with difficulty in air exchange. They were frightening uncomfortable spells which would last perhaps half a minute or less, before the spasms would begin to abate. I would get up on hands and knees to crow and struggle for breath. The precipitating cause, presumably, hiatus hernia, or a weakening of the lower sphincter of the esophagus. A couple of years ago, I ceased the satisfaction of my customary bowl of corn flakes before going to bed. Thereafter, I rarely had recurrence of these spells, except when taking 30 cc or more of liqueur at the hour of sleep – have therefore given up that little treat (which I had begun only a couple of years ago).

In September, I took a long trip to the Northwest to visit my sibs (Ookie, Duane, Vic, and Phil) and the children; also visited with my nephew Andre and his new wife, as well as with Grant Mosby. I carried to them the gifts of antibiotic and hand-made quilts. The visits with the kids are brief and generally unsatisfactory, in that we are too far apart philosophically. There seems little immediate hope for improvement in the near future. Their fundamentalist religious certainties are far too fixed and devastating. It doesn't seem likely that they will begin to get free of that, while I yet live. I have done what I can to oppose this; and to encourage them towards an intellectual honestly. Perhaps, in time, their darkness may turn into the dawning of a new light. Meanwhile I must persevere in my solitary search in pursuit of truth. I expect that it is best to keep my visitation among them to a minimum. And it seems certain that they will generally resist their any inclination to communicate with me. For, they know that I shall not deal indulgently with their mystic religious fanaticism either conversationally or by personal example.

The past six months I have been considering the possibility of enrolling into a psychiatric residency. I sent in my application to the University of New Mexico a couple of weeks ago. I estimate perhaps 25 to 50% chance of being accepted. Were that to happen, I shall then try to make arrangements with Las Vegas Medical Center to take educational leave and hopefully still to work some 10 to 12 hours weekly, to supplement the meager resident psychiatric stipend; and to continue my seniority status with the state; and to continue to be enrolled with the state employees health and dental plans. If, all of these pieces should come together, then I would probably accept a residency; and continue with it for at least a year. Depending on my then continued interest – and the congeniality of the program to me and my needs, I would decide whether to stay with the program, or simply return to my current occupation, to continue work towards a possible retirement by age 75 or 80 years. I have done very little on the Brasseur or Boepple genealogies in the past year. I have distributed out additional copies to various relatives – and my residual supply is meager. I would rather redo both, in typed and updated form, but can't see that I will have the time for that, this year. Bayloo and I attended the German Heritage Society meeting in Fargo, the past summer. Perhaps, will attend again this coming summer. I am currently considering spending some time in Québec province for a few weeks during some upcoming vacation time.

RGB

1993
1994

Summary for the year of 1994
by R. Garner Brasseur

nother year is finished. They seem to be passing ever more rapidly. Bayloo and I have lived comfortably together this whole year. She works a four day shift as a house monitor to juvenile delinquent Native American Indian teenagers in Santa Fe. When she is home, we eat one regular meal per day--and eat out only once a week. She is a good cook. She has her things to do (cooking, yoga, a few friends, walking, etc.); and I have my own things to do. I am preoccupied primarily with genealogy projects and correspondence. Bayloo has purchased a Bose Hi-Fi machine. I buy an occasional CD for her to play upon the device. It seems to give a fairly good sound.

We continue to reside in a plain one-bedroom, one-bath apartment that belongs to the hospital; and which we use rent-free. Neither do we have to pay any utilities. There has been some flack and class envy noise about this in recent months and we are tentatively to begin paying a monthly rent of $80 per month in the new year. But I have heard nothing more about this in the past two months and it may be that the whole thing would be forgotten as the new political party takes over the reins in Santa Fe. Time will tell.

Until last summer, Vi was getting and spending over half my pay. She then went out and signed up for the purchase of a new car whose total cost to me would have been over $21,000. I emphatically refused to be part of that; or to sign any papers committing to my responsibility for the expense. Seeing then how potentially dangerous economically is this separation status, I decided to go for a divorce, to get our financial affairs separate and independent; and to put the seal of finality upon our separation. But she

15

has been stalling the process and it is, amazingly, even now not yet settled. It was my plan to settle by mutual agreement if she would agree to $1200 per month, or even up to say fourteen hundred dollars per month. But she apparently has her sights on a bigger pickings. I intend for her to get definitely somewhat less than the more than 50% of my income that she has been using up. Meanwhile, a pay raise this year has boosted my income from $70,000-$90,000 and will bring me about $95,000 next year. If I can keep Vi from obtaining and wasting the money, I may be able to get some money put away in the next few years for retirement. And have at hand funds to assist the kids; and their large and growing families, when they encounter the various social economic crises of life. On the other hand, if what I am able to retain is only a relatively small part of my income, then I'll probably just forgo the struggle of an unrewarded occupation, to retire early upon some meagerly adequate Social Security income. That would at least give me some time in my life to do the things I wish in my final years. It seems likely that I may work another three years to become entitled to an adequate state retirement income of about $20,000 per year in addition to about $12,000 of Social Security. The past years I have accumulated and organized a lot of data concerning the Brasseur genealogy. I took a trip of three weeks alone to Eastern Canada and Michigan at about Easter-time. Then, in early July I attended a Brasseur reunion get-together in Kenosee Lake, Saskatchewan for three days. Then I traveled to Winnipeg to search there before attending the Germans-from-Russia convention in Pierre, South Dakota. And at the end of September, Bayloo was able to get enough off-time to take an extended month-long trip with me into West Virginia, New England, Ontario, Québec, and Michigan. There we spent a few days at a reunion of the Youmell-Brasseur family at the Brasher Falls in New York. An interesting and productive trip at the most beautiful season of the year; and we enjoyed almost perfect weather wherever we journey. Subsequently I had to put in a lot of time and effort organizing and producing the materials to add to the genealogy manuscript and have again been shipping out these manuscript materials to various distant relatives who indicated some interest in the project and who are beginning to contribute to the genealogy research project. The materials are getting too voluminous to handle by hand and I may have to begin to learn to use a computer. In the past several years I have gotten substantial assistance in the Brasseur genealogy project from Art Brasseur of St. Hyacynthe (now deceased): Yvette DesLandes of St. Dominique; Art Brasseur of Penetanguishene; Rene Limoges of Ile de Perrot; Youlanda Aubischon and her son Mike Aubuchon of Ile Bizard, Ron Joseph Brasseur of Buffalo New York; Alice Truste of Moose Jaw, Saskatchewan; Robert Brasseur of Québec; Francois Brasseur of Québec; Yves Brasseur of Newport, Vermont; Marcel/Jeanette Brasseur of St. Hyacinthe, P.Q.; Marlene Brasseur of Warden, P.Q.; Rita Thornton of Winnipeg, Saskatchewan; Frank Youmell of Brasher Falls, New York; Joseph Brasseur of Outlook, Saskatchewan; Teresa Robinson of Kinosee, Saskatchewan; Russell Brosseau of Afton, Michigan; Gerard Brasseur of Indian River, Michigan; Dr. James Brasseur of Saginaw Michigan ; Gilbert Brosseau of Ortonville, Michigan; Carl Brasseur of Cadillac, Michigan; and Lea Brasseur Bryan of the Palmer, Alaska, and Alva Brasseur of Las Vegas, Nevada. There remains a great many Brasseur persons whose families and names are as yet undiscovered; and many entanglements yet be clarified and explained.

I hope to make at least one more trip to New England and Eastern Canada this year, perhaps two trips. There is still some hard door-to-door leg-work that shall have to be done in Montreal and its suburbs, between Ottawa and Rigaud, and into the New York and New England. All of these things, just to fill the lists; and then there is the hope and effort of collecting biographical and autobiographical materials.

In the past couple years I have done almost nothing on the Boepple genealogy. More materials are being made available from Bessarabia out of the Russian archives, so it is possible that there may be additional work to be done with the Boepple genealogy soon.

Uncle August, aged 91, died of colon cancer at the nursing home in Glen Ulen. I had been out to visit him in North Dakota about three times in the past two or three years--last in July 1994. Upon the occasion of his death I wrote and sent to his family a poem--and later sent in a copy of the poem to the North American Open Poetry Contest.

DEATH OF AUGUST N

This humble man be nominate
Unto posterity as great
August he in thought and deed
Though not in ostentatious need

His light be lifted back on high
His load was borne with grace each day.
Courageous in adversity
Exhorted us along the way.

And tempted us to reasoned thought
Engagingly with candid talk.
Tended both his fields with care
This farmer and philosopher.

Gently place his frame to rest.
There to slumber with the blest.
Where we who loved him may restore
For strength, as pilgrims, yet once more.

R.G.B.
18 December 1994

Brother Duane and Georgia are coming down for a visit January 23 through the 30th of the coming year (1995). I will take some time off and show them about this interesting state. Then towards the end of February, Bayloo and I may take a trip of 7 to 10 days to California or Florida. And then, in March I have some tentative plans to travel into Mexico for two or three weeks; perhaps alone and via their bus system; or, perhaps, with Bob Brown. And again in the summer, I intend to attend the Germans from Russia convention in his Bismarck. And shall aim again for a long trip of 3 or 4 weeks into New England, New York, Québec, Ontario, and then into Michigan for September and October.

I entertained some thoughts about going up into the Northwest to see my children and grandchildren. Just yesterday, Pierre/Rochelle had a third son (Guin Luc) along with their now two daughters. I thus have now 11 Brasseur grandsons. And Real/Tina are expecting another child in a month or so. It would be nice to see them, but might be too much of a strain on a currently tenuous relationship. Too awkward. Perhaps in a couple of years, when they have had a chance to slowly adapt to the reality of the separation of their parents. But perhaps I ought run up to the Northwest anyway, to look in upon Skippy, Kate, mom, Ookie, Phil, and Duane . . . and my various nephews and friends.

I had applied for psychiatric residency training at the University of New Mexico last year, but was not accepted the past summer. In part, I am sure, because I didn't push them very hard about it. And I was half content that I have heard nothing more. Because, my income has increased nicely and I wouldn't want to have dropped back into the salary of a 'resident physician' for three whole years. Especially since earning my better current income will probably permit me to retire in three years. And the problem of psychiatry, interesting as it is, is hemmed in and plagued by legal political issues which are so ambiguous of definition, and concept, and of so dubious validity, that one is destined always to be caught up into unpleasant controversy and litigation. I am now quite sure that I wouldn't take a residency position, even if it were offered me tomorrow.

One's life expectancy is of course limited; and I don't really want to spend three long years of memorizing lists and doing scut work in residency when there are other definite things that I want to do with my life.

Vic was down to visit a few days in the past year, and I expect he may come down again in a year or two. But I have not seen Phil for over a year, though he has written a couple of brief notes. I have to suspect that he too may take some time to come down for a brief visit. He indicates that our mother's mental status continues to deteriorate, though the stuff of her physical being seems to be of better durability. In general I wouldn't think it likely that she will survive more than a couple of years. Philip seems to feel obligated to remain up in that area as long as she lives.

As to time off, I will have accumulated nine weeks of vacation time by a year from now. Again, I expect to earn and use compensatory time enough to give me about three months of leave scattered through the coming year. And there will also be about 12 weeks of sick leave accumulated by years end. If I can get my divorce settled, I expect then to get started on the purchase and the regular use of computer devices to process my information and correspondence; and to become more efficient in my collection of genealogy information.

The past year I've enjoyed excellent health. I usually jog 1.5 miles, three times weekly, posting times as small as 12 min. I generally eat but one regular meal daily and have been maintaining my weight at between 163 and 169 pounds. I always drink at least 1500 mL of fluid daily--usually somewhat above that. I try to do weekly push-ups and sit-ups, to maintain strength in my limbs. I do not, and never have smoked cigarettes. I first began to use a little liqueur at age 48--only one drink and only on social occasions about once monthly. A couple years ago, I began to use a daily shot of 30 mL of a liqueur such as 'peaches and cream' schnapps, but discovered that it gave me some esophageal reflux problems while sleeping. Therefore I only rarely use it any longer.

I have been somewhat hypertensive most of my adult life with blood pressure at 140/94 and pulse often at 90 per minute. But I neglected to treat the hypertension until about 12 years ago--and have treated regularly since then. I currently use prazosin 1 mg b.i.d. and Propranolol 20 mg q.i.d. That keeps my BP down to 130/78 and pulse regular. I have no angina or shortness of breath. I do have chronic tendency toward nasal sinus congestion and intermittent sinusitis, so that for many years I have regularly used one half tablet of Actifed q.i.d.; and on occasion have to take a several day course of nasal medications such as Afrin nasal spray and Beconase. Along with the sinus problem I am predisposed to frontal headache. For that reason and because I have chronic dorsal thoracic back discomfort as each day wears on, I commonly use 650 mg of aspirin four times daily. I often substitute a Fiorinal tablet for one of the aspirin. Upon occasion of about once every 7 to 10 days, I also use a Darvon compound capsule once a day, when the muscle tensions in my mid-dorsal back seem to be accelerating. I sleep quite well at night, 1:30 PM to 6:30 AM, often awakening once at night to take aspirin and Actifed. I use 2.0 gm per day of Niacin to keep my cholesterol level lowered; and use a multivitamin tablet daily. A year or two ago I was having some slowness of my urinary stream and occasional hesitancy. It was then that I started using Prazosin for the dual purpose of blood pressure control and for reduction of urinary symptoms. It has worked well for both. I have considered beginning to use Proscar to reduce an old man's prostatic enlargement, but haven't yet gotten an adequate dependable free supply to give it a year's trial.

About two years ago I painfully passed a renal stone in the local emergency room. I began then to regularly consume a minimum of 1500 mL per day of liquids; and it have had no recurrent renal stone episodes.

I am fortunate to enjoy rather good health. Because of years of untreated diastolic hypertension and tachycardia, I expected I to have some predisposition to slight cardiac wall thickening and potential for the arrhythmia.

I have refractive error that includes significant hyperopia and significant astigmatism. But these are well corrected with spectacles. I also have a modest exophoria and hyperphoria which are both well corrected with prism lens.

That I yet live and continue to work and function efficiently as I approach the age of 62 years is a tribute to the timely medical information and available medications; and to the fact that I have ready access to, and the use of these advances of medicine.

RGB
(Written at end of Dec.
1994)

Summary of 1995
R. Garner Brasseur

ragmented memories of what has been, continues to fold itself into one's memories of all past times. Changes have occurred . . . are occurring, in my life. I needs must try to recognize realities; and come to terms with them.

I have a full head of hair which is beginning to gray noticeably. My vision seems to remain good, though my spectacle lenses are badly in need of replacement; though perhaps needing not much change in power. My hearing is good. I have a mild arthritis of the lower thoracic spine; and the hint of a dowager's hump. I find myself stooping at the shoulders often. I have good motion in the limbs and joints; and good strength. It may be that I tire more easily from a day's work: is much more certain that I grow increasingly weary of the ministry to absurdities and perpetual increase of committees and of paperwork. And that I am perpetually cynical of their (reasonably?) well intended purpose.

My teeth are in current good repair and very functional. In the past year, my weight has been up as high as 176 pounds; but I generally maintain at 165 pounds. Once it dropped to 159 pounds and I should like to keep it there, but my appetite is too good to permit of that.

I have had mild hypertension for years and began to medicate for that about 15 years ago. In August 1995, the hypertension went quite out-of-control, and I am having to increase and adjust my medications considerably. I discovered that I was very sensitive to Propranolol (at a dose of 120 mg I begin already to get a little bradycardia). I have no history of any cardiac disease, but it seems likely that I might have a slight left ventricular hypertrophy account of many years of untreated diastolic hypertension. A couple years ago I had an occasional PVC, which responded to Propranolol. I have been jogging regularly 2 to 3 times weekly since about 1974 and find that my performance is down when I have any significant Propranolol aboard, as it seems to limit my heart rate.

I try to drink a minimum of 1500 mL of fluid daily since my single episode of having passed a renal stone some two or three years ago. I was having some nocturia and difficulty initiating urination a couple of years ago but this seems largely to have relented since I (first) gave up the regular use of Benadryl (for sleep and nasal allergies) and then began to take Prazosin (an alpha blocker) for hypertension a couple years ago. My current hypertension medications are: 1) Prazosin two milligrams four times daily, 2) Propranolol 120 mg extended release, and 3) Catapress 0.5 mg twice daily.

I have long been predisposed to skeletal muscle tensions – most especially in my neck and mid to upper thoracic areas. These, related to an old back injury of 40 years ago; and aggravated by a my occupational use of the slit-lamp (hunching in front of it to examine eyes). I have used Darvon compound for 20 years at times as often as two to 3 three times daily but try to keep it down to a maximum of one daily. I have used Fiorinal (butabarbital) once or twice daily over the past 10 years. In the past two or three years I have used an occasional 0.5 to 1.0 mg of Ativan per day since working at this hospital to relieve the various stresses and anxieties which are precipitated upon me. It has spared me endless hours of tossing and turning sleeplessly in bed. I guess I have owned some slight to mild predisposition toward anxiety since my years of medical school, but I first became aware of moderately severe episodes experienced while taking frequent airplane flights in about 1988 and 1989. Subsequently I have been able to discern ever more subtle variations of sleep disturbance and pangs of restlessness that one feels in the chest, neck, head, and mind. One is then the more aware of their vague but unpleasant reality when one takes one of these medications such as Ativan, Klonopin, Halcion, or Darvon. And then reclining to unwind, one begins in 15 min. to notice the progressive decrease in the tension of muscles of the extremities. And the excessive mental irritation begin to melt away the burden of this day's mental irritations which rest atop those of yesterday, and unwind the tensions within the chest cavity. These psychic manifestations of the anxiety are a very real and physical consequence of unrelieved psychic tension.

In the past year I was absent (on leave) from Las Vegas for a total of 82 days; on six different trips of variable length, from 3 to 31 days. Six days with Georgia and brother Duane: 15 days with Bayloo to Florida and Belize; 19 days alone into Mexico; eight days with sister Kate to the Russian German genealogy meeting, and 31 days alone to New York, New England and New France to gather more Brasseur genealogy information. Most of the rest of my spare time this year has been wasted and troubled by the harassments and dilatation from depositions, interrogatories, and court proceedings to the settlement of divorce—which I presume now to have been completed as of December 20, 1995, though I haven't yet received any formal papers to indicate that. Little by little, I acquired various pieces of information as to the outrageous impositions of the court—and eventual final disposition of my properties. Their confiscatory presumptions seem obviously to be incremental behind-the-scenes encroachments of the NOW gang in the past 20 or 30 years. It seems that the final disposition is pretty much a standardized court formula. The attorneys proceed as though the situation were otherwise, and charge exorbitant fees – as though this were all due to exertions on their part. Of course, the financial settlements are amazing in their double standard. It is a fact that nothing beyond the splitting of communal properties applies to the settlement of divorce. Except that in cases where one of the spouses is financially well-to-do; or (as in my case) where one is felt to have significant residual earning potential. And hence, my anticipated residual earnings have been neatly divided 50-50, as though the spouse had in some way been rigidly trained; and disciplined by dent of long hard hours of study and enforced experience, and was therefore equal with myself as to painful requirements of training/education and ongoing long hours of service, so as to make of her an equal contributor to acquired earnings. Patently a ridiculous presumption. Even if that much were true, there is yet the problems that I (alone) am required to be enslaved to continued earnings. No division whatsoever of the labor and expenditures of the ongoing hours of my labor – merely a splitting of income. The one must continue in the harness . . . the other continues to loaf fashionably in the Surrey with whip in hand and take control of the reins.

I need now to yet see copy of the final divorce decree and settlement so that I can plan an escape from this enslavement (into retirement) as expeditiously as possible.

And as the divorce seems even yet not completed I also note that in the past several months, the warmth and spontaneity of Bayloo has been steadily declining as the legal tensions mount: and subsequent to the final recent court judgment, she decidedly indicates she is leaving . . . . To return to Montana and work for a friend of hers in Superior, Montana. Since her children live in that area too, it seems a natural enough move for her. Yet, it doesn't explain her evolving dispassion. Her past two years with someone of my eccentricity moves us closer to something like a more complete explanation of her evolving dispassion. My children would say that it is obvious enough that my potential loss of income is a part of the explanation for her loss of interest in our relationship; and the fact that she was as stunned as myself (at my being cut off from earnings) then adds weight to their argument. In any case, she is free to go just as she chooses – either with or without any explanation to me. For, to me, our relationship has no significant meaning, unless it is co-voluntary and retains its human warmth. Naturally it is a little hard on the ancient ego to find oneself rejected, for we all like to maintain our delusions of some residual of personal value and human lovability. Yet, I tend to think of myself as having less of that egocentricity in these declining years. And I expect I am apt to get over these rejection pains relatively easily by virtue of long experience in the process.

I haven't seen any of my children or grandchildren in the past couple years; and have no immediate plans to do so. It is just that there is too much strain on these relationships, in consequence of the divorce. Psychological trade-off is that I am at least free of the strain of and unpleasant marriage that has been troublesome for many years. There are now 15 grandchildren – the youngest of which, I have not yet seen. And now, there are rumors to the effect that Miette may be planning to get married. That is good news, for she needs to continue into the fulfillment of her life's experience.

I needs must continue at my current job until (at least) February 1997, to assure myself the re-accumulation of a little saving and a somewhat enlarged monthly state pension check in my retirement. Even perhaps, I might consider some weekend outside hours of work, if I get an ACLS certification, and a pay rate of $60-$70 per hour. I might even yet work an additional year (until February 1998) for an even larger pension check—-if I can do so by working only half time, to get the full-time 3% added benefit. But all of this is yet in the early considerations stage of development. For I am actually wishing to retire as soon as possible to get on with the various projects I have planed to occupy my retirement years.

End 1995
RGB

1995
1996

SUMMARY 1996
(Written 1 January 1997) R. Garner Brasseur, MD

fter the Divorce Court hearings of 12/27/95 I considered just quitting my work and disappearing. Thought about it and spoke with Vic and Phil, then decided to take off a month and travel to the Northwest to brood and let things settle on my mind. Given the chaos of my economic status and current agitations of my mind, Bayloo decided to head up to Montana to be near her family and to work with her friend, Nancy Leigh in Superior, Montana in a halfway house. At the turn of the year I took a pickup load of her gear up to Superior and then continued with my trip to visit the children, grandchildren, and my brothers in Washington and Oregon. I thought perhaps I might just be getting depressed--tired and sluggish--in consequence of the stress and ongoing stagnation of the divorce proceedings. After visiting the families of the children, I then went on to visit my brothers in Washington. As I stopped over with Vic a couple days, my fatigue and need for sleep seemed to increase. Leaving his place I decided to take a motel room in Moses Lake for a couple of days to just catch up on my sleep and spend some time in cleaning and conditioning some of my equipment and getting ready it ready to sell. I can't be hauling this mass of unused equipment about with me forever, after all. And it looks as though I'd need the money in order to have the where-with-all required to make financial settlement on the divorce proceedings decree. A decree which I had expected to be forthcoming within a couple weeks.

Though I wasn't febrile and had no cough, I continued to be tired--desperately in need of rest. Surely--I thought--all explainable by my situational depression. I went on to visit a couple days with Duane on the farm. The need for sleep and the residual fatigue persisted. I drove to Spokane and spent a couple days there in a motel, trying to sleep off my long fatigue, before spending a couple days with Phi and Dot. It appeared for a while that I might there be able to sell some of the equipment, but that hope collapsed. I drove down through Carson City en-route back to New Mexico, and to work--returning to the job after a month's leave.

Work continued to wear on me; but I continued to drag myself through it. Sometime in early March, I began to develop some cough. And the intermittent aching discomfort of several weeks (in the right supra-clavicular area) became a bit more noticeable to me. I listened to my own chest with a stethoscope. It seemed to me that there were poor breath sounds in the lower part of my right chest. I made an appointment and visited Dr. Simpson. He detected no rales, no rhonchi, and no depressed breath sounds, but did find that my oxygen saturation dropped very precipitously with just a small amount of physical exertion. The chest film showed atelectasis and pleural fluid in the right lower chest. I took antibiotics and cough medications a couple more weeks but failed to improve. My dyspnea of exertion was becoming quite limiting to my activity. Perhaps my abdomen was gradually becoming a little distended?, though it wasn't a definite impression to my mind--too slow a process. And no one with me to notice it for me.

Toward the end of March, I entered the local hospital for intravenous antibiotics and further testing--was there 4 or 5 days. CAT-scan of my chest and abdomen showed an irregular spot deep in the right lobe of my liver . . . as well as a significant amount of ascites fluid in the abdomen (in addition to the chest problem). Breathing was becoming a little troublesome to me--especially when lying on my left side. Though I was beginning to suspect that I might have a cancer of the lung, bronchoscopy was negative. When I was told (of the CAT-scan) and allowed to see the "spot on the liver", I realized that I was rapidly approaching the end of my allotted years. By that time my thinking was beginning to become a little fuzzy and seemed to require quite a bit of concentrated effort. I called my brother, Vic, to see if he would come down to help me get my affairs settled before I passed over to the great beyond. He said he would, and he gave me some very relevant and cogent advice; to get my attending physician to refer me to the University of New Mexico Medical School for prompt and efficient diagnosis. But he would not be down for a week or two. It seemed to me that I was sinking so fast, that I was not apt to be around that long. And I felt that I absolutely had to get my financial affairs done and settled promptly. I had some valuables hidden away in several places; and very specific ideas of what I wanted it used for. Phil agreed to come down and arrived within a couple of days. Meanwhile, I called Bayloo in Montana. She too arrived in a couple of days.

I went home for a couple of days while arrangements were made for me to be seen at the UNM University Hospital the next week. I gave Phil personal instructions for the location and handling of my cache. And gave written instruction and authorization to Vic to be my guardian of personal health decisions and of my personals affairs.

Phi and Bayloo got me to the University Hospital for initial appointments. Arrangements were made then for me to enter the University Hospital on the following week to complete my diagnostic evaluation. By that time, Vic had arrived. I was told that my case was thought to be hopelessly advanced and that the general feeling among the University Physicians was that I must be content to return home for my final days.

Vic, however, is not that easily put off. And I credit him, for the optimistic and hopeful insight that led him to lean heavily on the medical and surgical team that was handling my case. Among the liver transplant team, a Dr. Hector Ramos thought that he might possibly be able to resect enough liver to get the entire tumor out. I was certainly agreeable to that effort, however addled my thinking had become by that time--as I was sinking fast . . . with no other options. Better far an anesthetic death upon the operating table than a lingering death of misery with terminal cancer.

On Good Friday, they took me down to near the gates of death with a general anesthesia, to perform the surgery. I wasn't a good surgical risk--with the atelectatic lung and all. When I arose to consciousness, it was Easter Morning. Pierre, Vic, Phil, and Bayloo were there. And post-surgical news seemed to be promising. But it was a long troubled post-operative stay before I finally recovered enough to be discharged. I had lost about 25 pounds.

While in the hospital, my appetite was so poor that I had finally to have a naso-gastric feeding tube--though it didn't function well. One night, I had a sudden episode of acute diverticulitis of the sigmoid colon area; and it began even to spread into a general peritonitis, before it finally localized and resolved.

While I was in the hospital, Vic had finally fired my original attourney (Baca) for his ongoing neglect of my case and obvious attempt to milk the confused status of my "estate" to his personal enrichment. Both Baca and my ex-wife's attourney continued to bother me with legal matters even while I was yet in the hospital. I was discharged from the hospital at the end of April. Soon thereafter I was required to be troubled by more legal difficulty.

At home, Bayloo saw to that I was properly fed and that my schedule of activity was regularly promoted. By early May, I was just well enough to attempt a trip to Cheyenne. Each small bump upon the roadway still gave me a little start. For the last 100 miles, I lay out flat on my back upon a bedroll and cushion in the back of the pickup. There, I seemed to adapt more readily to the bumpy ride. It suddenly became cool and began to rain. I scrambled beneath the covers for warmth. Dating from this sort of mystical occurrence, it seems to me that my vigor began to return more rapidly; and I was glad that I had elected to take this trip.

We had arranged to meet brother Phil in Cheyenne. He was bringing a load of Bayloo's things down to us from Superior. I didn't have enough yet of endurance to even consider attending Kim's graduation from nursing school in Laramie. I still had not recovered my appetite and had resorted to the daily use of 2 or 3 cans of Ensure, to maintain my weight. Phil and I took a room at Little America for a couple of days. It was my 63rd birthday--I hadn't expected to reach that milestone. After supper on that day, Phil gave me birthday card and dessert treat. He seemed to be as pleased as was I . . . of my advancing recovery.

As Bayloo and I returned home, I was making up my mind to go forward with plans for travel in the coming summer. We bought a tent to facilitate the necessary frugality of the anticipated travel. In late June, we drove to Montana. There I left Bayloo with her family while I drove on out again to see the children and grandchildren in Oregon, and sibs in Washington State. Vic and I took a trip into British Columbia via Marysville, where we visited a few hours with sister Ookey. Then, on to Kelowna, where we visited some of mother's distant cousins (Lechner's, Taichel's, Reimers, and Muellers). Their families had remained in Bessarabia, and ended up in Germany at the end of WW-II. From there they emigrated to Canada in the 1950s. We stayed at the home of Ella Traischel that one night, before returning to Yakima. I visited again with Duane, and then with Phil before I stopped back in Superior to pick up Bayloo; and we drove out to Cleveland, Ohio for the Youmell-Brasseur reunion at the home of Earl and Barbara Youmell. En route we stopped to visit with Dick Morgan in Washburn, ND--he was a classmate of mine at Dunseith ND in the 7th and 8th grades. After the reunion, we again journeyed into New England to do some genealogy before heading back to NM at the end of July to take care of some legal matters and to keep a follow-up medical appointment at the U of NM University Hospital. The exam was negative and I had regained my weight.

In early August, Bayloo drove back to see her children in Montana. And I attended a post-graduate education course in Albuquerque. I then drove out again to Medford, Oregon via AZ, NV, and CA. En route, I visited Jean Brown and Bob Brown in Carson City. He was a friend and a classmate of mine at the University of North Dakota Medical School. I then arrived in Medford to attend the wedding of daughter, Miette--to Bart Cunningham . . . on August 10th. It was a big affair--at a big church outside of Jackson, Oregon . . . at Rausch, I believe. I don't recall that I saw her after the ceremony that day. But I saw her briefly a couple days later before they departed for Florida. I gave them some cash to expedite their travel. A month or two later, I got a brief note from her. They had sold her nice Toyota car for a larger camper van.

I spent a couple days with Pierre in Cornelius, Oregon, before going back to visit with my brothers again in Washington for a few days. Then again came through Oregon, en-route to Nevada--and spent 2 or 3 days with Pierre and Rochelle and family, including a day and a half at the beach. Then on to Reno, Nevada, where I attended another post-graduate education course of two days in early September before returning home to NM.

In late September, I took a bus to Missoula, where I met Bayloo. We then drove up through Great Falls to Havre--where I had worked several years as a locomotive fireman on the Great Northern Railway in the late 1950's. We crossed over into Alberta, visiting my cousin Alice Trusty in Moosejaw, Sask. From there, we drove all across Canada to do some genealogy footwork in Ontario and Quebec Provinces before continuing out onto the Gaspe Peninsula. We next visited the Aubischon's and the Youmell's in the Brasher Falls, New York area. Then, on to New England before continuing down past New York City to Washington, D.C. to spend a couple days at the Smithsonian Museum and visiting the other sights of the Capital. En-route back home we visited Bayloo's sister in the Kansas City area; and her daughter, Kim, in Cheyenne; and then arrived home in early November. I arranged then to return to half-time work at the hospital, as of November 18th.

Meanwhile, my ex-wife and her atty. saw to it that I was properly harassed throughout the year with the trivia of time consuming and expensive side issues before (what I hoped was) the final appearance before the judge on December 12th. But at year's end, the final decree and final settlement had not yet come into being! In the 6 weeks after that, I make good progress in the writing of my autobiography. And I must soon now arrange to get this into typed and finished form. I was undecided as to whether I should get a complete personal computer, or merely just a word-processor . . . which was my only real need at that time.

In the past year, I had sent in a couple poems for publication. And I hoped to be able to continue writing at least a couple poems yearly.

Both the Brasseur Genealogy and the Boepple Genealogy scripts were now badly in need of updating and corrections. I would like to have gotten both completed within the coming year, but had doubts about the possibilities--for genealogy becomes eventually massive, as well as endless.

I would have liked then to update and complete my philosophy book, *"A Studied Impression of That Which Is".*

What projects after these? I didn't exactly know. Some sort of a literary project, I expect. I was under a sense of urgency about wanting to get on with my various projects, since I was now living on borrowed time. Who can say when this sarcoma problem will return to claim me?

I had heard that Las Vegas Medical Center (the psychiatric hospital) expects to turn over the management of LVMC to contractual arrangements with private enterprise about April. A thing affirmed by some and denied by others of the hospital staff. It certainly seemed like a real possibility when one considers that this trend was then currently common among many such state institutions. If that were to occur at LVMC, it could work to my advantage by providing me the real possibility of an early retirement settlement. Otherwise, I may well have been best served by awaiting retirement until about July of 1998--though I would rather have retired about July of 1997. So I was to hold my cards in closely and wait to see what developed.

THE END 1996
RGB

1996
1997

1997 SUMMARY
(Written in January of 1998)

More than two years have now passed since I first developed symptoms that one might attribute to liver cancer for which I had surgery in March of 1996. I had returned to half time employment at Las Vegas Medical Center on 20 November 1996, but continued to draw half time disability benefits through 1997 and on into September of 1998.

Bayloo and I had departed into Texas for ten days of vacation beginning December 27th of 1996. In San Antonio I was able to contact Mick Rosckowff--the first I had seen or heard from him for 11 or 12 years. His son, Garner, is now about 12 years of age--born at the time I was in Hobbs, NM. I was--at that time--helping Mick find a way to complete his medical education. Mick seemed pleased to see me, but rather chagrin, and his first statement was to the effect that he was apologizing for his failure. He has his M.D. degree from Guadalajara, Mexico, but had never passed his Foreign Graduate Medical Exams, so had never served his internship. He works now with a physician doing some research projects. We went out for supper with Mick and Carlotta. I have not seen nor heard from him since.

I looked up some Boepple people in Ganado, Texas, and traveled to Alice, Texas, to learn some additional information about John Boepple. We saw Big Bend National Park, and we saw a stage production in Austin. We stopped to look for the so-called "lights of Marfa", but the phenomenon was unconvincing. On 6 January 1997 Bayloo and I returned from our trip into Texas. I then required of myself to earnestly work upon the project of organizing, writing, typing, editing, and rewriting my autobiographical biographical history of my family and myself. When I suffered through my near fatal illness in 1996, I had been troubled and discouraged account of having made only poor beginnings on that project. On 18 January of 1997

I purchased a Brother Word Processor from Wal-Mart for $320.00 and about 4 months later had to pay out another $40.00 for a service contract on the thing. But I have put the equipment to good and steady work, and it has served me well, after a few frustrating weeks of reading the manual and on-hands bumbling experience gradually acquainted me with the operation of the device.

On 9 November 1997 I completed the final draft of *"Inheritors of a Few Years"*, and forwarded that manuscript to my brother, Phil. He and I had arranged in the early autumn to have it printed in Spokane. In Mid-December Phil called me to say that the finished manuscript was now off the press. He agreed to send copies of it to Duane and Pierre for me so that they would receive them by Christmas. I planned to take off a month beginning mid-January 1998, to drive to the Northwest to see my extended family in Oregon and Washington. From there I was to spend several days at Phil's place, mailing out copies (of the 80 which I had printed) of the manuscript to those upon my list. I intended to send copies to each of my 24 Brasseur derived nieces and nephews, to each of my 6 remaining siblings, and--eventually--to each of my 4 children and (then) 17 grandchildren. It seemed to me prudent to delay the mailing of these copies to most of my children and grandchildren until beyond the time of my death, or for at least several years . . . whichever come about first. But would I have enough determination of restraint to accomplish that delay? And how would I ensure that those eventual mailings would be accomplished after my demise. Something I needed yet to ponder well!

There are also a few cousins to whom I needs must send copy of my book. Also, quite a few--perhaps a dozen--to various distant relatives with whom I had become acquainted over the past 8 or 10 years of genealogy research.

My work on the manuscript had been often interrupted by my various periods of absence, upon my various trips, and by the necessity of frequent legal and attorney consultations concerning the slow and halting progress on the finalization of my divorce--which process had its beginnings in about September of 1992.

In February, son Jauhn and I spent a day together touring central New Mexico when he stopped by en-route to Austin.

I attended a post-graduate education meeting a couple days at the end of February in Albuquerque on "Spirituality in Medicine"--it was pretty hoaxy, and I had to speak that truth to the medical staff at Las Vegas Medical Center after one of the Psychiatrists had already spoken his praise of the nonsense. At that meeting, Dr. Ghosh affirmed my view of the thing. I attended a second Post-Graduate Education meeting in Salt Lake City for several days towards the end of March. Upon that trip, I first took a few days to drive out to California, and drove into Baja California, Mexico, to look up daughter Miette and Bart at Carmen Serdon. Later in the year, their son Josiah Isreal was born 4 September. But earlier--2 April--was born the seventh and last child to Real and Tina--a lad of many names who I call "Nombres" (Names) for the many names he carries. At that time, I then had 13 grandsons and 4 granddaughters.

At the end of May, I drove out to the Northwest again to visit my various family and friends. From there, Pierre and I flew out to a Brasseur Family reunion at St Valerian in the Province of Quebec on 5 June and returned 17 June, after visiting various distant Brasseur relatives in the provinces of Quebec and Ontario. My grandfather was born and raised in St. Valerian, and the gravestones of many of his relatives are to be seen in the cemetery along side its big Catholic church. In fact, I didn't see signs of any other church in St. Valerian or any other of those smaller French-speaking communities of the interior of the province. I then visited Vic, Duane, and Phil before returning to Las Vegas, NM on 22 June.

Bayloo attended the Marsh Reunion in early July. In mid-July I drove up into Montana and visited sisters Kate and Skippy en route to the Germans-from-Russia-Heritage-Society meeting in Jamestown, ND. Returning, I stopped a day to do genealogy research in Miles City, and had supper there with nephew Steve Kransky and family; and talked a while with Harold (Aloha's first husband).

In early September, I attended the 45th reunion of my high school class in Miles City. About one in ten seems to have passed away. Of those attending, I claimed the largest number of grandchildren (17) and was given a little prize for what fate had ordained. I saw Ed Neuhardt for the first time in 35 years. From Miles City I drove west to visit briefly with brothers Phil, Duane, and Vic before driving back home to NM.

October 18th I again departed to visit my extended family in the Northwest. En route back to work, Phil, Kenton and I stopped over at Fairmount Hot Springs near Anaconda, Montana.

RGB

Summary of 1998 Journal
R. Garner Brasseur, MD

The death of Dr. Don Beyers, psychiatrist, in early January from liver failure and coma beclouded my local situation. And Dr. Fisher, psychologist, died of brain cancer on 11 January--first diagnosed about the time I was diagnosed of cancer in 1996.

Early in the year I had my eyes checked and a new pair of glasses from ophthalmologist, Dr. Bell, though I usually prescribe my own glasses. On January 8th I received a copy of my manuscript, "*Inheritors of a Few Years*" and distributed 58 copies mostly to relatives and a few friends. I was very glad to have gotten it finished and am looking now toward other projects. Glad also to have had the miraculous reprieve from my liver cancer that permitted me the time I needed for the project. A medical miracle.

My health is good and I generally feel well, but I had developed a macrocytosis and had therefore been taking interval injections of Vitamin B-12. I was also regularly taking a multivitamin tablet, Prostatin, Folic Acid, Vitamin B-6, Selenium, Propranolol 40 mg. b.i.d. daily, Capoten 6.25 daily, and had switched to the use of acetominophen instead of ASA, account of the macrocytosis. I developed a pigmentary bruising of my lower abdomen--apparently related to my capillary fragility problem and the pressure from my belt that aggravated it. Or, perhaps, an allergic reaction to the rubberized band in my underclothing. I discontinued using a belt. Very slowly in the space of six months, the abdominal pigmentation and bruising cleared up though some spots of dry skin rash persisted there. For a while I was having a lot of flatulence and so began to watch my diet. Too much sugar or starchy foods tends to aggravate the problem, as does whole milk. Lactose intolerance is a not uncommon problem as one transits from youth into advancing age. And so, I cut down my intake of milk and that, along with the B-12 injections seemed to keep the flatulence under control. Also, to eat my daily bowl of oatmeal and daily apple seem both beneficial to my digestive processes. In the last two to three months of 1998 I had increased in weight up to 192 pounds--the most I have ever weighed, and I needed to get some weight off. On medications, my blood pressure was controlled at about 120/84 and pulse down in the 84 range.

In mid January, Bayloo and I drove to Las Vegas, Nevada and then toured a few days in western Arizona. From Flagstaff I then put her on a train to Santa Fe to return to her work while I drove on up into the Northwest to visit my children, grandchildren and my brothers. I also visited the Buchanan twins (high school classmates) in the Seattle area.

Earlier, in March, while in Spokane, I had purchased a Compaq Pressario 2200 Personal computer for $550.00, a monitor, a HP jet printer, and a cheap scanner. I worked with that equipment a bit at a time, trying to get acquainted with its operation. A slow and frustrating job. But I had been away from the apartment so much that I hadn't yet had any prolonged experience of it. In the fall, I therefore took a course at Luna Vocational Tech in Las Vegas, on the use of Word Perfect.

While in Spokane, Phil and I got most of my *"Inheritors of a Few Years"* mailed out. I then returned back home to Las Vegas 15 February to return to work 2 days weekly and continued to collect long term disability of $2,000.00 per month until they cut me off of those payments in September. I was surprised it went on as long as it had.

Back again in Las Vegas, I became tied up with Physician's Union negotiations, grievance writings, and politics most of the year. I thereby made some enemies among the administrative people, and they in turn have gotten around to making some difficulties for me. I was told at one point that I had been fired, but the union politics got me around that problem. Rather an interesting episode of conspiracy and intrigue which I have covered in other essays.

On May 13th I discovered that I have been now officially divorced since about February. What a long, arduous, and expensive proposition that had been. I was relieved to have done with it, though the economics of it seemed to promise forever to weigh about my neck like a millstone. Much better to be free than bear the burden of pretense to a marriage that had ended long previously. Much better to make a strong statement of one's philosophical religious views by a definitive act than to allow one's authenticity to wash away in unexpressed resentment of allowing oneself to be continuously inundated with sanctimonious pieties and persons.

Again, May 13 through June 6th, I took a trip up into the Northwest to visit family and friends. Phil and I took a brief trip up into the Canadian hot springs. We then attended the wedding of nephew, Dobbie Bassuer and Karen Kaufmehl on the 16th of May, north of Spokane--it was a nice family get together.

On June 10th, I found myself unexpectedly to be a candidate for president of the medical staff--an office that I didn't care to have. Yet, I consented to the nomination because we union physicians hoped in that way to keep that position of power out of enemy hands. In accepting the nomination, I informed the staff that I had no actual ambition to the dubious honor, but that--if elected--I would serve the term as kind of a lark. The political alignment against us prevailed, though I was surely not disappointed to lose the election. One of my friends then stood up to congratulate me on the success of my acceptance speech (in sparing myself the burden of the office).

On the first weekend of July, Bayloo and I were house setting for Carol Oppenheimer in Santa Fe, and we took in an opera and a Flamingo dance performance.

July 18th we headed again into the Northwest where BL stayed mostly with her family in Missoula and I spent a couple days with them at Flathead Lake, but most of the time with my brothers in Washington. She stayed in Missoula and I returned to Las Vegas to work on August 2nd. I departed Las Vegas again on the 11th of August to meet Bayloo in Terry, Montana. We left her car there at Skippy's place and drove to Bismarck to attend the Germans-from-Russia-Heritage-Society meeting a couple days. Departed Bismarck promptly at 8:00 AM on August 15th, to drive to the wedding of Bernie Brasseaur--the 22 year old grandson of my dad's brother (Amey). The boy's father, Jene Brasseaur, would be my cousin. I had never met either of them previously, but had been in correspondence with Bernie four of five years concerning genealogy information which he was wanting to acquire from me.

We left the twin cities and headed westward again, driving through northern South Dakota and back to Missoula. There Bayloo and I got married on August 21st at the court house.

While in Missoula these several times of this year, I have occupied myself in studying out the geological evidence to be found in Montana, Idaho, Washington, and Oregon. Evidence which pieces together a plausible and fascinating picture of the evolution of the channeled scablands which dominate the character of eastern Washington State and the Columbia Gorge. After our wedding, we drove through western Montana, into

Idaho, and Washington to follow out that course and geological evidence for those spectacular Spokane floods that carved out the Channeled Scablands. We then drove to Port Angeles and ferried across to spend a day and a night at Victoria, B.C. Returning, I stopped to find LeRoy Westover just east of Port Angeles (his mother, a Boepple woman, derived from the Teplitz community of Bessarabia). I gave him a book of Boepple Genealogy which I had sent to his mother a few years earlier--and which had returned account of no forwarding address. I thought she might have died, but her son says she now lives in Wenatchee. We then stopped over one night, west of Olympia, with Nancy Leigh, a friend of Bayloo. And then stopped over a few days with Vic and Marg in Yakima. With them we drove up to inspect the aftermath of the great Mt. St. Helen's volcanic eruption of 1980.

I arrived back in Las Vegas on September 5th--Bayloo stayed on in Missoula. I had a fair amount of business to tend to, including getting Bayloo onto my health insurance plan. From vacation time, I went immediately into a five month period of leave of absence. Not knowing how long my good health might persist, I had plans to take a fall trip back east, and to attend two or three Elderhostel courses. As those plans were firming up, my mother died at age 92 on September 12th. That day I wrote a poem to commemorate her life. The poem was read and was in the church bulletin of scheduled events the day of her funeral on September 17th in Coeur d'Alene. Before I got out of town to drive to that funeral on the 14th, there was some intrigue and the intent of administration was to fire me. An intent that was to use that action as a sop to the ire of Desert States Guardian Co. Each time some complaint is lodged against the hospital, the administration seeks to deflect the force of the complaint by accusing and firing some one of the 20 or 30 professional staff. I was to be the sacrificial lamb on this occasion. However, that plan seems to have been hurriedly withdrawn by the actions of the union--sort of interrupted by union negotiation. Instead of being fired I was given a note of assurance that I would remain in my current apartment until June 1999.

I stopped at Phil's place in Spokane the day before mom's funeral. Duane and Georgia were there too. I slept that night in the pickup, and drove over to Coeur d'Alene for the funeral the morning of the 17th, having visited mom's body the evening before, when we also visited among the relatives. The weather on the day of the funeral was fine. It was a nice church ceremony, where she had been a member for many years--perhaps fifty or so in attendance. She had outlived all of her own sibs and friends--as well as her two oldest children, Gene and Aloha.

I had agreed with Duane that we should solicit funds for the payment of those funeral expenses (over $5,000.00) from the various families of mom's children. Accordingly, Duane and I signed the letter of solicitation--which we passed out to the various persons in attendance.

A month or more later, as secretary treasure of the solicitation committee, I sent out a follow-up dunning letter to the members of the family. Thus, the funeral expenses were rather widely supported by family. Otherwise, as it seemed to us, the full burden of those expenses would have been allowed to fall upon the shoulders of brother Phil--who had already been the mainstay of the care and attention to our aging parents through these past thirty years. I was certainly not enough financially secure to handle the expense on my own, and I presume that neither was Duane.

On February 25th, I had a call from Rochelle that Pierre had gotten progressively ill the past few days, and had now been hospitalized with what seemed probably to be a ruptured appendix. I was worried and concerned, but there was no way to get up there prior to his surgery early the following day. I called Pierre at the hospital that evening and was relieved to hear the healthy bloom in his voice. He was out of pain and improved on medications, and his surgery was to go forth in about six hours. The surgery went well. He returned to work in about a week, then had a relapse and had to be grounded and treated with antibiotics again for a spell.

Curiously, only several months earlier, Jauhn's son, Jonah had been hospitalized and underwent surgery after an illness of several days. His problem was tentatively diagnosed by Michah--age 14, who plans to be a Pediatrician despite his mild moderate hearing loss problem (congenital?).

Shortly after his surgery, Pierre bought a well kept large station wagon, several years old, though he himself does not have a driver's license. In later December--they purchased and moved into a large five bedroom home of about $215,000.00 price . . . the first home they have ever owned.

In early June, I spent five days with Pierre and children driving about Idaho and camping before they went on to attend a Saur family reunion in Montana. In late September, Pierre, the kids, and I along with nephew Malcomb and his girl friend Sunny, spent a day climbing on the Timberline of Mt. Hood. Within a few days of that, I of course also visited with the families of Jauhn, Real, and Miette--all in Oregon. While visiting Miette,

Bart, and grandson Josiah on September 30th, the boy took his very first solo walk of about 8 or 10 steps.

I was in Medford October 1st and 2nd. There, grandson "Zelt" (Beaux) and I spent the better part of a day together first at the library, then in a rest area park where we got a little nap, and then visited with Bill and Idris White. I then heard that Real and Tina had been offered a chance buy the house they had been renting for the past several years at a price of only about $53,000.00. I had the impression that Real had more or less rejected the idea since he had no means or savings, and was about $12,000.00 in debt; a school loan ($8,000.00), credit cards (about $2,000.00), and hospital bills ($2,000.00). I long talked first with Tina and later with Real to encourage them by no means to allow this excellent opportunity to pass through their grasp. For the place being worth perhaps $90,000.00, would be essentially a windfall gift of $40,000.00 to them. I then discussed it with Phil and he wrote up for Real and Tina an offer to buy, which they were to send to the owner in Africa. That, they have not yet done even at years end, though I assured him I would lend him the necessary $5,000.00 for closing costs etc. This year since August, Real has been working at his first full time teaching job--the fifth grade at Hooser School in Medford with income of about $24,000.00 per year, plus benefits. He seems to like and to be inspired by the job. The depression that I have seen in his demeanor the past four or five years seems largely to have lifted. Their four oldest children are all enrolled in public schools this year, rather than in the home study program of previous years.

Pierre's children and Jauhn's appeared all yet to be home schooled.

In mid-October, Bayloo and I again met in our apartment in Las Vegas, New Mexico. After taking care of a lot of odds and ends of details and business, we departed towards the Northeast October 26th. We stopped first in the Kansas City area to visit a couple days with BL's sister, Carla and Lew Schroeber. We stopped then in Omaha to look up Bernard Chase, but missed catching him. We then drove on to Cleveland, Ohio where we spent a day and a night with cousins Earl and Barbara Youmell. And stopped next to spend a day and a night with cousins Larry and Margaret Brasseur in Buffalo, New York. Then we drove to Brasher Falls, New York where we spent the night with cousins Frank and Glenda Youmell. From there we crossed over the border into Canada and spent an evening and a night with cousins Yolanda (nee Youmell) and Andre Aubischon--and spent the following day at the French Canadian Archives at 1945 Rue Mullen, in east Montreal. That night we stayed at a motel in Grandby, Quebec

Province. The following day we headed south and stayed at Concord, New Hampshire. The following day we saw a show at the planetarium in Concord, NH and then drove on into Boston via Hwy 83, stopping at the Holiday Inn there about 2:30 PM. It was to be our home for the following week while we attended lectures and demonstrations at the Boston Museum of Science (and one day at Harvard's Museum of Natural History) where we also took all of our noon and evening meals. All of this as a part of an Elderhostel Program into which we were enrolled.

We had application into another Elderhostel Program in New Your City for the following week on a standby basis, but no opening developed for us. We therefore left Boston on November 14th, and drove into the Hudson River Valley and on into Pennsylvania, where we stopped over near Hazelton, PA. The following day we headed south on Hwy 81 through Maryland, into West Virginia. There we entered the Blue Ridge National Park, following the beautiful Skyline Drive southward. The mid November weather remained perfect for the entire trip. We stopped over a night at a Park Lodge and continued south the following two days. Then we continued southwest through the Great Smoky Mountain National Park and stopped in Chattanooga to visit some caves and spend the night. We picked up the Natchez Trace Trail road and followed it part way through Mississippi. On then through Arkansas and Texas, then back to New Mexico, arriving back home November 21st.

I had follow-up tests at the University of New Mexico Hospital--abdominal CAT scan, chest film, and lab work work--all looking quite satisfactory. Then met with atty. and attended to multiple other odds and ends before departing westward through lower New Mexico and Arizona. We spent a night in Deming, and then a night in Yuma, before entering California. We stopped at El Centro where we looked up an old high school classmate, Lynn Fitz, who works there as a pharmacist. As when I visited him ten years ago, he still lived alone in a mostly empty trailer home, though he has been married a couple times and has a grown son in Oregon. Lynn's father was the Presbyterian Preacher in Miles City. Lynn gave me copies of some essays he has written to the local newspapers through the years, and gave me a copy of some quite nice poems written by his father years ago. We had lunch and a long interesting conversation before we drove off to take a motel room.

The following day we drove into San Diego to the travelers Lodge Motel where we were to stay the whole week, attending another Elderhostel Course. We drove out to Sea World that day but the price of admission was an outrageous scandal, so we didn't enter. The Elderhostel program was on the general subject of "Consciousness". The accommodations were nice if one doesn't mind a constant diet of chicken, but the course was not well organized.

We departed San Diego Saturday the 5th of December and stopped over in Atascadero. There I again tried (the second time this year) to contact a cousin (daughter of dad's brother, Anthony) Stuart--they were away on a trip. We drove north on Hwy 5 to Medford where we took a motel and I then visited Real, Tina, and family. The following day I visited Real's classroom, then Tina and I drove over to Grants Pass to watch Cowboy play basketball. He is quick, decisive, and aggressive on the court. He is also quite interested in skate-boarding, and does it very well.

December 8th we drove north into Portland. There I put Bayloo on the train for Missoula. I stayed over at Pierre's. I was in a position to comply with his request for a personal loan to tide him over against his current heavy expenses. I then visited with Jauhn's family briefly the next day, before driving north through Seattle to Marysville. My sister, Ookie, had just had a hysterectomy and an AP repair and was now home from the hospital. I stayed with her a couple of nights and did some errands for her. One evening I visited with nephew Andre, his wife, Gretchen, and their six girls. He gave me a check for their branch of family--towards the expenses of mom's funeral . . . the sum of which I passed on to brother Phil a week later.

On the 12th of December I looked up a high school classmate, Grant David Mosby, near Yelm, Washington. Had a nice visit with him and his new wife, and had supper with them before departing for Portland about 8:00 PM. Pierre and family were just then moving into their new home. I stayed the night there and helped them with some moving that evening and the following morning before departing to spend some time at the library.

I spent the nights of the 14th and 15th at Jauhn's place. The night of the 15th, Bart, Miette, and Joss were there. The boy had chicken-pox. I played with him an hour or more while the gals went shopping and Bart, Jauhn, and the kids were outside playing football. The lad loves to play catch and has a pretty good arm. Miette is a bit thin and appears fatigued. She had thyroid surgery early this past year for a cold thyroid nodule and has been on replacement thyroid the past few months. She tells me she is pregnant again, too. On the next morning I drove Miette, Bart, and the boy to the airport--they are flying to Baltimore to see his mother and sister for a few days.

I then drove on to Spokane and spent a couple days with Phil concerning talk of real estate, Real's possible house purchase etc.

The 18th of December I arrived in Missoula, where Bayloo was staying at the home of her daughter, Annie, who had just given birth to their 4th child on the 12th. It was cold in Missoula. I and Bayloo stayed on with them a few nights. I spent my days in the city library. On a Sunday, Dean and I saw the new Star Trek movie, while Bayloo and Cindy see another movie at the same complex.

Preferring to spend my Christmas alone as an opportunity for reflection and creative thought, I departed Missoula on the 23rd. I drove to Phillipsburg to take a motel room there for three nights. My primary project was a poem that I must write and submit before the end of the year. I had time in solitude to relax, unwind, and take a few good naps. I also watched a little TV, read and did some writing. On December 26th I returned to Missoula en route to Spokane, the farm, Portland, and Medford. Bayloo preferred to remain in Missoula for now and to meet me in early January in Salt Lake City, en-route to our return to the Las Vegas apartment.

In Spokane I typed up my newly composed poem and sent it to the North American Poetry Contest in Owings Mills, Maryland as I had been doing annually since 1991. It is about the fifth poem I have written this year. One for Miette, one for Jauhn, one for mother, one for a poetry contest in mid-summer, and an extra one while in the mood for it. I attempted to write one for Pierre's birthday too, but it failed and I sent to him instead, only an outline of its thoughts. The writing of a poem is, to me, generally, a very difficult and time consuming thing. Despite its difficultly and the customary unspectacular results, I continue to be driven by this compulsion to something creative.

I was still trying to master the use of my computer--progress is slow. I knew that upon my return to work, I would be under the gun from administrative pressure. They continued their vindictiveness towards me account of my letters against them through the union activities. Also, they feel abused account of my exercising my right to be so long absent on leave; and because I have so often confronted them on many issues at morning report meetings and staff meeting.

RGB

Year 1999 Summary
R. Garner Brasseur, MD

I returned to work at Las Vegas Medical Center on 7 January 1999 after returning from visitations with my people the northwest. I was immediately confronted by administration-management allegations and intrigues. They were obviously determined to be rid of me. Indeed, they had believed they had already accomplished that in September of 1998, but with the help of the Union Doctors we squelched that at a Union/Management meeting on 10 October 1998. Pablo Vigil seemed awkwardly aware of that at a brief face-off meeting between us on 23 November 1998.

These adversaries had now had the time to concoct a new strategy against me. But I was aware of my rights as a state employee and as a citizen with union rights. And with the support of the union, I had full confidence in my situation.

In point of fact, I had full intention of retiring by May or June of 1999; and it was actually my hope that they would continue in their improper and unconscionable harassment against me without delay so as to have fully accomplished their evil plan before my intended date of retirement. A retirement whose intention I had kept from their awareness. The administrative management personnel were so uninhibited in their tyrannical audaciousness that they charged foreword--seemingly oblivious of any impropriety. I was astonished to finally own a clear paper-trail of the infamy they were perpetrating.

Upon my return to work I was accused of dereliction of duty in a half dozen specific instances and was reassigned to work exclusively in the hospital medical records dungeon, in order to protect patients from my presumed incompetence or neglect. I steadfastly endured the insult of these allegations and with the support of physicians Ghosh, Pembroke, and especially Stan Kaster, I set about the investigation of those patient's charts concerning whom charges against me were being alleged. Stan Kaster participated with me in the review of these charts. That review demonstrated that there was no substance whatever in the allegations against me. I then used my word processor to compose and publish a detailed and comprehensive self-defense based on the evidence of the record and the sequence of events which fully supported my counter-allegations of administrative pretext and charade in the heedless and malicious impugnment of my character and medical competence. On 24 February Stan Kaster and I presented my defense against charges before the LVMC Professional Medical Staff several days after getting my published findings and defense into the hands of each staff member. I was acquitted of all charges by a 13 to 3 vote--the administrative members of the staff being totally impervious to even the obvious fact that the allegations were nothing more than mere allegations without substance. Voting the intention of their malice, rather than the clear evidence. The four staff conspirators making the allegations had made no effort whatever to substantiate their bogus allegations which were in no way supported by the records--the baldest and most transparent of assertions. In the end, even one of my major adversaries--Dan Seagraves--is said to have been willing to testify that he had been present at meetings behind closed doors, where plans were afoot in conspiracy against me. And as medical staff president, he wrote for me a letter indicating that an exhaustive and comprehensive investigation of charges against me had ended in my complete exoneration from all charges. He is said to have resigned immediately thereafter to pursue further study goals afar, and was thus unavailable for testimony when I then initiated my legal countercharges against LVMC.

I returned to my regular medical duties 26 February. And yet I was not permitted to return to full time work as I had requested--though I believe that to have been my legal right under EOA regulations. Additionally, both Vigil and Perez (remembering the charges, but having forgotten the verdict) continued administratively to harass me by presuming to "supervise and oversee my professional work" just as though I had not been exonerated of the bogus charges they had manufactured against me.

On 3 March I first consulted Atty. Linda Hemphill to discuss the possibilities of initiating legal charges against LVMC. We elected to approach the situation as that of a retaliation against me for exercising my first amendment right of free speech. I had submitted to her a time-line form of instances in which I had (over the past few years) confronted dictatorial procedures and requirements posed by administration which I interpreted as being counter-productive to the best interests of patients and of other employees, as well as in opposition to the rights and professional prerogatives of we of the professional medical staff. As I had this record and documentation all organized and processed, our legal confrontation and negotiations to the settlement progressed quite rapidly to a settlement with administration completed on 22 April after I had submitted my letter of resignation on the 21ˢᵗ. Resignation effective as of 1 May.

Subsequently, on 30 March, there was a backlash movement against Dr. Perez concerning the incompetence of her handling of the trumped-up allegations against me. And I had my chance before the medical staff to thoroughly castigate her concerning this matter. Administration failed to follow through on sanctions against her (presumably because she had permitted herself to be the supple tool for the illicit acts of administration). Thus they and she were permitted a sort of face-saving. However--and behind the scenes--she later quietly resigned from her position as clinical director in about October . . . returning then to a staff psychiatrist post in out-patient clinic.

Meanwhile, as of 10 April, I went on leave to use up my vacation and leave time. On 22 April I headed up to the Northwest to visit my people. May 5ᵗʰ I began a long trip back to NM for another divorce hearing on the 7ᵗʰ. This nonsense and endless expense has been going on now since 1993 . . . with no apparent hope of ever any resolution. Reminiscent of Kafka's book, "*The Trial*". There needs desperately to be a remedy for the incompetence and injustice of New Mexico's divorce courts.

I learned that my nephew John Dalke died of sudden myocardial infarction 8 May. I hadn't seen him in 10 years or more.

We had until the end of May to get moved out of our apartment at LVMC. While making those efforts and plans, I was beginning the arduous task of putting the Brasseur Genealogy information into my computer. A process that was to occupy me intermittently until the end of summer, when I completed the project and finally submitted it to the Library of Congress for copy-write. I completed my 1998 tax forms with Bayloo and the CPA on 27 May. We then rented a storage unit in Las Vegas and hauled our gear into it. I return the key to 'the Transcendental Apartment' to the hospital administrator's office 1 June 1999, and then head off to the Northwest. Bayloo drove to Taos to stay with a friend for a few days and then worked a few days before following.

On June 4th I arranged with Phil to carry a 2nd mortgage on his home and we signed an agreement on the matter.

I stopped by Vic's place on the 6th and left with him--by previous agreement--my pickup load of personal notebooks, books, writings, and my computer and genealogy information. I then went to Portland where I left my Brother Word Processor to be repaired. I visited children and grand-children in Oregon and then stopped on 16 June to visit brother Duane and settle up with him concerning mother's funeral expenses. He and I agreed each to pay $1350.00 of what was yet owed to settle the bill.

On June 20th, Bayloo and I took a trip through Grand Coole into Kelowna, where we visited mother's cousins. Not persons that my mother had ever known, or known of: immigrants to Canada, subsequent to the end of World War II. We stayed with Wilma Lechner and her son Roy four nights and they showed us around the area. We then drove to the coast and down to visit sister Ookie and nephew Andre's family, as well as Bayloo's friend, Nancy Leigh. Then to Pierre's place; and back to Vic's, where I spent another five or six days working on my computer genealogy papers. I then drove Bayloo back to her family in Missoula and headed out alone to visit Harold and Steve Kransky in Miles City. I next stopped in Sydney to locate and speak with Blinda Larson--ex-wife of nephew Billie Ban (Skippy's son). I visited nephew, Bill Huft in Fairview en route to meet Pierre and Bam-bam off the train in Minot on July 8th. We three drove to Dunseith where we visited the graves of my Brasseur grandparents before driving south through Jamestown, to Aberdeen, South Dakota. There we three spend the next three days at the German's-From-Russia Convention. And then headed back north on the eleventh and stopped to visit an old classmate of mine in Washburn--Dick Morgan. We then stopped to visit the graves of the Boepple grandparents and other relatives in Beulah, before reaching Williston. Pierre and Bam-bam boarded the train and headed back home to Portland the following morning. I then drove to Miles City where I met brother Vic on the 13th, and we left my pickup with Steve Kransky as we two headed east in Vic's car on the 14th. We drove through Ohio and into the Adirondacks of New York to look at some Youmell graves in Tupper Lake. The Youmelles are actually Brasseurs, who have mistakenly lost track of that original name--strange as that seems. We then visited Frank and Glenda Youmell in Brasher Falls, NY on the 21st. Then visited Andre and Yolanda Aubischon on the 22nd; and then into eastern Ontario and Quebec to visit Brasseurs and look at cemeteries, before driving to Hampshire College near Amherst, NY on the 25th of July. There we spent a week at an Elderhostel course on Philosophy, living in a dorm and eating in a cafeteria. A course not overly satisfying as it dealt only with historical philosophical incidents; and old assertions and arguments. We drove a leisurely return through New York State, southern Ontario, Michigan, Wisconsin, and North Dakota to Miles City where I got my pickup and Vic and I parted company on August 5th.

I stopped in Missoula a few days and played a couple games of touch football with Bayloo's grandchildren: and visited with Glen Williams--a 7th and 8th grade classmate of Dick Morgan and I from Dunseith. I stopped then in Spokane where I ran into nephew Greg Krahn (one of Ookie's sons) and his spouse and baby at Phil's place. After visiting my children, I stopped to visit the family of nephew, Andre in Everett. I once again returned to Vic's place in Yakima, were I spend the next eleven days finishing my Brasseur genealogy manuscript list. From the 1300 plus page manuscript, I made three copies of three volumes each. Gave one to Vic, kept one for myself, and I later took one east with me as Bayloo and I departed Missoula on Sept 6th. We drove through Lewistown, Bismarck, and Michigan to Ontario and Quebec. We stopped at the home of Andre and Yolanda Aubischon in Isle Bizzard just outside of Montreal for two or three days. Yolanda wanted me to accompany her on her visit to an Ophthalmologist, and to help her make up her mind concerning cataract surgery and implant for her one good eye. We then drove south through New York State and Pennsylvania to Washington, D.C. There we took a motel room and stayed for a three day visitation of the sights. And I dropped off a copy of my Brasseur Genealogy manuscript at the Library of Congress. From there we headed west into West Virginia. We next spent a couple days recuperating at the home of Pat Lipscomb Maher in Buchanan--an old friend of Bayloo. Our next stop was in the Kansas City area for a couple days to visit Bayloo's sister Carla and Lew Schroeber. Then to Omaha to spend three days visiting a high school friend (Bernard Chase) and his wife. We passed on again to stop briefly through Missoula and Spokane. From there Bayloo drove out to Shelton, Washington to be with a friend, Nancy Leigh, who has cancer of the base of the tongue and is trying to learn what might be done to offer her some hope of survival from this complex problem. I drove out to visit family in Oregon, as well as an old friend, Dr. Larry Otis, in Grants Pass and cousin Dorothy Boepple-LaValle in Central Point. I then arrived in Shelton, Washington November 1st to drive Bayloo and Nancy to and from the airport. I left there with Bayloo on the 4th and we drove through Oregon and Nevada to Arizona. There we parted, Bayloo to Phoenix to spend two or three weeks with Nancy after Nancy was to have surgery to the base of tongue for the squamous cell carcinoma. I drove on to New Mexico and stopped in Las Vegas to talk with my divorce attourney, and get my mail, and talk with doctors Ghosh and Kaster. Then on to Albuquerque to rent a small one bedroom furnished apartment until Bayloo joins me. She arrived November 23rd, Nancy having returned to Washington State to complete her recovery there.

On 10 December 1999 we moved into a two bedroom apartment 15 D, at Valle Grande Apts., 8401 Spain Road, NE in Albuquerque--$600.00 per month. I set up my computer and my word processor in the spare bedroom. We had to make two trips to Las Vegas in order to cart our rag-tag possessions to our apartment. Then, once settled in, we departed Albuquerque for the Northwest to spend the holiday season with our respective families. I spent a night at the home of the Dean Mikes (Bayloo's daughter, Cindy) in Missoula, and then a few days at the home of brother Phil and Dot. I then spent Christmas Eve alone--my custom of recent years. I finished up my poem for the North American Poetry Contest at a motel in Phillipsburg.

I then arrived at the farm of Duane and Georgia near Ephrata at mid-day of Christmas Day to talk and dine with them. In the evening we watched a movie and Duane and I talked until late. The following day I drove to Yakima and spent the night at Vic's place. The next day I loaded my gear from storage at Vic's place and drove to Portland to spend the remainder of the year with Pierre and family, and Jauhn and his family. Miette was about for a few days at that time. I have been a little uncomfortable about imposing upon her in recent years, and she apparently didn't have time to look me up. I would have gone over to see her, but her mother was hanging out with her. A mother that has brought me so much grief through so many years--and who continues to make me so much mischief--that I hope never to lay eyes upon her again.

RGB 1999

Y2K Summary
R. Garner Brasseur, MD

MILLENNIUM
BY
R. GARNER BRASSEUR

The new millennium soon shall be.
Pray tell me what you then foresee.
Expectantly this jaugernaught,
They say may change the world to naught.

Search the writs . . . the sky . . . within.
Consult the oracles . . . omens . . . Zen.
Plainly say what shall have been,
When soon we pass millennium.

Doubtful what magicians say,
I see a century pass away.
And standing with descendants tall,
Miette enshrined upon the wall.

Like mine their years shall transit fast.
And what has been, shall come to pass.
Offspring join ancestral halls,
Of bygone lives upon the wall.

Portraits frozen in past time,

Remind to distant kith and kind,
The legacy of those depart,
Who lent them useful thought and art.

Perhaps in silence and enlight,
We merely hope we led aright.
Upon the nature of reality,
That was, and is, an e'er shall be.

R.G.B.
27 Nov. 1997

I was retired and unemployed this year--but hoped yet to get free from the entanglements of divorce so as to find the economic separation that would make it worth my while to return to work. Her intention, I suppose, to continue her court authorized permission for economic punishment, regardless of its pointlessness--apart from her vindictive satisfaction.

I arrived in the Portland, Oregon area about the 27th of December in 1999 and spent a few day there, It happened that I was at Jauhn's place on New Year's Day. It being a nice day Jauhn, Mich, Joe-joe, Norg, Bobby, Daniel, and I played touch football in their front yard. The game ended when I strained my ankle--the first time in my life that I have had that problem. I spent the next day with Pierre and his family; and we also stopped in to see nephew Malcomb Brasseur and his girl friend. Malcomb seems to have made an amazing turn around this year. He has been sober, working regularly, and is even thinking of getting married.

On January 3rd I drove down to Reedsport with the hope of seeing Miette and her family. I took a motel room there and then stopped in to see them a while on the following day. We all napped in the afternoon. I then brought in a pizza for supper so that they could be gone early to a church meeting as I returned to my motel room. They all seemed to be happy and well.

The next morning I drove on to Medford. There I visited Bill and Idris White for a couple of hours, before driving over to see Real, Tina, and the kids. Quite a noisy bunch, and filled with antics and all sorts of enthusiasms. I slept there upon a mattress on the floor in Cowboy's room. I stayed there another two days before heading home. They are still making vague plans for buying the house that they are living in, though their progress in that direction seems very slow. My last night there, Tina was having a card party while Real, I, and the kids watched "Joan of Arc" on the video.

On Saturday the 9ᵗʰ, I watched Cowboy play a basketball game at a local school gym. I talked then briefly with Real and loaned him a thousand dollars to keep his bills paid so as not to ruin his credit rating if he planned to buy the house. About noon I headed out Hwy 140 through Klamath Falls, over the Albert Rim Fault into Nevada and on to Carson City. I located my old friend, Bob Brown at work in the emergency room at the Fallon Hospital and had a chance to talk with him about fifteen minutes before I retired to a motel. The following morning I headed south through Nevada and stopped over for the night at a casino motel just south of Boulder City. Yes, indulged myself with a big steak dinner and a plush bed in which I sank deeply into a death-like slumber. A rare deviation from my general rule of Spartan frugality. And I arrived home in Albuquerque the following evening.

On January 13ᵗʰ I straightened out the accounts between Bayloo and I in accordance with our pre-nuptial financial agreements. I re-initiated my daily walks of about two miles and continued them throughout the year. We immediately set up the computer and the word processor and I spend progressively more time with it each day. A lot about it required plenty of fumbling about before I got the knack of the various uses I may put it to. Bayloo seems to have the knack and patience for getting various programs on line and for the getting systems back on line as it was doing its frequent nose dives. Far to many nose dives. I finally decided to add more memory--an additional 64 Mb, bringing the total up to 80 Mb. It functioned more reliably after that.

Bayloo is working four-day shifts in Santa Fe. On her return trip from Montana in early January, she hit a deer and put some wrinkles into the fender and breaking the right headlight. I was able to install a new headlight on 14 January. She indicated that her car has been using a little oil and the clutch has had to be re-adjusted. With her car now 17 years old and her having to drive to work in Santa Fe, I suggested the possibility of getting her a replacement vehicle. So we looked at comparative costs and quality of cars in Kipplinger's Magazine, and then proceeded to check out some local used cars. Evaluating those costs suggests that the low to medium price cars cost $14,000.00 to $15,000.00 new. And that those selling such similar (but) used cars are asking prices that follow a consistent sort of pattern. The asking price is generally about $1,000.00 less per one year of age of the vehicle, regardless of the age. So, if on the average each car costs about $1,000.00 per year of usage, then we might just as well buy a brand new car to begin with, knowing that either a used or a new car is going to cost one the same $1,000.00 per year. Hence, we would seem to be well advised just to proceed to the purchase of a new car. And we did so. On 25 February we stopped at Garcia Motor on Central Ave., and picked out a new 2000 model Honda Civic four-door white auto with air conditioning, CD player/radio, electronic locks etc. at a cost of _____. As I was thinking of risking some capital into the venture stock market, I thought it might be wise first to invest some of that cash into the cost of the new car, so that even if I were to end up losing out at the pig-trough, I would have at least something to show for my money. And so, I put $5,000.00 of my cash into the down payment of the car. The remainder to be paid in monthly payments at 4.9% over three years.

I then proceeded on a program of stock investment by opening an account with Ameritrade.Com, and made my first stock purchase on-line on February 18th. For the past couple of months, and then upon an ongoing basis I was reading some books and magazine information in an effort to comprehend the basics of investing. But there seem to be various notions of how one should invest, and where. For the past couple years I had noticed that there were significant week-to-week variations in prices of some of the stocks. Volatile wide fluctuations that seemed to be ongoing already over several months. It seemed to me obvious that if a trend such as that were so regular and so ongoing for so long a time, one could just purchase a ticket and ride the ups and downs to one's financial advantage. Buy cheap, and sell dear--how tidy. And even while thus cycling up and down, some companies such as Intel and Microsoft seemed to have a general upward trend that historically progressed to "splits" such as to enhance their potential value. Still it was my intention to pick out a few stocks that seemed upward bound and ride them upward. But, as things happened, I ended up riding the gyrations of price change. However, just as I was getting invested in the Nasdaq tech-boom, the market experienced a minor crash and I was involved in buying and selling in order to try and make up for the 30% loss I had thus accumulated in March and April. I seemed to be doing fairly well at first and was a little euphoric with the action. In order to make it work the better, I was using progressively a large portion of "margin" loan funds. Of course, I was aware of that as being risky. But the market had just made a bit of a crash, and was now recovering. And so, I thought I might continue using this margin allowance for only yet a teensy little while in order to get a bit of a toehold of financial assets of my own. Then, I would back away from the risks of margin leverage and rely principally on my own enlarged nest egg. By mid-July I was holding stock purchase investments of up to nearly $120,000.00--though half of that was margin financed. Still, from my original total investment of just over $43,000.00, my equity was up to about $60,000.00 at times. And then (of course) the whole fabric of my financial hope began to fall apart--"all at once, and nothing first--just as bubbles do when they burst". I had been "saving at the spigot; wasting at the bung". But the net result of the bursting bubble was the same whether it came about all of sudden and all at once, or if it came about in slow motion.

Soon after I first entered the market on 2/18/2000, the Nasdaq reached an all time high of 5,048 on 3/10/2000, just as I was getting my purchases secured; and then reached a low of 2,350 in early January--a decline of 54%. [For a more complete discussion of this situation, see the section named Economic Reality, beginning on page 354 of my book, *"A Studied Impression of That Which Is".*]

RGB

Summary 2001
R. Garner Brasseur, MD

The (non-)settlement of my divorce proceedings goes on into eternity with no progress, or prospect for closure, though I met with my divorce attourney 1/3/2001; 5/1/2001; and 8/21/2001. We seemed to be snagged on getting a response from the PERA attys.

I had attained the ripe old age of 68--unlikely as that would have seemed six years ago. Because I lost all my right lower molar teeth with its bridgework in August of 2000, and because I was beginning to develop some problems with the left lower teeth, I had now to consider getting some dental care if I was to be able to keep on eating. I considered the possibility of getting some dental implants (right lower) which I already knew to be expensive. Before investing in that, it seemed prudent to get a thorough medical reevaluation to be certain that I was not harboring any residual evidence of cancer. I was seen by Dr. Morris of the UNM Oncology Department to be examined and get studies on 12 March; 3 April; 5 April; 4 May; and 10 May. There appeared to be no evidence of recurrence of cancer and my general health seemed to be good. And so I made arrangements for dental care, the first evaluation being 11 April. I had to have old crowns removed off three lower left and one upper left--at a cost of $2,648.00 above the $2,000.00 annual allowance of the Concordia Dental Insurance plan. For implant work, I was informed, it would cost me perhaps the equivalent of the cost of a new car--for three or four Titanium implant pegs and their subsequent chewing crowns. Quite pricy! And I have an income sufficient to only subsistence levels. The only way I could afford that would be to go back to work. Which, I may well have considered, as (in discussion with my atty.) there is a problem about getting a retirement income for Bayloo from PERA (after my eventual demise). The atty. proposed to put forth a motion to permit me to work enough to provide my wife an annuity without having to share (with my ex-spouse) the income I would need to earn to accomplish that. The cost of that annuity would be considerable--perhaps(?) something like $150,000.00 to $200,000.00 over a couple of years. Nothing very magical about that if one can get something approximating 7% with an I-bond. We were still awaiting information from PERA before the atty. could actually propose any such motion to the court. Thus, you see, two big reasons that I might at least have given consideration to the possibility of going back to work.

I had some preliminary contact with BIA to inquire into the possibility of working a government job on one of the Indian reservations in the Dakotas, Montana, or New Mexico. I would have to submit application and await developments on that matter.

Meanwhile, I had to take three post-graduate education courses that year. I took the courses 21 April; 2 May; and(?). And I also had to pay out cash for license renewal fees to NM, to WA, and to ND. I finally decided to let my Idaho medical license lapse because they were now applying a totalitarian requirement of necessary sworn statements that is far too repressive to suit my sensibilities.

On 13 March I began to go through the usual agony of compiling information for filing my tax returns. I met with CPA Johns, in Las Vegas on 13 April, 19 April, and 1 May before finally getting those done about August 19th. The whole process was very complex and difficult as I had to submit long lists of information about the disastrous stock trades I made in year 2000. I also had to send in corrected tax reports to both State and Federal for 1998 and 1999. The CPA bill was pricy.

But, we received NM tax refund of $312.00 for 1998; $624.00 for 1999; and $1,846.00 for year 2000. And we got a $600.00 tax relief refund from the IRS. And on November 19th, a federal tax refund of $1,600.00.

Throughout the year I had was preoccupied with reworking my manuscript, "A Studied Impression of That Which Is". Its second section, ("Old Lamps and New light") I completed in mid-February, intending to send out copies to various relatives soon thereafter. It was the heart of my thesis, and I wished to be sure to get it distributed before giving up my ghost. And yet, in mid-May, I made a tentative completion of the whole manuscript and subsequently distributed another 13 copies (lists in these journal books). I am yet working now to complete still another section of this slowly growing manuscript which I hope to bring to completion by this year's end. None of it is apt to be well received by my few select readers for my writing skills are yet in need improvement, the subject is complex, and the material will not likely be well received as it opposes the prevailing outlook.

I wrote a couple of brief letters to keep in contact with grandson, Cauxby Brasseur, this year.

I have seen and graded 46 movies this year, and have completed the reading of 29 books.

Bayloo's friend, Nancy Leigh, was out to visit twice this year, in conjunction with the follow-up care and evaluation subsequent to treatment for squamous cell carcinoma of the base of the tongue. It began to appear that it was going to have been cured.

I made four major trips in 2001:

1--11 May through 29 June
2--13 July through 10 August
3--10 September through 24 October
4--26 November through 28 December

The above said third trip, I have recently summarized into a 21 page manuscript ("Travel and Visitations; the Summer of 2001") I sent its sections out by e-mail to many friends and relatives. I have given hard copy of it Duane, Vic, Phil, and Jauhn.

The first trip was taken to attend the graduation ceremony of Cindy (Scott) Mikes from Pharmacy School in Missoula on 19 May. Bayloo drove up into eastern Montana to visit her friends and relatives before that date. I drove up separately in the pickup, taking a western route to enable me to visit my own friends and relatives. She and I met in Missoula and hung about there for a couple of days. On that trip, I visited Duane, Vic, Phil, The Mikes, and Adams family, Pierre, Jauhn, Real, Miette, Jerry and Anita Fisher, Karen and Doby Bassuer, Tom and Barbara, Larry Otis, and Raymond Horton. On the return trip I visited Garberville, California and Soquel, California, looking for genealogy information--but didn't actually discover any.

Son, Real, was married on June 30,2001 to Catheryn Anne Conant nee Crenshaw at Jacksonville, Oregon. This was the second marriage for both of them. She and Real have one child born 28 December 2000 in Medford,(Clair Noel Hope). Cathern has three previous children, Rachel (b. 4 Dec. 1990), Brianna (b. 19 Oct. 1993), and Chad (b. 1 Sept. 1995). I was unable to attend the wedding. On that day, Bayloo and I were visiting her friends, Marilyn and Bernie, in Taos.

My second trip was 13 July through 10 August. I had previously informed Pierre and Tina/Real that I was to attend the Germans from Russia Heritage Convention in Pierre, SD. They were agreeable and so I was able to take both Fancois and Xavier with me on that trip. I drove up to Medford where I picked them up. We tented as we drove along across southern Oregon, southern Idaho, northern Wyoming, and into South Dakota. We enjoyed perfect traveling weather. At the genealogy convention, we took a motel room where the boys got their fill of indoor swimming and playing cards. We all took a few dance lessons and attended a dance in the evening. Upon departing Pierre, SD, we drove up into North Dakota, where we visited the grave sites of my Boepple grandparents in Beulah; and my Brasseur grandparents, in Dunseith. We visited cousin Elmer Neuberger in Beulah, an old classmate, Don Richard in Bottineau, and old classmate, Dick Morgan, in Falkirk, ND. We camped out with the mosquitoes at Lake Metagoshe, at Lake Sacajawea, and in the Badlands of western ND. We visited Bill Huft in Fairview, and Belinda Larson in Sidney, Montana, as well as sisters Skippy and Kate in Terry, Montana. We stopped over in Miles City, Montana to visit with Steve Kransky and spend the night at Harold's place. In Billings, we stopped to visit Carl Eaton and go through some of Aloha's old collection of photographs. In western Montana, not far from Superior we stopped to visit with one of Phil's friends, Kenton Lewis at their little religious commune, "The Heavenly Fold", and he put us up for the night. En route back to Oregon, we then stopped a night at Phil's place, a night at Duane's place and a night at Vic's place. I dropped the boys off at Portland where we visited with Jauhn's and Pierre's families. I then drove up into western Washington when I stopped to visit nephew Andre, his wife Gretchen, and their six children. There I ran into Vic's family (Marg and Yvette) Brasseur, as well as young Garner's wife (Krista) and my niece, Adrienne (Andre's sister), I then visited with my sister Ookie at Marysville and spent a night or two at her place. From there, I drove to nearby Monroe, Washington to visit Gerhardt and Tillie Saur, who live with their daughter Glenna and Eddie Skartvet. As fate would have it, Ervin Gaetz and Christine were also visiting there, and I even got to see Julie, Judy, and Jolyn Gaetz. (It was my impression that Tillie was probably near death at that time, and upon my return to Albuquerque, I discovered that she had died.) I drove over to Yelm to visit old classmate, Grant Mosby, and spent the night at his place before returning to the Portland area the following day. There I had a visit with Ookie's son, Mark Krahn. He, his wife Shelly and their six children were visiting at Jauhn's place. Their children are Sarah, Eliz, Anna, Esther, Johannes, and Joshua. Mark and I had a chance to talk as we took a bit of a walk together. I stopped again a couple days in the Medford area. *I a*lso had a visit with Larry Otis in Grants Pass. We discussed my book and the Philosophy subject. We also discussed possible plans for driving together through Central America to Panama in the coming January. En route home I again traveled across the "Winnemucca to the Sea Highway" and across northern Nevada into Utah, to arrive home 10 August 2001.

Concerning my third trip, which occupied me 10 Sept. through 24 Oct., see my travelogue, "Travel and Visitations; the Summer of 2001". That trip was devoted to genealogy research and that search was fairly productive. The month between that trip and next was occupied in updating my genealogy and in writing the travelogue.

My fourth and final trip of 2001 was 26 Nov. through 28 Dec. Bayloo had three weeks off and was to return to work by 19 Dec. I thought I might ride with her into eastern and western Montana, and then take the bus to Spokane where I might borrow one of Phil's cars, to visit my relatives in Washington and Oregon. But Bayloo had plans for spending so much time in eastern Montana that it would cut me far too short of time. Hence, I left several days before her departure. I drove through Flagstaff to Page, and encountered rather severe weather. It was too cold to sleep in the pickup, so I had to take inexpensive sleeping quarters in Kanab and again in Ely. I tried to contact an old high school classmate, Grant Mosby, in St George, Utah, but he was not around. That trip took me through Medford, to Grants Pass, to Portland, to western and eastern Washington through Yakima and back through Portland and down the coast on 101, into California, through San Francisco, and Atascadero; through Los Angeles and then eastward on Hwy 8 and 10 to Deming, through Hatch, and then via Hwy 25 to my home in Albuquerque.

I visited at Real's place a couple days and also stopped in to visit Tina. I saw all of their youngsters, but only briefly. In the Portland area, I had a chance to play touch football with all of the Portland area grandchildren a couple times--once on each passage through the area. Even the smaller ones play quite well, so that though I got a lot of running in, I did not often see the ball. It was a great time. Michah had gotten too fast for anyone to catch up with on the open flats. He is in his second year of college courses at a small Junior College near their home and is doing very well. He is looking about for scholarships in various universities as he will have to transfer in the coming year to continue his preparatory studies for entrance into a medical school. The rest of Jauhn and Massey's kids are continuing their schooling at home. They are all getting some music training and are active in various sports. Jauhn does some coaching in his spare time. He also carries 9 credits of college courses in Geology and Archeology while still working half time with Intel. When finished, he may eventually leave Intel to work in Archeology.

Pierre is working full time at Intel. Jackie comes in each day to put some order into the household. I talked a bit with each of them. Perhaps they will yet get married, but there seems to be some reservation on that in the mind of each of them. There were a few get-togethers of Jauhn and Pierre's families that included Jackie so I gather that Jauhn's previous reservations about the possibility of that leading to matrimony has now somewhat relented. I saw Miette only once and briefly when she and her mother were in town on my first passage through Portland at Jauhn's place. She and her mother are so often in one another's company that there is rarely an opportunity for me to see her in the past few years. Nor has she ever invited me to her home, though I have dropped in to visit them on several occasions and even stayed a night on a few occasions. It is obvious that we are worlds apart, nor is there any evidence of a softening of her attitude towards me. But then, what does she need me for, at this time in her life? Naturally, I love her well, but I have no enthusiasm for the thawing of our relationship unless and until there is some evidence of reciprocity between us. Nor will I accept any "forgiveness" for the managing of my personal affairs as I deem necessary (for whatever reason I have owned). Nor will I have any interaction whatever with her mother, unless or until she finally gives up her course of legal harassment and bothering my economic life.

Real and Miette seem to have formed somewhat of a bond in the past couple of years, with Real, Catheryn, and kids occasionally visiting at Miette's place on a long weekend. I hear that Miette and Bart have recently purchased a home in Reedsport. He still works at contracting odd jobs there. And so far as I know, is still trying to establish his own congregation. I wish him better luck with his followers than I have ever had with mine.

I am relieved to note that Real seems currently to be quite content in his new marriage, for he appeared previously to be rather depressed over the past several years. I like Catherine and her previous three children. My limited observations suggest that she is congenial and has a pleasant disposition. But I am not yet well enough acquainted with her to have come to any firm conclusions. The two of them are in economic straits in consequence of their divorces, but few divorced persons can avoid that. Both are still working as elementary teachers in the Medford Public Schools System and I look for that to continue. Trouble comes when these churchy people start getting overly involved in their goody two-shoes of fundamentalist religion.

I stopped to visit with Tina whenever I was through Medford. She had full custody of Real's kids just a Catherine's ex-spouse had full custody of her previous children. Tina also got remarried this past summer to Perry Miller, and they bought a big house on Diamond Street in Medford. Perry works with the Postal Service at Grants Pass and has two teen-age children, Danny and _____, who live with them. Nine children in that busy household.

In Hillsboro I usually stopped to see Rochelle who lived in her own apartment; the kids going to her place every other weekend? On my third trip through, she came over to Pierre's place and started a row with him, seeming to try to get me involved in that. It was my impression that she is much belatedly having second thoughts about her separation from Pierre, as her share of "community property" assets stock also took a great nose-dive this past year and her prospects for funds throughout life are much diminished. I believe she was under the influence of alcohol on that occasion, which bodes ill for her future as she is said to have had an alcohol problem earlier in her life.

The End 2001
RGB

2002 Summary
R. Garner Brasseur, MD

I arrived home from the Northwest on 28 Dec. 2001 and found myself at home as the new year commenced. I was preoccupied with the reworking of my manuscript of *"A Studied Impression of That Which Is"*. In fact, that project has occupied most of my time and attention while at home throughout this year also.

I have continued to enjoy good health the entire year. I continued throughout my life to be vexed by chronic nasal and intermittent sinus congestion, and have continued my use of Actifed to a half tablet, twice daily so that the nasal congestion does not interfere with my sleep. I also occasionally use Beconase (a steroid) nasal spray. I don't believe I have actually had a headache all year. It may be that my hearing is slightly diminished, though that is uncertain. I do find myself straining to hear at the slightly lower volumes that Bayloo prefers.

In years past I have had intermittent episodes of acute apnea caused by spasm of the vocal chords and which resulted from reflux of gastric material into the esophagus. But this year, no such episodes at all--and only one or two the previous year. Neither do I have heartburn. I have no problem with constipation in the past year, though I have had some such occasional spells in past years. I drink plenty of water and I usually have an apple each day. I also usually have a few graham crackers with honey each day. I am sure that those things contribute to my regularity, but one's digestive system runs on "autonomic", so that it doesn't communicate much of its goings on to one's intellect. The past few years I have had to get along without molars in my right lower jaw. That would cost me about $12,000.00 more of less. Beyond my means. I suppose I ought to go in and see if I could be fitted with a partial denture.

I have an occasional night or string of nights in which I am troubled with "restless leg syndrome"--seemingly a bit more intense in the right than in the left leg. One or two mg. of Ativan relieves that. If I don't take it (or Halcyon) it keeps me awake for unpleasant hours. And there are spells when recurrent thoughts or concerns will keep me awake until the last hour before arising. The Halcyon resolves that problem, but if the episodes of insomnia are repetitious night after night, for more than three or four nights, I will sometime use 125 mg. of Doriden in its place for a couple nights. These spells of insomnia do not often occupy more than 5 or 6 nights in sequence and I have only had such strings of sleeplessness perhaps 4 or 6 times in the past year. Perhaps two or three times that many occasions of a single night of insomnia. It seems to me that the insomnia episodes are generally related to such times as I am spending myself in heavy thought, on writing essays, or reworking manuscript.

I walk two miles or more per day, though I sometimes miss that exercise when I am traveling long miles. In Portland I commonly get involved in playing basketball, football, tennis, or soccer with grandchildren. My joints seem yet limber and I remain fairly agile. I have no tremor, except an occasional transient tremor of a few minutes in one hand or another when I am tired. In the past couple years I do have some seemingly progressive discomfort in the left sacroiliac joint. Seemingly a mild form of arthritis--a common ailment. The discomfort of it affects my posture for a couple of minutes after I arise from a slumping position of sitting on a couch for example. I can avoid this happening by keeping my weight shifted on the opposite buttock while I sit. I take 200 mg. ibuprofen 3 or 4 times daily to keep the discomfort and inflammatory component minimalized

I have a bit of slowly progressing narrowing of stream from prostatism over the past 6 to 8 years. Pretty much the norm as a fellow advances in years. I sometimes get up in the night to relieve myself. On rare occasion, may get up 2 or 3 times, as when I am cold. For several years I have been taking Saw Palmetto in lieu of any more definitive hope of retarding the process of prostatic enlargement. In the past year of more, I have taken to also using one mg. daily of Cardura, to facilitate emptying and reduce hesitation. Medical check up last May revealed that my PSA titer was up just a smidgen, at 4.1.

I am hyperopic and presbyopic with also rather high astigmatism and I wear bifocal glasses since my mid-forties. My allergies occasionally cause me spells of ocular irritation.

For many years now I have been taking Propranolol 40 mg. twice daily and Capoten 6.5 mg daily for control of blood pressure and account of a long tendency toward tachycardia of about 80-84 per minute (even though I have been active all my life and even jogged regularly until six years ago). Walk rather than jog, as I am getting older. Currently on meds, my blood pressure tends to run about 129/80 and pulse at 68 to 70.

I have a past history of eczema as a child and I have a chronic dry skin problem with very poor sweating of hands--am probably a carrier (one gene for) of cystic fibrosis. In the dryness of winter there is a tendency of the skin (especially at the tips and sides of the thumb about the nails) to fissure, and also at the heels of my feet at the edges of the soles. And the skin of my hands, forearms, feet and legs is chronically dry, so that I do best by keeping the skin of these areas lubricated with vasoline.

I easily gain weight, and the more so when I travel and visit among friends and relatives where I am often overly fed. My weight has been as high as high as 192 pounds this summer. When at home I limit myself to one main meal daily--in the early evening. For breakfast, a slice of banana bread and part of a banana. For lunch, an apple. Through the day and evening I often snack on a set of two graham crackers with honey on them. Watching my diet thusly, I am now again after two months, back down to 171 pounds.

I have read only about twenty books this year, in addition to those I study as I do my writing projects. And once every two or three weeks I spend four or five hours at the city library to peruse journals such as Scientific American, Science News, Popular Mechanics, the Humanist, US News and Business Report, Time, Discover, and National Geographic. When I visit at Duane's place I spend a large part of my time reading his accumulated magazines such as the Libertarian, Chronicles, some economic letters, and Time. Also at Phil's place I review his accumulated stack of news magazines. At Vic's place I often read a book or two that he has on his shelf.

At home in the evenings, I usually watch 4-6 hours of TV during the week--News, various interesting PBS specials, Seinfeld, Cheers, All in the Family, Spin City, and BBC news. On Sundays I often watch part of a couple football games. And then, I am usually up until 2:30 or 3:30 AM working on manuscript and reading.

This was the first year in the past ten or twelve that I have not made a genealogy trip to New England and New France.

My sister, Skippy, (22 months older than I) passed away at age 70, on 23 January in Terry, Montana. She had been bed-ridden with multiple sclerosis the previous ten or fifteen years. On the 24th, I traveled alone in the pickup to be with family in Terry at the time of her funeral. I stayed a couple nights at their place. From there, I drove on into Washington and Oregon to visit my family--and then with friends in California, before returning home on 14 February. I then spent some time making job application and watching the web for possible employment. Bayloo was gone every other week to her job in Santa Fe.

I attended post-graduate education courses two days in March, one day in April, three days in May, and one day in October.

In response to a call from Pierre in April, I headed towards Portland on April 14th after finishing and mailing in my IRS tax report. Pierre was having legal problems with divorce and issues of custody of the children. He wanted me about to give testimony if needed--though I can't conceive that the court would be much impressed that a father would have fine things to say about his son. En route, I again burned out a generator and had to get it replaced in Medford. While in Portland, I stayed part time at Pierre's place and part time at Jauhn's place. And I spent a couple days repairing a few pieces of furniture at Jauhn's place. Of course, it all gave me some couple weeks to spend time with the grandchildren. I got back home April 30th.

In May I reported to UNM to get a follow-up CAT scan and other tests subsequent to the liver cancer problem of 1996. Reports were all negative.

I finally completed the 4th draft of my manuscript May 15th, before again heading out on May 16th to be with Pierre at the continuation of his divorce legal problems. I spent a day with Real in Medford. Then arrived in Portland and again had opportunity to spend some time with the grandchildren. I had the chance to walk and talk alone with Jessica about forty five minutes one evening. I even got to see Miette and her two children briefly one day as they stopped over one night with Jauhn. On May 28th, I drove up to Marysville, Washington and spent a couple nights with sister Ookie. I had supper with nephew Andre, Gretchen, and their family in Everett; and niece Yvette and nephew Tom where there. The following day I looked up nephew Garner and Kristain in rural Bellingham, and stayed over with them after going out to supper. He is gone a week at a time at his flying Job in Alaska. I had a nice talk with Garner as I tried to figure out his slant on life and philosophy there in Sudden Valley, not far from Bellingham. From there, I went on to visit brother Vic in Yakima. After three nights there, I drove out to visit Duane on the farm and spend three nights with them before moving on to Spokane to yet another three nights at Phil's place. And then I returned once more to Portland area for a couple nights before heading south on June 11th, stopping one night at Real's place and the following day and night at the home of long time friend Raymond Horton in Redding. Then across Nevada and arrived home June 14th. Bev Susag and her granddaughter Angie were visiting with Bayloo from Missoula. The following day, brother Vic arrived from Yakima. He and I visited, drove about locally, and looked at some real estate, as he was considering the possibility of moving down here to Albuquerque. He departed June 25th.

July 20th. I began work on a summary essay concerning the economic realities of the stock Market game in light of my past three miserable years of experience with it. I finished it and sent out e-mail copy to relative and friends. July 30th I began an essay on Zionism, to be added to my next edition (draft) of "That Which Is" manuscript.

On August 2nd, I headed up to Medford and arrived after thirty hours of driving and a couple spells of brief rest in the pickup at rest areas along the way. I stayed the night at Tina's place and on Sunday the 4th, Poco, Cui, and I headed east for the German convention in Bismarck, tenting and picnicking along our way with great economy. We spent three nights at the Raddison Motel where I attended a couple lectures and used the research room for my study of genealogy. I found very little additional Boepple genealogy material from that research. I have not now done much genealogy work in the past year.

After the GRHS convention, we stopped over to see Dick Morgan at Falkirk, ND before visiting the graves of the ancestors first in Beulah and then in Dunseith. Then, en route westward, I dropped off the grandsons at the Saur Reunion Camp near Red Lodge after we first toured Yellowstone National Park. We also visited sister Kate and brother-in-law Ed Ban in Terry, Montana. There the boys pitched their tent and slept in Kate's back yard. We also dropped in to visit Harold Kransky, Steve, and Steve's two girls.

Bam-bam had a bad hand infection for which he was hospitalized a few days in Helena while Pierre and the rest of his family attended the Saur Reunion. Pierre and family stopped by briefly while I was visiting Phil and Dot in Spokane on August 18th. I was then back again to the Portland area through the 27th. I helped Boo work on the fence repair about the house and spent some time with the other grandchildren. Then, again I drove up north to visit with sister Ookie on her birthday and take her out for a hamburger and an ice cream. Stopped by again one evening to see Andre's family. And then spent another four nights at Vic's place before again stopping another three nights visiting Duane at the farm. He has been troubled the past year with some vague arthritic symptoms subsequent to a bout of shingles, but he appears now to be feeling and looking better. He preoccupies his time working on equipment and following his investments in the penny stocks.

I then spent another few days in Portland with the grandchildren before once more passing through Spokane and heading toward the 50th class reunion in Miles City. I stopped over to spend the night with Roxie and Jody (the daughters of sister Kate), who have just moved into a nice little house being purchased now by Jody, who works there in Hardin as a teacher. Roxy lives with her and works there doing accounts in the local hospital. The next morning (12 September) I toured Custer Battlefield before driving on into Miles City. I met and visited with many old friends and acquaintances, and left some copy of some of my manuscript writings with several members of the class--including a couple of them in the ministry. Knowing of course that if they get around to perusing the material they will be a bit irritated by the substance of my comments on the OT and NT historical details. But, it will be good for them to be aware that there are other views on history and religion than their own biased and self serving views.

Raymond Horton was also at the reunion--having recently had cataract surgery on his one good eye. But I didn't see much of him before he departed early to visit his family in South Dakota. The morning of my departure, I saw Dennis Blunt--badly crippled and perched awkwardly in a big wheelchair, subsequent to surgery for dissecting aortic artery problem. I also talked a bit with B.J. Dawson and Helen Raymond. And then on that 15th day of September, I headed south through Broadus and Wyoming to arrive home the morning of the 16th, to settle in for a couple more months of revising my manuscript. Finally, on the second of November, I printed off a copy and sent it in to Vantage Publishing Inc. of New York, to learn if they might think it worth printing. No word on that yet when I departed for the Northwest again for the remainder of the year on December 4th.

I responded to a copy of a letter for Atty. Schwarz which had been sent to my atty the 17th of September. On October 28th, I again met with my atty in Las Vegas, trying to get him to expedite progress on the settling of my divorce (now in its seventh year with Him!). Before I headed out after Thanksgiving, I called the office of the atty. and got word that the divorce re-hearing might be(?) in about Mid-January?

Lew and Carla Schroeber visited with us September 20th, through the 24th. One day we toured Salinas National Monument. Another day, we visited and hiked in Tent Rock State Monument.

October 13th, Bayloo fell going doing down the stairs at work. She suffered a compound comminuted fracture of the tibia and fibula just above the left ankle. It would appear that she first badly sprained the right ankle and then fell to sustain the fracture. She was carted off to the hospital in an ambulance and under general anesthesia, the tissues were cleaned and plates and screws set across the fracture sites to maintain position and stability. I brought her home the 15th, and she was then on crutches, but without a cast. I drove her out to her intermittent doctor's appointments for follow-up of the very slowly healing fractures. A month later she was able to drive herself. It seems that she first learned this year that she has osteoporosis--which, presumably, contributed to the fracture and is related to the retarded healing process. She is supposed to be on an especially potent bone building calcium supplement--Fuosimide--but she says it gives her heartburn. An so she has switched to some other related medication which is not nearly as highly recommended.

Actually, on the day of her injury, I was logged in to a web site and therefore the call concerning her injury did not get through to me for three of four hours. When I arrived the hospital about 10:00 PM, she was just getting out of the recovery room. While at the hospital, someone broke into the rear of my pickup and carted off my little bag of tools. Can you imagine anyone taking the risk and the trouble for so little gain? I parked the pickup near the place of her employment and drove her car home for safe keeping.

And so, Bayloo has not worked now for the past two and a half months, and it looks like she may not get back to work for yet a couple more months. However, as the injury is "industrial" and insured, she gets workmen's compensation pay and the medical expenses are covered by insurance. She is able to take care of the household chores. I usually make the bed and sometimes haul out the garbage as my token of contribution to the running of the household--and try mainly to stay out from under foot.

She, Carla, and Lew flew out to Arruba the 29th of November to spend a couple of weeks with Bayloo's daughter, Kim and Wes Mikes. I did not feel comfortable about imposing myself on anyone for that long and so I chose rather to make another trip to the Northwest to visit friends and family. Before departing however, I spent three or four days of intense effort to complete a new draft of my book. Then I made a double-spaced copy to send in to Vantage Press in New York, to be considered for publication. That done, I loaded my gear into the pickup and headed out alone December 4th.

I was a bit reluctant to make the trip, because I had had a falling out with Real subsequent to a nasty e-mail note he sent me on October 15th. He had berated me with allegations of harassment and economic warfare against his mother. I? . . . harassing her? Who was intruding on whose life and livelihood, after all? Real's perceptions, of course, without having taken the trouble to actually inquire into the facts and details. His ire apparently having been inflamed by the uninformed and slanted whinings of his mother. Cockamamie complaints and allegations of the nature of hearsay. In reading between the lines of Real's diatribe, it seemed apparent to me that she has been pouring her tales of woe out upon all of the children. And I further gathered, that as they would get together in various small and larger gatherings, they discussed these alleged issues based on the one-sided (mis-)information from her petulant fantasies. I get the vague impression that they seem gradually to have come to a sort of informal judgment against me. I am tempted to suspect that the contents of Real's nasty note of condemnation to me, was actually an unofficial expression which represents a sort of collective input from them all. Thus did I have a certain reluctance about my usual custom of dropping by to see them one by one. Concerning this problem, Real sent me two long notes; and I sent him two long notes of rebuttal. I dealt harshly with him but not abusively. Perhaps I may even have cast some shadow of doubt upon the bogus certainties within his biased mind? And I indicated that I was trying to think of any reason I might have for ever again looking him up. Not at least until or unless he were to take the time and trouble to disabuse himself of some of his self imposed error and self-righteousness.

In finally deciding to continue with my plans for a trip into the Northwest, it seemed most likely to me that Real had fully shared his mischievous letters and my rebuttals with all of his siblings, and that they had all thus shared in their ill-informed opinions much as they had all had their share in the ill-formed accusations and judgments against me. All of this, without my having actually had to confront any but Real. And so, as I pass among them--avoiding Real--I must only be watchful of the temperature of cordiality and adjust my interactions and length of stay accordingly. Even were they all to prove themselves too cool for my domestic comfort, yet, I have siblings, friends, and acquaintances with whom I can pass away my time in the great Northwest.

Miette and Pierre have already made themselves at least slightly cool and distant in the past few years. And I recognize that all of this family junk is basically of the nature of a religious war. I doubt that they themselves have yet fully arrived at that conclusion.

But why fret? Perhaps something good may yet evolve from all this ado. And, after all, I never had it in mind to raise my children and keep them in servitude to my notions and affections. My job was to raise and nurture them along into their adult years of full citizenship, from which point I had hopes of them being able to support themselves, raise their own families, and come to their own conclusions concerning things known and unknown. Of course I had and still maintain hope of their being able to discern reality and coming to accurate conclusions. If we are not interested in the possibility of accurate conclusions, then we might as well spare ourselves a lot of fuss and concern and be content with coming to our point of view by the flipping of a coin at each junction of our diagnostic comprehension.

They all survived into adulthood, Now let us see if they will ever display the wit, and the courage; and find the time and determination--the interest--to plumb the depths of philosophy in quest of what is probable and what is knowable. I have made mistakes; and it is inevitable that they do so also . . . and shall. Not much for me to do but to strenuously pursue my own quests. And stay out from under foot while they learn (or fail to learn) from hard reality and their own offspring.

Meanwhile, after my return from the class reunion, I hustled about with determination to make corrections and alterations upon my manuscript. And then printed it out in double spaced lines for review for possible publication. On November 2nd, I sent it in to Vantage Publishers in New York. At years end, I was still waiting to hear from them.

I have spent a goodly amount of time the past year in searching about the web for leads to possible employment, thinking that I might give up the rigors of retirement if I could find work that paid me enough to make it worth my while. That is to say, if there would be any significant expendable cash remaining to me after all of the state tax, federal tax, FICA, alimony, etc. And there still seems at least slight hope that a judicial decision or a settlement might make that option viable by setting me free from the grasping clutches of a vindictive ex-wife. The other problem however, is the reality that there are plenty of reasons that state, federal, and private employment possibilities are more or less closed to the elderly. This, despite well known laws intended to curb all forms of discrimination for job openings. Not wanting to employ the elderly, the potential employers simply come up with other reason for eliminating the elderly by specifying qualifications that the elderly physician can not meet. Hasn't had a recent residency (despite already having worked in the field); hasn't worked in the past two or three years; insurance premiums for the old doctor would be to formidable; not enough hair on his pate; etc. What seems a lead to a possible job does turn up occasionally, to fire one's hope, only to evaporate like a mirage as one approaches to inquire further.

My pickup truck is aging and I may have to think about finding a replacement for it if I am to continue my travels. The odometer is no longer functioning, having quit at mile 324,000 or thereabouts on the day after 9-11-02. I estimate that by this time, I have about 365,000 miles on it. I faithfully change the engine oil and filter regularly. And the engine runs well, giving me somewhere about 32 miles per gallon. The alternator needed to be replaced in April. In August, I had to get a new set of tires. Not long after that, it began to seem clear that my clutch was slipping and it seemed inevitable that that was going to cost me another $600.00 to $1,000.00, so I put it off. And still, I nursed it along, finally having to stop over at the farm a few days including Christmas, to get Duane's mechanic to replace the badly worn clutch plate. He did the job charging me only $25.00 per hour--the full cost coming to only $351.33. He tells me that I was within a whisker of ruining the differential and burning up the rig, as the transmission seal had failed and leaked out most of the grease. Since then, the pickup has continued to run just fine. Who knows, perhaps it will last another year of two. Perhaps it will out-last me.

In any case, my last trip of the year began 4 December and I did not return home until early in the new year. My stops and visits along the way with Raymond Horton in Redding, Tina and Real's kids, Larry Otis, Pierre's family, Jauhn's family, Jean Bertholate in Belview, Ookie, Andre's family, Jerry and Anita Fisher, back with Jauhn's and Pierre's families, with Duane and Georgia, and Tom and Barbara. Then with Phil and Dot in Spokane and once again to Fisher's Place in Vancouver, where I also has a nice visit with their son, Richard Fisher. Then once again to the homes of Pierre and Jauhn briefly, one more night at Tina's place, two nights at Raymond's place, and finally a stay of two night in El Centro to visit Lynn Fitz. I also saw Miette and her two sons on December 18th when I stayed over at Jauhn's place.

Thus has passed another busy year of retirement. I strive to maintain connections with my many family members and old friends and acquaintances through personal visits and by e-mail. An still maintain my journals and work at writing projects.

RGB

Journal Summary 2003
R. Garner Brasseur, MD

I arrived home to the apartment in Albuquerque the 7th of January. I was still pursuing the declining possibility of returning at least to part time practice of medicine. Towards that end I have been keeping up with post-graduate education requirement hours and maintaining registration of medical licensure in New Mexico, North Dakota, and Washington. And have been scanning employment sites on the internet as well as investigating directly into various employment possibilities as I travel. It being close to a year since I applied to Bureau of Prisons concerning job openings, I was rather surprised to get a call from them on January 9th and discover that I am the only applicant to a job opening for one of their facilities in West Virginia. Being agreeable to that possibility, they sent me a packet of forms to complete and return to them. They would need to have thoroughly investigated my background and scrutinized me for reasons of security. And I would need to prove physically capable as well as mentally alert to be of service. I completed the forms. In mid-February I drove to the Altoona, Texas prison site for interview. A few weeks later I was informed that I had not been selected to fill the available vacancy--though I was the only applicant. The reality seems to be that the BOP and other governmental agencies needs must "consider" my application and process my information even though they full well know that they are not going to hire me. Unless they go through the motions of pretending to give serious consideration to my application, they could be leaving themselves open to the charge of discrimination in their hiring practices. And they might thus be leaving themselves open to a devastatingly expensive civil rights violation suite. It turned out that they have an informal code (as explained to me by brother Vic) that actually prohibits me being hired unless able to work enough years to eventually have earned some retirement benefits from the agency. Thus, they must process my application etc. to be sure that they find something (either by objective scrutiny or subjective testing) that will somehow disqualify the applicant they do not wish to hire (on the basis of their unstated informal code) for some cause or pretext based upon firmly stated and written criteria. So much for the possibility of getting employment in government work.

In the course of the year my search for employment has also demonstrated to me that there is essentially also no possibility of my being hired into any of the private practice openings. For any such group as might otherwise wish to hire me would be prohibited from doing so by the prohibitively enormous premium price for malpractice insurance on a physician of my age who has not recently practiced in more than a year or two, and who has not maintained board certification status. Though I might buy my own insurance to protect myself and that private group against malpractice claims, the cost would be such as to largely nullify any earning I might hope to glean. And so the idea of my returning to the practice of medicine goes by the board. And toward the end of the year, I got an e-mail message from a woman employed as a physician recruiter in Washington State, in which she specifically (informally) indicates (and becries the fact) that many physicians in my precise situation are thus disbarred from returning to practice.

Bayloo having broken her right ankle the past November, and unable to return yet to work in a BOP contracted halfway house for juveniles, was encouraged by her former IYC employer to reside in Santa Fe, and take two or three of their young wards into our home to be under her care and guidance. The pay to her would make it quite worthwhile. And so, Bayloo took some of her retirement funds to purchase a nice three bedroom house in Santa Fe. The 27th of February, we moved into the place. Nancy Leigh, from Washington State flew in to help us with the moving. I parted with the remainder of my 33 1/3 speed record collection finally, as it was too burdensome to haul about; and it isn't likely I would ever be in a situation to find either the time or the equipment to listen to those records again. Moving always entails this process of sorting and culling through the beloved articles of yesteryears. We now live just outside the city limits and not far from the airport of Santa Fe. A nine hole fenced-in golf course is two or three blocks distant and I have made it my habit to take my daily walk two miles or more along its fence line. On my hike, I pick up stray golf balls which I bring home to toss into my growing collection in the back yard. As I do not golf, I have no use for them--just something to have, and the small thrill of finding each one hidden away in some unique spot. Like hunting Easter eggs. My walks are mostly solitary, as one or the other of us is generally required to be with the foster children in the home.

On the 23rd of March, the 19 year old Heather Yazee and her two or three day old Angel, moved in with us. She is a Navajo Indian under now the care and guidance of Bayloo through the IYC.

On April 1st, Chelsea Montewine moved into the third bedroom of the house. She is a 16 year old Native American Indian girl of Ute and Pueblo extraction, from Nambe (between Santa Fe and Espanola). The two girls are doing GED schooling and are integrated into the IYC program of counseling, working at part time jobs, and intermingling with the integrated goings on of the half dozen group homes and private foster homes of the IYC program, which in turn is overseen and policed by the BOP. Both girls are in parole programs which hope to place them back into society as private citizens once they are self-disciplined, trained, and organized enough to have some hope of being able to manage their own personal lives. If they do not comply with the strict overseeing and training program, they are subject to a prolonging of their length and terms of parole, and relocation to jail or to housing arrangements that are more harsh and unforgiving than the relative ease they enjoy in our private household.

In point of fact, I rather enjoy having these three young people around. Bayloo keeps occupied in running them around to this or that activity and in completing reports on them to and for the IYC and the BOP. One or the other of the girls is often left at home with me for an hour or two. And our limited social life involves us in occasional get-togethers with the youth and the overseeing IYC staff. Nearly all of the young folks are court committed to the IYC program, and are of native American Indian ethnicity.

I like the two girls and they are both warm and cordial to me--seem to look upon me sort of as though I were their grandfather. And their cultures generally regard grandparents with respect. The youngsters and Bayloo are generally gone for the day before I generally arise at 8:30 AM or later. We four usually have a quiet supper together without disturbance from radio of television so that we can dine and share a little conversation. Heather is rather outgoing and always cautiously impatient to get free and be able to get on with her own life. As her baby has begun to evolve from his infancy, I have become quite attached to him and often spend an hour or two with him daily. Watching him, holding him, bouncing him about, trying to get him to smile or laugh, or roll over etc. When he gets too tired to be easily pacified or becomes in need of a diaper change, I of course turn him back over to the care of his mother. She seems more than happy to tender the child over to my care each day and it seems to please her that I should take such an interest in the little tyke. My obvious interest in the child seems to fortify the warmth of my relationship to Heather. She likes to kid me a little, just as she notices that I spoof her with a little patter of conversation. A little game has evolved whereby she will occasionally steal up close enough to suddenly startle me--and I do not take care to avoid occasionally startling her by the silence of my stocking footed tread about the house.

Chaco (Chelsey) is younger than Heather. More a self-conscious teenager, and more inhibited. She has a beautiful smile which amazingly fascinates the Angel. She and Heather seem to have become somewhat alienated from one another--I know not why. She has family in the area and often spends some hours or a day with her young aunt. She and I seem to have a more reserved relationship. I try to encourage her sense of humor. Her youth and feminine sensitivity as well as her solitariness and strained relationship with the more dominating Heather tends to keep her more towards the periphery of our family unit. She too will occasionally try to startle me, but I exercise more caution about incidentally startling her. It would be more natural and easier for her to feel comfortable--I suspect--if Heather would permit her an easier access to the Angel.

It is true of course, that my relationship with these foster children is relatively easy since I am not their watchdog and stern disciplinarian. That, is Bayloo's job. A job for which she is trained and experienced; and more especially--for which she is 'certified' to the satisfaction of the agencies and organizations through which she is paid for this work and responsibility. In the American society of our times, one must, after all, be properly brainwashed and browbeaten in order to be 'certified' to do anything at all. A doctor can not be employed as a nurse, because he is not 'qualified' nor certifiable to that narrowly defined occupation. A person can not be employed as a licensed barber unless fully educated and then certified to that occupation. The theologians will not permit God to be a god unless he meets their particular vague criteria.

In mid-March I looked up Paul Lewis and Jackie (Phalen) who are old acquaintances of mine from Miles City. She is the sister of one of my high school buddies, Jim Phalen. Paul was a high school classmate of brother, Gene. The Lewis's spent their career as airplane maintenance mechanics to a Christian missionary support group in Brazil. And they retired back to the USA and into Santa Fe about 1986, when he had a heart problem that required surgery. I often visit them for two or three hours on Saturday morning or afternoon. We discuss old times and old acquaintances, as well as some current events, but it seems generally understood between us that we will not discuss religion and that only mental infirmity; or a personal message from God to me would ever require me to retrace my steps back towards the Christian religion from which my roots have loosened. And that they are likewise certainly not apt to move in the direction of my religious and philosophical leanings.

Now, again, in the first half of this year I spent a good many hours and days in further revising my philosophical manuscript, *"A Studied Impression of That Which Is"*. And in sending "query" letters to publishers with but the vaguest mere hope that one might be willing to publish it for me. But I have been fully aware that that would be highly unlikely. After all, who am I? I am a nobody. I am not even schooled--let alone certified--by any school (or even any course) of Writing, Theology, Philosophy, Religion, Humanities, or Literature. No. I did not expect nor did I receive any acceptance nor any encouragement whatsoever in my writing or written manuscript. But I viewed it as my right, responsibility, and obligation to make the effort; since I have legitimately arrived at my personal views of the nature of reality by dint of honest effort in wide search and based upon my own wide experience of life and reality. Though my hopes are disappointed, I am certainly grateful to have had in my life sufficient health, energy, time, opportunity, and freedom to have been able to set forth my views into at least rough manuscript form. In fact, there was one publisher (Vantage) that did offer to produce it in book form for somewhat over $20,000.00. But I do not have that kind of money; nor am I so naïve as to believe that this offer was anything more than the publishers offer to keep himself in employment. But it was an actual good-faith offer. But there was nothing to suggest that there was anything of intrinsic merit or possible wide interest within the manuscript itself. Now--for the record--it is to be noted that very few ever get any offer of publication except at their own expense. Those that do, are primarily, known and previously published authors. Know too, that rustic (or even professional) philosophical manuscript materials generally sell poorly to the public at large; in that regard, much the same problem as with books of new poetry. The reality is that hopes are not promises, nor are promises by any means commonly fulfilled.

In early May the state of Oklahoma found a way to extort $140.00 from me regarding an old traffic violation of 1991. They are now linked by computer with the New Mexico Department of Motor Vehicles in conspiracy against the common honest citizen. My NM driver's license could not be renewed until I had settled up with Oklahoma. I presume that this bespeaks a reciprocity of evil between these and other states.

On the 15th of May I headed up to the northwest and was able that night to view a lunar eclipse from western Utah. I briefly visited the grandchildren in Medford where I watched Zink (Ribs) and Zelt (Beaux) play baseball on the same team--they both do quite well. They won the league championship and also the league tournament this year. I then visited the grandchildren in the Portland area before next traveling with brother Vic to Dunseith, North Dakota for a Memorial Day gathering at the town cemetery named "St. Louis". We traveled the blue highways as much as possible. Followed Hwy 200 all the way from Great Falls into eastern ND on this trip that took us seven days. In Bottineau I checked into what seemed like a possible medical practice opening which later fizzled out for reasons discussed earlier in this essay. Within a day or two of the time I left Vic in Yakima, he and Marge received word that their son, Jay, has developed acute myelogenous leukemia. A fine young man, and another great tragedy. I rather suppose that his chances of survival beyond five years is uncertain, though oncology research drugs and other therapy may have or shall make a breakthrough in the treatment of the problem.

I visited brothers Duane and Phil a few days. In Spokane, a young woman with Brasseur ancestors had recently contacted Phil. I looked her up to gather the genealogical information from her. She is descended from a Napoleon Brasseur from Anaconda, Montana. I happened to have with me a copy of his death certificate, as I had been trying for a few years to run down additional information on him.

I returned again to visit with the families of Pierre and Jauhn in Portland for ten days. Then stopped to visit an old high school classmate in Bellvue as I was en route to attend the wedding of Kirsten Brasseur--daughter of Gretchen and step-daughter of nephew Andre who lives in Everett, WA. Being married to a nice young man, Ben Skelton. There I encountered quite a few members of my extended family. Then again I stopped a few days with Duane and briefly again in Spokane with Phil before returning to Portland in time to visit with Mark Krahn and Shelly, and their family of six children. He works with the U.N. computer operations from their home in Vienna, Austria. They had a planned one day and night stop at Jauhn's place. Mark is one of sister Ookie's sons.

Next (en route home) I picked up Zelt and Zinc (ages 12 and 11) from Tina and stopped briefly with old classmates in California before arriving home in Santa Fe on 7 July. Concerning those three and a half weeks I spent with two grandsons, I have previously composed a ten page summary which I sent to their parents by e-mail. After returning them home, I returned immediately home, arriving July 26th. There were many overly warm days with no cooling rains--which I endured with a rather low quotient of ambition. Meanwhile, I was making plans for another extended trip to begin September 5th. But, before I could depart, I spent eight days laboring to lay 168 one-foot square concrete blocks to serve as a patio in the back yard. Three hours a day is about all I could handle of that hard labor in the rising heat and sunlight of each morning.

I actually departed for the Northwest on the Sept 3rd--earlier than planned, as Pierre wanted me to stay with the kids, while he was preoccupied with some personal problems. I arrived in Portland at 5:00 AM on the 5th. Each day I accompanied the kids home after school for a week; and played some football and basketball with the families of Pierre and Jauhn on the two weekends I spent in Portland.

Though I had registered to attend the German Convention in this time, I cancelled that plan to help out a bit at Pierre's place. On the 14th of September I drove to Spokane, where I stayed over with Phil and Dot at their apartment. Phil began to consider the notion of flying to the east coast to spend a week of travel with me. I tended to some business on the 15th before driving into Missoula where I had supper with Tom and Anne Adams' family; and then watched a TV football game with Todd Scott before I retired to sleep in Tom and Annie's camper trailer. In the morning I arose to have oatmeal and then drove on into Hardin, Montana, where I stopped in to have supper and to spend the night with Kate's daughters, Roxy and Jody Davis. They had colds and retired early after I met Roxie's boyfriend, Kevin Cain. I stayed up late to read and got up the next morning to have cold cereal after they had gone to work. Leaving town, I picked up a hitch-hiker who rode with me as far as Rapid City. I stopped to sleep in my nest in the camper shell, at a rest area near Canistoda, SD that night in the wind and rain. I recall a time in the late 1940s when mom and dad had been away from home for a week as they traveled to Canistoda where I was told that dad had undergone some 'treatments'. In the morning I inquired of the locals what sort of medical facility had been in Canistoda; that anyone might come there for treatments. Not a thing that they could recall except a couple of Chiropractic doctors. As I again headed east, I picked up a hitch-hiker whom I dropped off before I arrived in Omaha, Nebraska. There I stay the night with Bernard Chase and his wife. The next day (the 18th) I continued east on Hwy 80. I stopped an hour at the Amana Colony in Iowa to get some pastries and then made it easily through Chicago and into Indiana, where I spent the night at a service area in my pickup camper nest.

On the 20th I followed first Hwy 80 and then 90, to arrive into the Amish country of northeastern Ohio. There, at Orwell village, I chanced to stop at a mom and pop restaurant where they had a folksy singer entertaining we handful of diners. Quaint and pleasant. I then stopped at a rest area to nest for the night, after taking my exercise walking its perimeter. I again slept well and the weather was fine. The 21st I drove on into Buffalo, where I found the 75 year old Larry Brasseur, cheerfully sweating at his work project on the house and climbing a ladder to the eves. I visited 45 minutes with him and his wife before continuing eastward. They insisted on sending a sandwich along with me. I stopped the night at a service area to get my two mile hike, eat my sandwich, and sleep the night away. I arose the next morning to continue on Hwy 90 through Syracruse and up Hwy 87 to Watertown, where I spent a few hours at the library to look there for Brasseur connections--none found. Continuing then on Hwy 11, I reached Brasher Falls, where I stopped over to have supper and stay the night with cousin Frank and Glenda Youmell. The following day I crossed over into Canada at Cornwall. There, I encountered the usual immigration "service" snooping and overkill in order to provide their overly large force with a pretext of having something important to do. I stop at Cornwall a couple hours to search for new genealogy information at Nativity Catholic Church. And then to the city library before I stopped at their Wal-Mart to get an oil change. And there, I also park to spend the night in their parking lot.

Again, on the 25th of September, I spent the day doing genealogy at Hawkesbury before driving to Plantagenet where I took a motel room and walked about the village for exercise. The next day I had to locate the new home of the French Canadian Genealogy Library in Montreal and discovered very little new information before then driving east across the St. Lawrence on the high bridge to arrive at Grandby, where I took an inexpensive hotel room. That night I had a remarkably excellent supper at a nearby restaurant. As their genealogy center was closed the next day (Saturday), I drove on south to cross back into the U.S. at Newport. There, I looked up Yves and Yolanda Brasseur, who seemed quite pleased to have me come by again. Yves and I walked about the town and they had me stay for supper and spend the night with them. Four or five of the 13 children dropped by to visit that evening. After breakfast in the morning, I then drove about 20 miles to locate and arrive at Jay Mountain Ski Lodge about noon to sign in and take my room for the six day Elder Hostel course. It was a very genial group of about thirty senior citizens. We ate wonderfully at the lodge and had lectures on Beethoven's music, astronomy, and on writing. I had time each day to take a two mile hike and to get a bit of a nap. The course was finished on Saturday the 4th of August. I drove back to Newport and stopped at Louise's store of Fabrics (she, a daughter of Yves). I used her phone to locate a place to lodge in nearby Troy for $30.00 per day at a bed and breakfast place. I stayed there three days, spending my time reading, writing, and getting my daily walk. For I was now only biding my time to await the arrival of brother Phil on the 7th. On that day I drove south to Haverhill, MA and spent a couple hours there doing genealogy before driving the other 35 miles to Boston's airport where I picked up Phil at 9:00 PM. He and I then drove back north to take a motel room in southern New Hampshire. The following day we had time for an extended walk in picturesque Burlington, VT, prior to our ferry boat crossing of Lake Champlain. We stopped at Ausabe Falls, and then on to Malone, NY, where we took a motel room. The next day, we stopped to visit Frank Youmell in Brasher Falls. He got me a replacement for my gas tank cap before we crossed over into Canada at Cornwall. From there we proceed into Vaudreuil and stopped at the cemetery. And then on to St. Ann de Bellview by the locks, before we continued over the high bridge from Montreal and on to Granby. In Granby we got an inexpensive quaint room in hotel 400 in the center of town. That evening we walked the Avenue Principle and stopped for a fine supper at the restaurant.

Next morning (the 10th) we drove to Roxton Pond to visit Bernard Brasseur; and then surveyed the Brasseur homestead site of 1832 along Rhond Egypt. Our direct ancestor built this road and settled the four homestead sites which subsequently went to his four sons--one of whom was my own great grandfather, Francois Xavier--a name that was also passed on to my grandfather. We stopped at cemeteries in St. Valerian and St. Dominque--communities from whence our grandfather, F. Xavier, emigrated to North Dakota in the late 1800's. We drove then through St. Pie, through St. Hyacinthe, and out on towards the Gaspe Peninsula, stopping to visit Quebec City that afternoon, and taking then a motel room. The next morning we continued on eastward along the peninsula. We stopped for the night at Riviera du Loop and the following day, into

New Brunswick and into Maine, where we visited the well preserve old Fort Knox on the Kennebec River. As we continued south, we got signals of alternator failure and had to stop in Augusta, Maine to get the alternator replaced. On the 15th of October, I dropped off Phil at the Boston airport and then drove on west into NY. I arrived in Kansas City on the 17th, to attend the wedding of a nephew (John Schroeber) on the 18th--son of Bayloo's sister, Carla. We stayed at the home of Lew and Carla. Bayloo flew back to New Mexico where I arrived a day or two later in the pickup.

Heidi Begay is now residing at our home in Santa Fe, while Heather and the Angel have returned to live on the reservation. I miss the child--he was just getting interesting.

October 24th I attended a post-graduate medical education course in Albuquerque and there I met Dr. Keifer, who seems to think I might find work in her urgent care center? Perhaps I shall contact her after the first of the year. I helped Heidi with a couple of her complex home-work school projects. Her mother and aunt visit with us a couple of times. I set some loose floor tiles in the hallway with mortar and hauled in some land fill for a sunken spot in the front yard. Chelsea is preparing to leave the program and move out about Christmas time.

At the UNM in November, my CAT-scan follow-up was reported normal and I was referred to a Urologist for evaluation concerning genital tract minor bleeding, but I won't finish up with that investigation until next year.

I was home for Thanksgiving and we had plenty of pumpkin pie. A call from Pierre brought me up to Portland again on the 1st of December. I hung around his place to encourage and push the children to keep up with study programs he wishes to impose upon them. Bah now lives with her mother. Belle is oppositional and defiant, and precipitated a bit of a crisis that brought in the police for a quick call. Pierre and Jackie have indicated they plan to marry. It is my belief that it will not turn out well and that it will only cause addition stress to Pierre's life; and I am concerned that he is already near the limits of what he can endure--so much for my opinion. Belle's defiance finally precipitated her moving in to her mother's place just before I left on the 20th to stop at Jauhn's place. The next day I drove north on Hwy 5 and stopped at the home of nephew, Andre, but he wasn't about; so I continued on and stopped at Duane's farm in the Columbia Basin for several days and over the X-mas holidays. Phil and Dot, too, arrived at the farm on the weekend after X-mas for three days of talk, walks, and playing cards.

On Monday, the 29th, I arrived in Spokane in time for supper with Phil and Dot. The next day I took care of some of my personal business and spent a couple hours trying to make a genealogy connection.

I thought I might stop by at Andre's place in Everett, but snow and storm conditions were threatening and so instead, I drove down through the Tri-cities and through the Columbian Gorge to arrive at the home of Jauhn and Massey the evening of New Year's day.

I hear that Real is again separated from his wife and living with his mother. Not a big surprise to me. I had stopped to visit a few hours with Tina en route to Portland. She was contemplating a move to the other side of Medford as the economics of her recent divorce were coming were bringing on that necessity. She still had full custody of the children, but was giving consideration to the possibility of going to joint custody with Real. Tina seems now on the verge of entering into a new romantic relationship with a fellow who sounds to me rather unstable--and potentially troublesome besides being unemployed and seeming not eager to return to work.

RGB

Summary 2004 and 2005
R. Garner Brasseur

What is the reason for the writing of this essay? I have gotten into the custom of doing an annual summary in order to reflect and remind myself of the events of the past year, while also considering what ought to be my course for the new year. But at the end of each of these two years, I was so preoccupied with preparations for; and now having to work four days a week; and--filled with new hope--was once more revving up my efforts to get my book published. For now a couple of weeks--before I have to get involved with the income-tax filing troubles--I have a little time to catch up on this (till now neglected) project.

Improbable as it seems, I did recover from cancer surgery performed on Good Friday of 1996 and am still chugging along ten years later. And I returned to work on a half-time basis six months after surgery. In November of 1997, a year and a half after recovering from surgery, I had completed and published *"Inheritors of a Few Years"*. It was done with some sense of urgency, not knowing but what my survival may be only temporary.

Taxes and court ordered excision payments--of my then limited income--to my estranged spouse left me with but about $600.00 per month on which to live. In 1998 the prolonged court proceedings finally granted my divorce petition. But the draconian judgment still left me with very little income. So little that it did not seem to me at all worth my while to continue to work beyond the age of my full retirement at age 65, and I immediately filed my intention of retirement with Social Security to become effective in May of 1999.

By June of 1999, Bayloo and I had stowed our gear into a storage facility and then spend about a year traveling about the country while I continued with my genealogy projects concerning both the Brasseur and the Boepple families. We eventually settled into an apartment in Albuquerque and Bayloo went back to work. I continued to also work on a pet writing project which had its conceptual origins in about 1975, and which I had been slowly writing and transcribing into manuscript form since about 1982. In its now finished form it has come to be entitled "*A Studied Impression of That Which Is*".

At the same time, I began to look about for the possibility of finding employment so as alleviate my meager financial status--thinking that my ongoing court-ordered financial enslavement to my ex-spouse might yet somehow be considerably moderated by the court or by mutual agreement. For, after all, the crippling of my ability to make some reasonable income in no way financially facilitated her economic situation. Such, however, was her animosity and sense of entitlement, that she permitted the legal wrangling of the economic end to the divorce settlement to continue. Perhaps it was yet her fervent hope that I might just go back yet to work and allow her to suck me dry economically even though there be but the most meager of financial benefit to myself. The legal fees of this ongoing wrangling were costing me considerably, and costing her about twice that much--as best I could determine.

In February of 2003, Bayloo bought herself a nice little 3-bedroom house using some of her retirement funds, and we moved from an Albuquerque apartment to Santa Fe. From there she is able to contract with IYC, to take into the home two foster children--for which she is reasonably well paid.

The divorce wrangling continued, month after expensive month into about ten years. New Mexico is supposed to have a 'no-fault' attitude towards divorce--that is to say, neither party is "guilty" nor therefore "punishable". But I saw not a hint of that in the attitude of this judge. His foot dragging neglect over these many years of disjointed proceedings, and a number of his several comments made it obvious that this judge who was (mis)guiding the course and outcome of the case did, and fully intended to use his authority over me in a punitive manner. Where was 'the level playing field' referred to so eloquently in the long course of these proceedings? It was for me, sort of like playing a game of football against the opponent while all the game officials are wearing the uniforms of the opposing team.

Year after year, I continued to pay out my time, energy, and funds to gather postgraduate education credits and renew medical licensure--with now only vague hope that I might some day be able to return to the earning of a better living income.

Finally, in April of 2004, the ex-wife, too, must have gotten tired of paying out endlessly to the support of attorneys. And was so self-assured of the favoritism of the judge on her behalf, that she audaciously demanded some four hundred dollars monthly above the settlement that had been awarded--and I must finally accede to those demands just for the mere hope of ever getting free of her and this self-righteously bigoted judge. Manumission, at all costs! Mine, now, for little more than what I had been paying out in attorney fees on a monthly basis. At this certain additional cost of a few hundred dollars monthly, she seems to have found it expedient or necessary to accede to my financial independence. I could hardly believe it, after all these years--yet, there it was.

But it had now been five long years since I had worked, and there seemed but little probability that I might yet find work in my advancing years. Even so, what a breath of fresh air--just to be free entirely of all the strain and havoc that she had raised into my life these past twenty plus years! And to be free from court ordered constraints upon my life and from the overseeing of my life by any court of such prejudicial incompetence. And now too, actual--though limited--hope of the possibility of a return to the earning of a decent living standard.

In 2002 I spent a goodly amount of time traveling about to visit with friends and relatives, and spent some time with a couple of my grandchildren. Towards the end of that year I began earnestly to pursue the possibility of having my manuscript published (*"A Studied Impression of That Which Is"*). I looked up the addresses of publishers and sent out a dozen letters of inquiry towards that end; but, alas, was unable to drum up any interest among them. It is at least some small consolation to have learned that even many now well known books have been turned down many times and by many publishers before finally finding their way to publication. I did, in fact, get an offer from Vantage Press to publish the book, but I myself would have to pay them over $24,000.00 to do so. Many writers have finally had to resort to such an arrangement. If I had that kind of money available, I would do so too. I do not have the patience to pursue publishers endlessly. And so, I tired of the project and set it aside, though it continued to weight upon my mind. Perhaps I might yet find a job that would enable me earn enough to bring the project to fruition. Thus, I continued to cast about for some part-time employment.

At long last, in April of 2004 it finally came to pass that I was freed of the accursed burden on ongoing legal entanglements of the divorce. It was settled--at some not inconsiderable cost. But settled, nevertheless. And now with manumission, I first bought myself a new pickup to facilitate my travels; and then began my search for economic revival more vigorously. Once again--and foremost in my mind--was the hope I might finally manage to have my manuscript published. I already had the contract for its publication in hand, requiring now only my signature and the economic where-with-all to set the process in motion.

It is not the case that I imagine my manuscript would be likely to find any significant number of purchasers or readers. Nor even the case that I suppose it to be especially well constructed. But it is the case that I have deeply invested myself in the project as a matter of self-enlightenment for nearly half of the years of my existence, and I yearn for the opportunity to publish my say. For in this country, and in our times, it is my right to have my say; though I am fully aware that there is no one who has any obligation to either hear or read what I have to say. It is my hope that at least some of my own people might yet be touched by its content, which I suppose to contain a considerable of philosophical and historical validity. Not to engage in the pursuit of ideas is to live like ants--instead of like men, as Mortimer Adler has put it. And Ingersol allows that the most noble of all occupations is the search for truth--would that it were easy to make a living at it. And, for the record, I would not wish it be supposed post humorously that I had affirmed any opposing point of view as my final testimony on the matters of which I write: or that it might some day be said (when I am no longer around to refute those allegations) that in the final hour, I had "received Jesus into my heart" etc.

In the course of a conversation with Dr. Kiefer a year earlier, I had explained to her that there seemed little chance of finding employment at my age and under my circumstances. She owns and staffs an urgent care medical facility in Santa Fe, and was in the process of setting up a second one. She was interested to learn that I had worked in such a facility for a few years, and led me to believe that she might well be able to use my part time services. I now looked her up to discuss this with her, at her suggestion. But the reality was that I should first have to take an expensive 10 day 'refresher course' for emergency medical physicians, and pass the update certifying examination of relevant trivia and details. As though it were a sort of minor detail--though she herself was prepared for the "easy course" by virtue of a three year residency training program. It seemed not to be a realistic possibility for me at this time.

I was now decided to make a door-to-door job search in North Dakota, and I set out upon that task in the earliest part of May 2004. I stopped over a couple of nights in Terry, Montana to visit with my youngest sister, Kate. A month later passing westward into the Northwest, I stopped by to chat with her a few hours again. It was to be the last time I was ever to see her, as she suffered a massive heart attack and died 23 July in a Billings Hospital. From Terry, I moved on to Bismarck to search their library and to check with the state Medical Association and the Board of Medical Examiners. They seem to know nothing of such matters as job openings. I stopped in to visit briefly with Dick Morgan in Falkirk, and then proceeded to comb first the communities of the western part of the state. Talking with hospital administrators and pharmacists, I picked up leads which I explored from town to town. I had just missed an opening in Elgin. I learned that there was an opening with potential in Glen Ullen--for the physician there had had his license suspended in some game of medical politics precipitated upon him by a local hospital. There, in Glen Ullin, I found a roomy and adequate apartment to rent for twenty-five dollars a week, and I make it my home base for the larger portion of the four weeks that I stayed in North Dakota. I had just missed one of the two annual Advanced Cardiac Life Support courses offered in a Bismarck hospital, and learned that the other was to be in September. Had I arrived a week earlier and completed the May course, I would undoubtedly found immediate employment at the hospital in Linton, for the administrator and the physicians there seemed very pleased and ready to avail themselves of my part time services. I planned to return then and take the September course--by that time, the opening in Linton had been filled. In the meantime, I borrowed from the hospital library the textbooks I needs must study and proceeded to prepare myself for the exam. Every evening and on the days that I was not traveling for interview, I studied the ACLS materials. While there, I also paid fee and made out my application for DEA registration (federal drug certification) which arrived to me at home later. I continued every day to take my fifty minute hike about the pretty little town. I had groceries from the local store from which I prepared my meals.

Among the various places I was eventually to visit in my search were; Bismarck, Minot, Center, Hazen, Hebron, Bottineau, Rugby, Beulah, Elgin, Mott, Glen Ullin, Killdeer, Washburn, Stanley, Rolla, Cando, Crosby, Linton, and Trenton--some, on more than one occasion. I visited cousins Elmer and Gordon Neuberger, and cousin Mike Rempfer. In Montana I stayed over a night with Bayloo's brother Bill Huft, in Fairview and visited in Miles City with Dr. Winter, and my ex-brother-in-law Harold Kransky, and nephew Steve and his two high-school age daughters, Tia and Lexie. I stopped in Fishtail and Manhatten to try without success to locate a former high-school classmate.

I arrived in Missoula on 4 June 2004 to join Bayloo who had arrived by plane for the graduation of her granddaughter, Nicole, from high school. We stayed with Bayloo's daughter, Cindy and Dean Mikes and also visited with her other two children that live in Missoula--Annie and Todd. I stayed there four nights and then headed westward alone after dropping off Bayloo at the airport for her return to Santa Fe.

I stopped over with Phil and Dot on the 9th and the next day headed down Hwy 395 and 14 to arrive into the Portland area after stopping to renew my state of wakefulness and soul at the Chamberlain Lake Rest Area--my favorite spot in the Northwest. I surveyed its magnificence and slept a contented hour and a half before continuing. I stopped by at Pierre's place along Hwy 26, west of Banks, in anticipation of the high school graduation ceremony of grandchildren Jessica and Francois, who were to graduate from Century High School the following evening--11 June. The morning of that day I stopped by to visit with Jauhn and his family; and in the evening I drove alone over to the outdoor stadium beside Hwy 26, beyond Lennox School. The jam of traffic in search of parking was so furious that I simply parked a full mile distant from the place and walked the rest of the way. I should have brought my binoculars, for as part of the huge throng of spectators, I was a long way off from the action. Foreseeing the chaos of the disbursement of that mob, I only stayed long enough to see Jessica and Francois get their diplomas--and then beat my hasty retreat ahead of the snarl of exit traffic. Later that evening, Michah and I had a nice little talk on Literature and Philosophy that went on till nearly 3:00 AM.

I had tentative plans and arrangement for making a camping trip with Bam-bam (Pierre's son) and Beaux (Real's son) of several days duration to acquaint them with some of the geology of the Northwest. As I tried to solidify that arrangement with Pierre a day or two earlier, he seemed rather more evasive than usual. But while breakfasting and talking with Massy the morning of the 12th, she informed me that Bam-bam had called from his mother's place to indicate that he was ready to get started. Now immediately comes a call from Tina, telling me that Real had unexpectedly taken the kids from her home yesterday while she was out. Apparently Rochelle and Tina were in accord with the plan for our trip, while other motives were afoot to defeat that intention. Tina informs me that Real insists that I call him concerning the trip on which I had expected Beaux would join us. But Real and I have not been on speaking terms for the past two years. Skeptical of even my own skepticisms, I did call Real. But it was an exercise in futility. He seemed to have had some notion that I would crawl and beg to his authority in the matter; and of course he was not about to turn the boy over to me. Between the lines, it seems to me most likely that he and Pierre have a united plan to keep the lads away from the evil influence of grandfather. I could see cause to expect that their troublesome mother was undoubtedly situated somewhere in the middle of this plan of minor betrayal--and she was due to arrive here at Jauhn's place within this very hour. And so, I grabbed my gear and headed out on Hwy 26, and then northward on interstate 5. Thus it was, that I must reluctantly abandon my little plan for some fellowship with the grandsons at this time.

Unable to find Grant Mosby at his place in Yelm, I continued up and caught Hwy 90 over Stevens' Pass. I stopped to nap an hour at a rest area west of Ellensburg, then had a bite to eat at George, Washington before arriving at the farm of Duane and Georgia about 9:00 PM. We ate some strawberries and talked a while before they retired about 10:30. I retired to the bunkhouse and read a few hours before turning in about 3:30 AM. I remained there nine nights on the farm. Whenever I arrive at the farm, Duane has a pile of books and articles set aside for me to read. It adds to the base of subject material upon which our discussions sometimes wander. Each day I get a two and half mile walk about the perimeter of the farm, and two or three meals with them so that I get in about two or three hours of conversation with them each day. I use the rest of my time writing, reading, and enjoying the luxury of a pleasant nap undisturbed by a telephone. Doby, Karen and their adopted son, Tyler were also there a couple of nights and on the 16th we had a birthday party for Tyler. That was the day that nephew Andre showed up with wife Gretchen as well as Anna, Emma, Clair, Laura lee, Kirsten and Ben. Whether by pure chance or planned that way, I know not. The table was all set and extended for the birthday dinner. As folks pulled themselves up to the dinner plates, I ducked into the library so as not be uncomfortably included into any ring of prayer to gods unknown to me. Thinking I had cleverly escaped, I paused a while before pulling up to table. But there seems to have been a sort of silent conspiracy to trap me, as they then joined hands in a circle about the table. The only escape for me then was to decline the enjoinment in the circle by joining together the hands of Andre and Gretchen who were seated on either side of me. It is often difficult to preserve one's honor in these things.

I departed the farm on the 21st and drove to Yakima to spend three nights at the home of Vic and Marge; to presume upon their hospitality; and to catch up on conversation and news. Though Vic and I discussed the matter, I neglect in this letter to say much about nephew, Jay--for Vic seems to have a great reluctance to readily share out information which he considers to be his private worries and concern. Sorrow can perhaps be enjoyed more profoundly when unshared. From Yakima, back to Portland on the 25th and spend the night at Pierre's place in the back of the pickup--as they had a houseful of boys staying over for a birthday party. The next day I stopped over at Jauhn's place, now that his mother was departed. I lodged there in the comfort of their attic room until the end of the month. From there, I have ready access to local libraries in the day and return to the base in the evenings. Some evenings we played basketball, and other evenings we drove out to watch JoJo or Norge play baseball. One evening at a baseball game, I ran into granddaughter Belle in Forrest Grove. July 1st I headed south, stopping en route first to visit Larry and Nancy Otis in Grants Pass (we were in residency training together, in Panama), and stopping a couple hours to visit cousin Dorothy LaVallee (nee Boepple) and Joe in Central Point. About 10:30 PM I stopped at Tina's place and talked a bit with her before I headed out to the Wal-Mart store about midnight. There I take a 50 minute hike before rolling into the sleeping bag in the camper shell about 1:30 AM for a quiet night of rest. In the morning I picked up some fresh donuts to supply myself some breakfast as I continued south on Hwy 5 to Redding. I stopped over three nights to visit with my old friend Raymond and Betty Horton and their son, Jim, who is currently living with them. I always enjoy my long conversations with them, and the rational tranquility with which they seem to bear life's burdens. I continued south on July 5th about 500 miles to arrive at mid-evening at the rest area near Boron on the high Mojave Desert. One of my favorite stop-over areas. There I built myself a sandwich and took a hike of about two and a half miles about the grounds. In addition to the trucks, 20 or more other wayfaring units have seen fit to stop over here for the night. All of these rest area facilities get very hard usage from even decent citizens, to say nothing of the ever present small proportion of vandals. I catch up on my journal and pause at length to reflect about the mystery of being; and of the Universe, as I peer into the depths of the night sky. Consider the relative good fortune that has been my lot as I am obliged to share in the universal agony that is proportioned out to all we mere mortal creatures. Strange how our short troubled lives delimit us from all but the tiniest proportion of all of "that which is" and from what goes on even in our own brief time of existence. How tranquil and fine is my solitude and time for reflection here in the high desert beneath the stars this night. I turn into my sleeping bag about midnight for a long quiet night of 9 hours rest with temperature about 70 degrees. In the morning I have another ham sandwich and finish the potato salad provided by the Horton's, and I then continue along Hwy 58 to 395, where I pick up a hitchhiker to drop him off at Hwy 15, where he heads on to Las Vegas and I continue on south through San Bernardino to Hwy 10 east, past Loma Linda and out to the open desert to catch Hwy 68 into El Centro on this rather hot day at about 2:00 PM. I take about a two mile hike inside the air-conditioned Wal-Mart and then park in their lot beneath a shade tree to snooze a bit in the comfort of my air-conditioned pickup cab. At 6:30 PM I drive over to the apartment of Lynn Fitz just as he is returning from his pharmacist job. We go out for an expensive hamburger and have mud pie desert, and then take a pleasant swim in the pool of the apartment complex. We talk of old acquaintances, current political situations, religion, and philosophy before he turns in about midnight and leaves me to read an hour before I flake out on his living room couch. Having slept poorly in the night, I napped a few hours in the day after spending some time at the library. After a second night at his place, I head east on Hwy 8 and 10 on another rather hot day. There is some scattered cloud cover and cooling later in the day as I get beyond Tucson, and I stop in the late afternoon at a mountainous rock enshrouded rest area to have a sandwich, take a two plus mile hike, and then get a nap in the pickup camper shell. And then on east to Deming, where I take the Hatch cutoff to Hwy 25 north and drive steadily until I am home in Santa Fe by 2:30 AM on July 9th.

I catch up on my mail and e-mail, chase about upon some local errands, tend to some business arrangement with brother Phil, and get my daily hike and daily nap as I settle again into the quietude of the retired life while hoping for some possible word of job opportunity from my recent long trip and the ongoing searching out of leads. On the evening of the 13th, Valerie and I attended a Berliotz Opera in the magnificent opera house north of town.

On July 22nd Phil called to tell me that sister Kate had been hospitalized with a massive MI. On the 24th he called to inform me that she had died. The grim reaper is beginning to catch up with us. I leave my legal documents to the care of Bayloo so that she has easy access to them and the settling of my estate, should I soon find some unexpected exit from the cares of this world. Just after midnight on the 25th I head north on Hwy 25 to attend Kate's funeral. It is 935 miles from Santa Fe to Terry. Up near Pueblo, Colorado about 4:00 AM I bed down in the camper shell for a four hour rest. Later, I leave Hwy 25 at Douglas and drive up north through Gillette and through Broadus to reach Miles City about 7:00 PM, where I get a bowl of chili to eat before arriving at Terry about 8:15 PM. Phil, Dot, Jody, and Roxy are at Kate's place organizing her meager worldly possessions for distribution and disposal, and conspiring as to where to unload her 8 or 9 cats. None for me, thanks--for I am not a cat lover. People problems more than adequately preoccupy my any small excess of time and patience. About 10:30 PM after thoughts have been unburdened, I turn into my camper shell, parked at the front curb for a quiet night of peaceful slumber.

Phil and Kate being only a couple years apart in age, have always been on close terms all through the years, and he is taking the lead in advising and helping Jody and Roxy with the funeral arrangements and in getting the estate settled. I have visited with Kate many hours in the past 10 or 15 years, and as best I could tell, her system of religious ideas was not assuredly any different than my own state of agnosticism. But she and Skippy were the closest of buddies all through the years and under that influence, Kate was a nominal Catholic in her adult years. Because of that, funeral arrangements were to be conducted by the local priest, and the day prior to the memorial service, Phil, Dot, Jody, Roxy, and I met with the priest about half an hour while he made a effort to become somewhat acquainted with the person of Kate. After that meeting, the girls were frustrated, for they could see that the priest was not going to have much to say about Kate. I pointed out to them the obvious--that the priest's agenda is primarily that of furthering and maintaining the interests of religion and the church upon the occasion of the death of this mere mortal of the flock. It fell then finally to Phil, to agree to stand up and say something specifically about the person of Kate. He had also gotten roped in by the priest to the reading of a bit of scriptural verse and he heartily agonized over being caught up into that duplicity before he was finally able--at the last minute--to pawn the task off on to some other poor pilgrim of deeper religious persuasion.

Phil, Ed Ban (Skippy's spouse), and I had supper together at a local café on that second evening, then Ed went out to play a few hands of cards.

About 10:00 PM I wandered over to Ed's place to talk a bit with him and spend the night there. Though hard of hearing, he is genial and pleasant; and since he regularly works about town at small jobs of yard work etc., he retired to bed early and I read a few hours before turning in. I was up about eight in the morning to take a shower, and then Ed made me a bowl of oatmeal for breakfast. Ed tells me that Billy Ban (Skippy's son) is currently working over in war-torn Iraq. Back to Kate's house about 9:00 AM as people begin to arrive prior to the memorial service to be held at the local mortuary. Nephew Mike Kransky, Jan, and their son, Gerik arrive from Billings along with Carl Eaton (Aloha's 2nd husband). Harold Kransky arrives with Steve and Steve's two girls, Tia and Lexy. Walt Davis--the father of Jody and Roxy--also shows up in support of the two girls. It is the first time I have ever seen Walt. After the memorial service, we followed the funeral parade to the cemetery, where Kate's urn of ashes was buried beneath a shade tree to rest in eternal peace while a few ceremonial words and motions were occasioned to facilitate the dispersal of the crowd. Later, Phil returned to the burial site to slip a silver dollar into the burial site for Kate's possible use as a grub stake in some possible card game in the great beyond. There followed a little socializing over some locally provided food at the VFW club before folks set out for home in the early afternoon. I was back home in Santa Fe by noon of the following day.

For the next several intervening weeks, I kept busy with study in preparation for the coming ACLS and BLS courses I was preparing to take--with the hope of thereby facilitating my prospects in hunting down some form of part time work. I intersperse that with also some further work projects including genealogy, re-writing parts of manuscript, and doing some leveling on the patio. On 4 August I drove Bayloo to Albuquerque for some day surgery for the removal of the hardware from the ankle she had fractured a couple years earlier, wanting to have it done before I headed out on my next trip.

On the second weekend of September 2004 I take the Basic Life Support course at Santa Fe Jr. College. With my senior citizen discount, it cost me something just under five dollars. On the 15th of September I get out of town about 2:00 PM, heading north on Hwy 25. About 5:00 PM, I nap just under two hours at a rest area near Pueblo, Colorado before continuing north and being then assured of getting through the traffic congestion of Denver at something other than the heavy hours of traffic. At Ft. Collins, I picked up a hitchhiker dressed in short pants and short sleeves on this rather cool evening and he fell asleep as I drove him as far as

Cheyenne; and about 1:30 AM, at the Lusk rest area near Douglas, I climb into the sack in the camper shell for the night. The next day, I traveled north to Gillette, and then east on Hwy 80 and up Hwy 85 through Belle Fouche and on into North Dakota. I stop at Glen Ullin about 7:00 PM to rent the apartment from Ted and Mary LeMay for $50.00 per week. The following day I got in my 2½ mile hike, and then stopped at the local newspaper where, for $139.00, I arranged to have my job application ad run simultaneously in every newspaper in the state--offering to work 20 to 30 hours per week at any locally owned and managed health care facility in the state. Late afternoon I drove to Bismarck to attend the evening session of a post-graduate education course, and returned to Bismarck also the following day for the full day session, and spent my extra time reviewing my information in preparation for the ACLS course to follow in several days.

Meanwhile, there is an alcoholic pipe fitter from out of Chicago that keeps hanging around the apartment while Ted LeMay is supposed to be working on his broken down automobile in the garage. They have already had a run-in with the guy and don't want him in the house or on the premises, neither will they work on his car until he has paid them. He is a con-artist and tries to gain an ear to the story of his self-inflicted hardships and promising assuredly that he is quitting the bottle. I try to deal with him in a civil manner, but I don't wish to waste my limited time getting caught up into the futility of the details of all of his psychopathology, full well knowing that he has no valid intention of put his own life back into order. So I circumvent him and keep the door locked so he can't just walk in--as he is prone to do.

On September 22nd and 23rd of 2004 I took the two day ACLS in Bismarck. It is really quite a drag going through all these simulated emergencies and a trying to drag out from one's memory all of the various doses and their sequence of usage for drugs one has never in the course a lifetime had cause to use--and most probably never will. Internists and ER specialty doctors are really the only ones that have much call for their usage. I expect one could get used to their use rather easily once caught up into the situation that regularly required it. And I don't have an actors disposition, so that I find all of these games of pretend to be a bit distasteful. And, the survival rate in these games of pretend is a whole lot better than what happens in the real life situations. In any case, I managed to blunder through to ACLS certification, and I don't expect ever to have to go through that again.

I relaxed in Glen Ullin on the weekend from the burden of repetitious study that had occupied me. Then on Monday I traveled out to Elgin to visit with Dr. Hsu. He told me the history of his battle with the state board of Medicine concerning his contest with Elgin Hospital and the bogus charges that had been leveled against him. His license is temporarily suspended pending a further hearing, but he expects to get free of this difficulty in perhaps three or four weeks. He seemed to have some interest in working me into his organization at perhaps half-time when his affairs are straightened out. He has had independent clinics in both Elgin and Glen Ullin for many years and a large patient load. This is currently being handled by his nurse practitioner and physician assistants who are being supervised by a physician that comes in one day a week. The Elgin Hospital wanted to buy out his clinical practices and when he would not agree to sell on their terms, they began to churn out allegations to the board of medical examiners. I told him I had seen this sort of thing happen before. The big hospitals in the area are ever eager to string out their trap lines of clinics into the rural communities in order to keep rural patients flowing through the hospitals for extensive testing and specialists visits. In general, I prefer to work in a free-standing clinic and not be a staff member of any hospital--unless the hospital itself is going to pay my salary. I left my address, phone number, and e-mail address with Dr. Hsu should he decide he might wish to utilize my services. I expect that he was very much surprised, when his license was later permanently suspended. And I never again heard from him.

I was around Glen Ullin a couple more days awaiting the arrival of my DEA federal drug certificate which was overdue. I asked Dr Hsu to foreword it to me when it arrived and on 30 September I departed to reinvestigate some old and new job opportunity leads. Up again through Minot, over to Rugby, and down to Jamestown where I stop to call Keith Prentice. His wife informs me however that Keith died of a massive stroke a couple of years ago. I elect then to head out on my genealogy trip to New England and New France.

I head south through Aberdeen and arrive in Watertown in mid evening. There I have a bite to eat and then out to the Wal-Mart, were I take my 2 ½ mile hike in the rapidly cooling evening before climbing into an extra layer of clothing and into the sleeping bag for the night. In the morning, I look up some of Raymond Horton's family. First, his brother William, and then his sister, Betty, whom I had known in Scobey and in Miles City, back in the 40's. By noon I was headed south on Hwy 29 to look up Bernard Chase, expecting to find that his wife had by this time died, as she had been discovered to have Pancreatic Cancer when I was through last year. Jackie had passed away in February and I am given to understand that Bernard had taken it hard, as I learn from Barbara Waite who was residing with him at the present time. Barbara was a year behind us in high school in Miles City. Bernard and she were in e-mail contact since her husband had also passed away. They have decided and are in the process of getting themselves a mobile park home in Vancouver, WA and plan on making a life together. In fact, will be heading out there within the coming few weeks. I am a little surprised at how short and irritable he is with Barbara at times, and I notice that he has a few sub-dermal bruise marks upon his arms. Is he in the prodromal phases of dementia? Or is this from overuse of alcohol? We three went out to eat, and again I note a few occasions where he is uncharacteristically rude in responding to her conversation. I stayed over with them, and Barbara made us some bacon and eggs in the morning. We talk a few hours of old times before I head out a little after 1:00 PM. A bit after three o'clock, I stop at a rural cemetery on this fine afternoon to get a hike of about 2 ½ miles before driving on into Illinois along Hwy 34. There, at about 8:00 PM, I stop at a rest area to nap a couple hours before continuing eastward into Indiana where I stop at the first rest area on Hwy 94 about 2:00 AM to crawl into the camper for a nights rest. Up at nine the following morning to continue eastward. Stop at Crawfordsville library to check my e-mail and then continue eastward. I was stopped by the highway patrol, for no reason that I could ascertain, just before crossing over into Ohio. I was merely one in a long line of ongoing traffic. I presume that perhaps his attention was caught by my yellow New Mexico license plate, and that he might have thought I was carrying some drugs. Not even a threat of a citation after we went through the identification routine; and his not discovering me to be nervous when he wondered if he might look into the camper shell.

I got into Cleveland that evening and looked up my distant cousin, Theophile Boepple, who had contacted me a few weeks earlier by e-mail concerning some questions he had on genealogy. He ordered out some pizza which we consumed as we talked a couple hours and I then left his place about 11:30 PM thinking it a little strange that since he had contacted me, he would not have asked me to stop over the night at their big and mostly unoccupied home. I got out of the city and drove south about an hour to finally find a well-lighted rest area on a blue highway where I spent the night in the pickup camper.

The following day I was driving the Hwy 90 turnstile and finally stopped at a rest area near Schenectady to spend another cool night in the camper after walking the grounds about an hour for my exercise. From there I called brother Phil in Spokane to find out if he might still be interested in flying out here to spend a few days with me upon my wanderings. He declined, being preoccupied with the details of trying to get a house built. Early the next day I arrived at Haverhill, MA to spend the next three hours in the public library looking for genealogy information, and later that night settled in at a Wal-Mart parking area near Salem, NH to spend the night after getting my exercise in walking about the parking lot and adjacent areas. The 9th of October I stopped a couple hours for research in Nashua, NH and then proceeded up to northern Vermont to visit my distant cousin, Yves and Yolanda Brasseur in Newport after first stopping in to the store to say hello to their daughter, Louise, and enquire about her parents. Their son Michael came by to talk a while and we four then had supper together. About eight-thirty I headed west on Hwy 105, 78, and 2 to reach New York on a gusting rainy night and stop at the Wal-Mart in Plattsburg to take my exercise and then bed down about 1:00 AM. The following day I drive up through Malone to Brasher Falls where I stop in to visit distant cousin and friends of several years (Frank and Glenda Youmell). That evening we three along with Glenda's Mother and brother drive over to Potsdam to visit the daughter, Terry, who is married to a Dermatologist, Jay Schlecter. They have a couple small children, Jacob and Ely whose antics we enjoyed as we ate and spent the evening together. We then returned to Brasher Falls where I read a couple hours and shower before getting to bed. The following morning we have oatmeal for breakfast and talk a couple hours before I head down Hwy 11 through Waterton, NY and down Hwy 81 to reach interstate 90 to head west. About 4:30 PM I stopped at a service area on this cold and blustery day to get my exercise by walking the lot and out upon an adjacent stubble fields. A passing patrolman stopped me as I shambled along in headband and worn clothing to ask if I needed any help. Later that day I stopped at a rest area near Toledo to end the day and return to the vagaries of the dream world. I drove all the next day getting through Chicago and the Twin Cities before stopping about 5:15 AM at a rest area near Winnona, MN to get a few hours of sleep and arise 11:00 AM. About 8:30 PM I reached Glen Ullin and arranged to stay a few days at the rental apartment of Ted LeMay, where I turn in early with a slight transient illness and an accumulated fatigue. I do my laundry and unwind in solitude a day, and the next day drive out to Trenton, ND, on the northwest edge of the state. They had responded to my newspaper job ad and seemed quite interested in having me do some work there. It all looked very promising, but in the end--a few weeks later--they became aware of the obstruction to that possibility by the realities of insurance costs. Heading back to Glen Ullin, I stop by at the café in Hazen, thinking I might run into cousin Elmer Neuberger there. It was a good guess. He insisted on buying me supper before he departed to play at the dance that evening; and I head back to Glen Ullin. I spend a couple more days there and speak again with Dr. Hsu before heading north to Minot and to again visit the medical situations in Stanley and in Trenton. From there I head west into Montana, stopping over to visit and spend the night with Bayloo's brother, Bill Huft and Marilyn. Their son Scot with wife and two children come by to eat with us and talk a while. He is now working as butcher in the family grocery store. Next day I stop in Miles City to visit briefly with Harold Kransky and Steve; then continue west and stop in Fishtail to visit briefly with Janet and Ray Potter. I get as far as Butte that night, and stopped to sleep at the Wal-Mart. The following day I stop briefly in Missoula to visit Bayloo's daughter and family before continuing on to Spokane to stop over with Phil and Dot. The following day, the 22nd, Phil and I drive out to visit Duane and Georgia on the farm as they are contemplating an arrangement for the selling of the farm. We spend the night, and then return to Spokane the 23rd. Having spent the maximum three nights with Phil and Dot, I drive north to Chewelah on the 25th, to visit with Raymond Horton and his family; and then on to visit with nephew Andre, Gretchen, and family on the 26th in Everett. There, I talk with Ben Skelton who is flying out to Alaska to inquire about an EMT job possibility. Anna, Claire, and Emma demonstrate for us their evolving skill in the Scottish dances. Delightful little girls. As they keep their home warmer than that to which I am accustomed, I convince them that I would actually sleep more comfortably in the pickup which I park alongside the house. They provide me a fancy breakfast in the company of the bubbling little girls before I depart at mid-morning the next day. I drive north on Hwy 5 to Burlington, where I stop in visit with sister Ookey. After talking a bit, I set out on my 2½ mile walk about the town and stop a bit at the city library to check my e-mail. Return to her place and a fine quiet nap before we drive out to have supper together. She is early to bed, while I read a few hours before sacking out on her fold-away couch bed. And the following day, I head south and stop in Bellevue to visit Jean Buchanan a couple hours. She offered to put me up for the night but I am under some sense of urgency to keep moving along upon this already overly long journey; and in getting out ahead of the heavy traffic of the area. Heading south, I nap a couple hours at a rest area in the gentle rain before continuing on to arrive at Pierre's house about 9:30 PM. They were already abed and arose long enough to show me to a lodging in the extra room. The following morning I had an oatmeal breakfast while talking a bit with Bam, Beans, Sam, and Chris before they head off to school. Nephew Malcomb was there that morning doing construction on the outside deck of the house. I talk a while with him before driving over to the home of Jauhn and Massy. I drive granddaughter, Stan, to her classes at the nearby junior college, where we catch granddaughter Jessica and talk with her a few minutes also. From there I spend the day at the Hillsboro library and spend some time at the goodwill store to pick up a few books. Supper at Jauhn's place before we watch a video movie and then play a card game with Jauhn and the kids before I retire to the attic den to read a bit before retiring. On the 30th, I attend the U of O football game with Jauhn and family down in Eugene. On the evening of the 31st, I spend a couple hours escorting Bam, Beans, Sam, and Chris on trick-or-treat rounds through the streets of Banks and then spend the night at Pierre's place. I depart the Portland area the 3rd of November and drive to Medford where I take my exercise and spend the night encamped at the Wal-Mart parking lot.

Tina appears to be in the process of moving and I don't where she is now living. I am up early with a plan to locate her. I drive to McLaughlin school hoping to catch Beaux on his way to school. I inquire about him at the administration desk, and then wait outside. The security officer was nervous about my hanging about the school and he was urging me to get lost. About that time, Tina drove up to put an end to my search. I spend most of the day with her in chasing down one or another of the grandchildren at the various schools. I even got a chance to speak with Cowboy a few minutes at about supper time. And then, I drove to Grants Pass where I stopped in to visit a bit with Larry Otis and Nancy en route to Reedsport to look up Miette. I slept that night in the pickup a few miles outside of the town and planed to run her down in the morning. I stopped at the funeral parlor where they supplied me an address for Bart and Miette. I arrived at their place about 9:30 AM into a situation that was entirely civil but stiff enough that it seemed best to continue south under some feigned sense or urgency after a brief visit of four or five hours. At half past midnight I stopped for the night at a Wal-Mart just north of Santa Rosa. There I had an almost mystically restful sleep of more than eight hours and was reluctant, even then, to arise. I had a little breakfast and then followed Hwy 580, which crosses the bay and skirts the eastern edge of the east bay community to give me access to Hwy 5 south. In a few hours I departed Hwy 5 eastwards to pass through Wasco and reach Bakersfield, and then out upon the Mojave to spend another night at the rest area near Boron. I arrived at Loma Linda the next day about 1:00 PM, where I locate Michah and talk a bit before I get my nap in the pickup across the street from his apartment. He was entertaining himself at the piano when I found him, and late in the afternoon we hiked over to the athletic field where I watched his intramural team play a game of softball. I took him out for supper and we returned to his apartment about 8:30, where I continue reading my book while he works at his study tasks. I get a shower before bedding down upon the couch about half past midnight. Up shortly after seven in the morning and Michah makes us a mess of eggs before I head out Hwy 10 past Indio and down Hwy 68 to Brawly by late morning. There I locate Lynn Fitz working in the clinic pharmacy and arrange to meet him at his apartment in El Centro after his work shift. At age 70, he is still working full time, though he has been threatening to retire for several years now. Though single now for at least 20 years, he seems always to be helping out some needy acquaintance or another with financial problems. We eat out and then talk before he turns in about 11:00, leaving me to read a while before retiring to the couch for the night. We have some cold cereal in the morning before I head out about 8:00 AM, and I reach home in the late evening of 9 November after an absence of about eight weeks. Bayloo and the girls managed to somehow get along without me.

When I visited the dentist on November 16th, he reminded me that I might still have 3 or 4 dental implant plugs placed into the right lower jaw, and that it wouldn't probably cost me much more than about the price of a new car. If I believed I might still have a lot of years ahead of me, I might consider it, even though my frugal nature rebels against the very thought of such extravagant expenditure. After all, I remind myself, brother Phil has gotten along just fine with his false teeth for now at least some thirty odd years.

I generally manage to get six or seven hours of sleep each night , getting to bed generally about 2:00 AM--and generally a nap of a little over an hour in the late afternoon. I wish I could sleep more, but after only those limited hours of sound sleep, my mind begins to churn upon one or another the various projects that confront me and which I dearly intend to complete. An hour or so of that churning state of unproductive fragmented mental effort forces me to acknowledge that I might just as well give up the vain hope of further sleep--for now--in favor of the wakeful state of more productive mental effort upon such projects as continue to haunt my intentions. Every week I find myself several hours in pursuit of a job opening by e-mail, letter, or phone--unlikely as the project begins to seem. Both the Brasseur and the Boepple genealogy books need reworking of their tattered pages. The manuscript which I hope to publish needs corrections, changes, and additions. There are more books that I want yet to read and study. There are several subjects upon which I need to study and write--in order to clarify an opinion to myself. I need to listen to Charlie Rose and Rush Limbaugh, to keep abreast of what is happening in the world. I would like to write a poem or two. I long to listen again to some of my favorite music, but the siren call of its melody distracts me from my writing and reading. I managed to read 46 books in 2004; and 50 in 2005. How many books can one read in a lifetime? I haven't read but perhaps about 1300, in addition to the many textbooks in my 24 years of schooling. In 2004 I also managed to see just less than a hundred movies which I carefully select, and many well worth seeing. In addition to these things, I regularly go through several journals each month in the public library. And I almost always take a fifty minute walk each day. All of these things take time, energy, thought, and determination. In the past few years I have taken to working some crossword puzzles by way of diversion. Little of all this would be possible, except that my general health remains good and appropriate medications control what would otherwise be rather distracting symptoms. I strive to keep method in these advancing years of my geezer-hood. As to purpose, that is entailed in the objectives towards which I aim. "Revolving ceaseless night and day, the lives of mortals wear away. As summer's torrid solar beams dry up the ever lessening streams."

Bayloo flew out to visit her family in Missoula for 5 days during the X-mas holidays while I enjoyed my preference for solitude and reflection. So much for the year 2004

RGB

2004
2005

Entering 2005, my course, plans, and objectives remained essentially unchanged. A couple of job prospects faded away as I expected they would. When one is job hunting, the answer one gets is almost invariably, no. On the other hand, that reality fades into insignificance in the face of another and overriding reality--that one needs must find only that one rare and elusive, yes.

I was dreaming up other angles of what I might do to bring in the cash I would need for the publication of my manuscript. And I was rewriting and adding to the text, in order to have it ready the moment opportunity should arrive. This being around home and under foot is a hard business for a fellow intent on making progress. I would rather be up and doing, to produce evidence of there being something accomplished. Or, it would be nice to get out upon another long road trip where I could combine the business of the job hunt with visitations upon those with whom I am acquainted. But I have just gotten back from a road trip and there needs to be a decent interval before I presume to impose upon their hospitality again. Besides, I need to get the income tax work finished before I dare leave again. I gave some consideration to working as a substitute teacher, but the remuneration was rather scant, so I didn't want to rush into that.

Near the end of January I looked up Dr. Tomlin and visited with him. It has been 6 or 7 years since I had seen him and he is now past his mid eighties. He was still alert and didn't seem to have changed much. We worked together and had common cause in various grievances when we were employed at Las Vegas Medical Center.

Val had been back on the Indian reservation a few days at X-mas and a few day ago had come up with some insect bite marks upon her person. She happened to be taking down a few old pictures off her bedroom wall when she discovered an insect behind one of them. I got out the insect field guide and discovered it to be a bedbug. I hadn't seen one of those in many years. None of its brothers or sisters were ever discovered to be hiding about the room. One of those creatures can survive an entire year on one good blood meal. On that same day, I heard the first peal of thunder for the year.

In February I printed out the most recent revision of the manuscript upon which I had been working more long hours. Would this prove to be the last laborious revision? Time would prove otherwise. Both Val and Heidi have afternoon-evening hours of work. Bayloo gets to bed usually by 10:00 PM and she gets up at five or six in the morning. As she is heading to bed, I drive out to pick up the girls from their places of employment. During the day hours, the girls are usually in school, one in high school and the other in GED program while also taking some college courses.

It is common for people in our dry northern climates to be somewhat troubled in the winter season with dry and itching skin. My back itches relentlessly and most especially in the evenings. I use a kitchen knife or a wooden backscratcher to thoroughly work it over once or twice daily. And then I use the knife to spread Vaseline over the rough and reddened skin to prevent the loss of too much moisture. The scratching routine is a very pleasant and satisfying relief, but the relief is only momentary and one is driven to go over the whole acre again and again. The workout must be judicial lest one leave the skin broken and subject to weeping and infection. Related to the dry skin problem (the winter crud) is the hyper-allergic state of eczema that flairs up or is set off periodically by a host of non-specific triggers of various foods and environmental conditions. Even after all these years, mine again flares up periodically to disturb my tranquility with yet another source of irritation--mostly on the hands, arms, and anti-cubital areas. I had been given a couple of handsome woolen shirts and had taken to wearing them a few weeks in this winter weather before I became fully cognizant of the eczematous disturbance they were bringing on to my system. I hardly noticed the new source of itching and irritation because of the then more intense itching of the winter crud upon my back. But the sum of misery had indeed increased before I recollected what I had long known--wool is one of the substances known with certainty to excite or precipitate a bout of eczema. Off to the Goodwill store went the shirts, but it was many weeks before the eczema finally abated.

In early March I finally got my Federal Income Tax Report filed, leaving me free again to roam about the country now that most of the winter was departed. On the 8th of March, after helping Heidi a few hours with her homework, I called Lynn Fitz in El Centro to warn him to expect my arrival and about 11:00 PM the 9th, I headed out to spend a couple nights at his place, traveling long into the night before stopping at a rest area in Northern Arizona to sleep about four hours in the pickup. On the 12th, I stop by to visit grandson Michah in Loma Linda. I leave with him some of my useful medical equipment and a few medical books. We eat out, and then I read a few hours before crashing on his couch. Michah and I have scrambled eggs for breakfast before I head north about mid-morning. I would stop over longer with Mich, but I don't want to intrude upon his schedule of hard study in his first year of medical school. A pleasantly cool day with even some rain and fog on the high desert, and I stop to get my 50 minute hike followed by a peaceful nap at the Boron Rest Area, and then drive on the whole day to arrive at Red Bluff in the wee hours of morning. There I located the Wal-Mart where I slept about six hours in the pickup along with about twenty other overnight camper units. I arrived in Medford the 14th, to find Beaux home with Roseola. I drove Ribs out to his baseball practice and watched the action. He is very attentive to situations of play and accomplished with his glove and arm. I am told that last season, he and Beaux played on the same team, and that they took the citywide championship, and even went on to win at a state level of competition. We return to Tina's place by 6:00 PM, and make ourselves some sandwiches for supper. Tina and Gordon take a night out to attend a movie while I stay about to watch the kids and I do up a load of dirty dishes. I talk an hour or more with Tina before she is off to bed, and then watch TV basketball a while before I bunk out in one of the boy's room about two AM. The morning of the 15th, Beaux and I drove out to Central Point to visit a couple hours with cousin Dorothy LaVallee nee Boepple and her spouse Joe. About 5:30 I drive Cui to meet with his councilor, and then try without success to locate Cowboy. Back at the house, I remove the broken screen door which is about to fall off of its hinges. And then have a meal of pasta with them, before Tina and I get in an hour of conversation. She fills me in on what is happening to whom. I get to bed about 2:00 AM and then head north in late morning. I nap a couple hours at the Aurora Rest Area in the late afternoon of this rainy day, stop at Burger King to dine on one of their fine hamburgers, and then arrive at Pierre's place in the west hills beyond Banks, Oregon about nine PM just as Pierre is arriving home. We talk of politics and things about an hour before Jackie, Sam, and Chris arrive home. They are all in bed by 10:45, and I read a couple hours before getting to bed about 2:15 AM in the spare room. The following day I spend time in Hillsboro Library and then over to Jauhn's place in the late afternoon. There I get my 2¼ mile hike and then watch some NCAA basketball before we sit down to the meal Massy has prepared for us. In the evening we play some cards and then Jauhn and I tell the younger boys some of the tales of our life experiences before all get to bed in the early hours of the morning. On the 18ᵗʰ of March, Michah flew in for a few days of vacation from school. While staying at their place I spend my days at the library to study and keep out from under foot as the youngsters keep preoccupied with their chores and home schooling assignments. In the evenings we generally play cards or some board games, and sometimes watch a video movie or some sports event. Some afternoons or in early evenings--especially on the weekends of holidays--Jauhn, the kids and occasionally even some of their cousins play basketball or football in the front yard. In the late afternoon or early evening there is often a game of soccer, or baseball to play for one or another of the youngsters, and we go out as a group to join the spectators. Late evenings we may talk a bit with the youngsters who are, one or another, at the computer in the large all-purpose upper chamber room. And when they all have retired, I usually stay up until about 2:00 AM to read. A short stack of full width mattresses with pillows and bedding is kept in a nitch on the floor, beneath a window, of the all purpose attic room. There, myself or many another relative has often nested comfortably at night.

March 22ⁿᵈ, I depart Portland and chase off in search of my high school classmate, Bernard Chase, who lives somewhere in the Hazel Del area, north of Vancouver, WA. I searched about an hour before I finally located the place where he and Barbara Waite--both now widowed--are attempting to make a life together in their golden years at a trailer home park. I spent the day and the night at their place, and she made us a big supper. But as the day moved along, I noted many clues that suggested they were not settling comfortably into their recent arrangement. Bernard seems to have an avid preoccupation with wine, and from some of the literature lying about, I deduce that Barbara is a tee-totaling LDS member. There were a number of uninhibited brief, but hot exchanges and vague accusations between them. Still, we managed to fill the evening with conversation about old times and mutual acquaintances. Barbara appears to have contact with a great many of her school chums from through the years, and she must have called a dozen of them that evening, wanting even me to say hello to some of them--like Jean Buchanan, Lucy Heiss, and Janet Potter. But the long term prospects for their companionable association did not seem bright. The demon alcohol seeming to be a part of the dysfunction between them--or, perhaps, a consequence to it. But it was not my place to make any comments about that to them. Only something drastic is likely ever to bring him to grips with the reality of that seemingly troubled relationship. Only a few months later I picked up rumors that he and she had gotten into a heavy domestic altercation, and that he had spent some time in jail and then into a treatment center at Ft. Vancouver. I contacted him by e-mail just a couple months ago and I get the impression that he may have gotten back control of his life and freedom from the bottle. He is renting a room in a private home and it sounds as though he is beginning to take interest again in the world about him.

Next day (the 23rd) I dropped in to visit the family of nephew Andre and Gretchen in Everett, WA and arrived just in time to take supper with them. They are a very hospitable family and never seem to mind setting another place at the table. After supper, they were heading off to their church where Laura Lee has recently gotten a good position as church music director, and Andre and Gretchen participate in one of the instrumental groups. Naturally, I was not enthusiastic about getting involved with their religious avocation, but since it was only a musical practice session with no preaching or passing of the plate, it seemed like it might be a good opportunity for a first hand impression of where the saints are heading these days. I did spend some time observing the musical practice session and then spent part of the time with Anna, Emma, and Claire playing ball in the foyer. I have come away with fresh observations and formulated impressions with what is going on in their supermarket church, but that is a subject for another essay. Back to the house by 10:30, we have a little ice cream, Baileys Irish Cream, and conversation before everyone heads off to bed. That night I sleep in the pickup alongside the house in preference to the offer of their spare bedroom, for I don't want to impose on facilities overcrowded with women folk.

Andre is a sort of human dynamo of good will and cheerful disposition, urging and encouraging his people along on their individual learning and practice sessions in schooling, music, and dance. I gather that he is in the top echelon of the engineering staff at Boeing. He is also working on a masters degree in management. The affection he lavishes upon his householders seems well reciprocated. His behavior seems a very near image to that of his father (my brother, Gene), except that one can talk with him, without being 'talked down to'. Alone with him when the family is in preparation for bed, I note that he has a marked predisposition for some deep and philosophical ideas that he is wont to penetrate. But the hour is late, time is short, and he must arise early to work, so we do not long pursue that course at this time.

The next morning I head north to visit sister Ookie who now lives in Burlington--just north across the river from Mt. Vernon. En route, I stop at the Wal-Mart in Marysville to get an oil change. I have long considered the possibility of perhaps doing some refractions and contact lens fitting at one of these chain store outlets. Limiting my Ophthalmology practice to these simple procedures. It is obvious however, that these positions are being filled exclusively by Optometrists, and it seems not likely to me that they would be open to the use of my services into what seems to be one of their private domains. Still, with time on my hands while awaiting the servicing of the pickup, I decided to pop in to their vision center to make enquiry. Talking with the optician, I was surprised to learn that the ODs in these stores are often looking for someone to fill in for them for some occasional shifts of work. He took my name and E-mail address and promised to put it out on the Wal-Mart web site for such as might be looking for help, and promised to get back to me concerning the possibility of finding some work shifts in this very store. Visiting Duane in the following week, I enquired at the Wal-Mart in Ephrata and discovered that they were looking for someone right now to work in their facility. But their local and area managers were not available at the time I was in the area, so I never actually had a chance to get together with them. Not long after that, Bayloo sent me word that a manager from the Wal-Mart in Santa Fe had seen the information on the e-mail blurb and wanted to get in touch with me to talk about some possible work arrangement. I began to suspect that there might be possibilities for such work all over the country, though I would naturally be limited to those few states in which I had been maintaining my medical licensure. The thing seems to have some possibility, but I am aware that the insurance industry will surely stand in the way of this--directly, or indirectly.

I then arrive at Ookie's place and we talk a bit before I take my usual hike and stop at the library to check my e-mail. In the late afternoon we stop by Hastings large grocery store and make a supper from their deli food bar. She retires early, as is her custom--like about 7:00 PM--and I spend the evening watching some NCAA basketball and reading until about 1:30 AM. In the morning after breakfast she and I poke about in a couple Goodwill stores for books and other second handed usterets, before I head back south about noon. I stop in Bellevue a couple hours to visit Jean Buchanan a couple hours before moving out ahead of the heavy traffic about 3:00 PM with the snack she sent along with me. Then eastward over Steven's Pass, stopping at the rest area west of Ellensburg to get my nap and then eat my snack before I arrive at Duane and Georgia's farm just before 9:00 PM, where we talk for 1½ hour before they retire and I settle into the bunkhouse were I can be out from underfoot and manage upon my own time schedule. We breakfast together in the morning and I am made privy to the nature and details of the impending divorce and details thereof concerning Tom and Barbara. A marriage that has been a series of minor and major crises since its inception some 6 or 7 years ago. From what I am told, it seems obvious that Tom is severely depressed and even suicidal. During the seven days that I remain on the farm, I have plenty of leisure for reading and study of the various books and other materials that Duane has accumulated for my perusal. We discuss other matters as well, but they are naturally preoccupied with Tom's problems and the disruption it threatens to further precipitate upon him.

April 1st I left the farm and drove to Chewelah to visit Raymond Horton as I stopped over at their place a few days. I am always amazed at how much we have in common and the parallel interests that has occupied our thoughts throughout the 50 year interval between ages and 15 and 65 in which there was no communication whatsoever between us.

On the 4th, I stopped by to visit Phil and Dot in Spokane. There I do my laundry and have the use of Dot's word processor to work out a writing project. Word comes from Kate's daughters in Hardin, Montana, that Roxy has bought the house next door to Jody's place where she and Ken will be living. They are to be married 21 May. Phil has been out to Hardin not long ago to help her make her decision on the purchase. Roxy lived with Phil and Dot for several months, a few years ago. Also, while in Spokane, a call from Bayloo informing me that Jarvis (of Wal-Mart Optical) wants me to get in touch with him.

I left Spokane on the 7th, and arrived at the Tri Cities where I stopped to take my evening meal. I tried then to locate nephew Mark Krahn (one of Ookie's sons) in Pasco. Stymied in that effort, I had to stop at a local library to research the question before I finally arrived at their door in the early evening. His wife and the 2 younger children were out of town, and the older girls were just in the process of rustling up the evening meal. We watched a very good video movie (Gandhi) and then they put me up for the night. The next morning after breakfast, Mark and I had a walk and philosophical talk together before I head out to Portland about 1:00 PM. En route there, I stop--as usual--at the Chamberlain Rest Area on the

Washington side of the Columbia to revel in its magnificence and then get my day's nap before continuing on to Portland. I learn from Jauhn that Gerhardt Saur has recently died and his funeral was a couple days ago. A plain man of unusual excellence of character and quiet disposition. I had last visited with him a couple years ago in Monroe, the day his wife, Tille, slipped into her terminal coma a few days before her death. I stop at Pierre's place for the night. The next morning, Pierre and I and his neighbor step out together the property line between them that threatened to be a source of dispute between them. In the afternoon, I drove up to Alpine Rose to watch Norge's team play a baseball game. I spotted Miette in the opposite bleacher (with her mother). Miette, Joss, Izzy and the baby (they call her Moria Joy) came over to chat a while with me, and I had a chance to hold the youngster in my arms for a bit. Back then to Pierre's place after stopping with Jauhn and family to have a hamburger. Another call from Bayloo to inform me of another call from the Wal-Mart people in Santa Fe--they must have at least a solid intention of wanting to give me consideration for employment.

On the 11th, I relocate my base to Jauhn's place, getting out from under foot of the noise and commotion of some construction work at Pierre's place. Though it seems to me a virtual certainty that the biological mother of Pierre's children is of full blooded native American stock, she was adopted into the family of the Ashby's as an infant, and has never taken an interest in pursuing the question of her genetic heritage. Massy and I discuss at length the matter of the possibility of getting funding for the education of Pierre's children. If my supposition if true, Pierre's children are fifty percent native American ethnicity. If that were to be established with proper documentation, these grandchildren might elect to obtain their individual (proof) "**certificate of native American blood**" status; and be then eligible for enrollment as tribal members. That would make them eligible for the wealth of financial aid, grants, and scholarships to which tribal members have full access. That, I believe, <u>would alone be adequate to entitle them</u> to a plethora of grant and scholarship funds (even without having to be actually enrolled as a tribal member). A matter of current and practical significance to Jessica and Francois who are obstructed from their opportunity to obtain financial funding for college education. The minimum requirement for the above said "certificate of native American blood" would be that the name of mother's biological mother be known. One would then be able to obtain the necessary proof by obtaining birth certificates from Oregon's Department of Vital Statistics, or from Klamath

County. Even though the adoption courts may have put up obstructions to the actual facts (to the public at large), either Jessica or Francois, or their mother--as immediate concerned family--does have a right to access that information. The necessary steps do not seem to me to be formidable obstacles. "Life is short, and time is fleeting . . . ." To obtain this information concerning the mother and maternal biological mother, one would first need to present a certified copy of one's own birth certificate. One would then write for this information to:

DHSF
Dept. of Vital Statistics
P.O. Box 14050
Portland, Oregon 97293

OR, apply in person at:
800 N.E. Oregon Street
Suite 205
In Portland, Oregon

AND, one must supply them with the following:
-Current driver's license
-Full name
-Date of birth
-Place of birth
-Mother's maiden name
-Your reason for needing these birth certificates

While in Portland at this time I pursued this question more intently and put forth my best effort to get this information into the hands of those who are legally entitled to obtain the necessary information and documentation from state and tribal archives. Would I be able to get any of these people to lift a finger to expedite such a project? The mother? The grandmother? The father? The children themselves? It became discouraging unlikely. To each child this question has a potential financial value of perhaps up to $250,000.00. Is that worth reaching out for? What are the actual probabilities that even a concerted effort at this project might bring it to fruition? I do not know, but I do know that if it were me, I would give it my unstinting effort with the utmost of perseveration. For what--after all--are the chances of a young person getting hold of this amount of tax free money by dint of working long shifts slinging hash in some café? How probable--we might ask--might it have been that the Mahatma Gandhi could have had so wide an influence on the events of Africa and India during the course of his life?

I stopped by Portland State University in downtown Portland to further inquire into the subject on behalf of Boo and Bah. The Native American Indian Center there is a fine large building on the edge of the campus. They referred me to Rose Hill, who is the native Indian advisor to Indian students on campus and I finally located her in room 425 of Smith Hall. She reminds me that to have eligibility to native American Indian funds, the kids will first have to be enrolled in the tribe and then funds ought surely be available to help them, for the availability of funds quite exceeds that which is actually drawn upon, each year. She advises me to have each of the two children make an appointment to come in to talk with her, and she will do what she can to help them along. I passed that word along, but I have no way of knowing if they ever acted upon it. With tedious persistence, I finally got a call through and managed to talk with the elusive Rose Treetop of the Klamath tribe in Chiloquin near Klamath Falls; to find out specifically what steps must be taken to get the kids enrolled into the tribal register--and thus eligible for those minority loans and grants. And I left word with Pierre that the next step is to find out from Bobby Ashby whatever facts and details she can recall from the adoption process that will be of assistance in putting us upon the right trail in the quest for relevant information. He tells me that in the ensuing summer he did stop by to talk with the adoptive grandmother, but from what I am told, she seems not to have much exerted herself nor taxed her memory to be of any much help in the matter. Nor is likely to--we may safely presume. One thing seems certain; the mother of the children is not about to lift a finger to be of any assistance in the search.

Rose Treetop informs me that the requirements for eligibility to enrollment in the Klamath Tribe are as follows:

- Must be at least one quarter of Native American Indian blood.
- A parent or biological grandparent must be or have been an enrolled tribal member.
- One must obtain a birth certificate of the enrolled ancestor (biological grandparent).
- One must fill out an enrollment application (can be obtained from Rose Treetop).

- One must then complete a family tree to as far back into your native American Indian ancestry as is possible.
- Obviously one would need to know the maiden name of the of the biological native American grandmother (and/or the N.A. grandfather).

Late morning of 19 April, Massy serves me some eggs and toast before I head out to Yakima, stopping again en route at Chamberlain rest area to refuel my soul with wind, sweet dreams, and inspiration to further endurance. I arrive at the Vic's place about 4:30 PM. He and I take a hike before Marge serves us a tasty salmon loaf and pasta. And then... a call from Bayloo. She informs me that Phil has been trying to reach me to inform me of the death of our nephew, Tom Bassuer last night. We chew on this and make our tentative plans, and I make calls to Phil and to Jauhn as the grapevine serves its purpose. And of course I reluctantly made my call of condolences to Duane and Georgia, not knowing what exactly to say.

Yes, the 19th of April 2005 saw the death of my nephew, Tom Bassuer, by his own hand in the prime of his life. A great loss and sorrow to his parents, Duane and Georgia. Tom was a talented and husky fellow with a bachelor's and master's degree in engineering; and employed as a locomotive engineer with the Burlington Railway, in Spokane, Washington. His long troubled marriage was about to end in divorce; and he leaves two daughters behind. I had just spent the last six days of March with Duane and Georgia on the farm and during that time I had become privy to their view of the details of his troubled life. Being aware of his troubles, they had regularly been in close contact with Tom by phone, and had been spending weekends with him in the hope of helping him to work through his problems. During my stay on the farm, there had been so much discussion of those problems, that I presumed they were interested in knowing my views and in hearing any suggestions that I might have. One evening, Georgia even had me speak with Tom by phone for about 20 minutes. The situation seemed grim to me. I told Duane and Georgia of my impressions in this matter and outlined a proposed plan of action both in conversation--and in writing--so as to be certain that they understood the graveness of my concern for his very life. Through the years, I have personally only seen and spoken with Tom on perhaps only a dozen or two scattered and brief interactions; so it is not the case that I had anything like a personal relationship with him. I was nevertheless deeply suspicious already for several years that there were things about his behavior and lifestyle that were badly in need of reform, long before the current crises of this situation. I wish now that I had taken the trouble to write him a pointedly thoughtful and perhaps somewhat offensive letter a year or two before, for, from what little I knew, things were already then going from bad to worse. Was it any of my business?, since his parents were already in contest with him over the mismanagement of his life. An idea that they seemed unwilling to accept or entertain, was that the major problem was that of alcohol--and that Tom had, in fact, become an alcoholic. From what I could gather, it seems as though he was even in some danger of now of loosing his job. A life disintegrating. The issue of alcoholism was the elephant in the room.

But Tom is gone now, and some of us from his immediate and extended family have ongoing regrets, for it is entirely possible that the fatal outcome might have been otherwise. What use now, for us all to berate ourselves in endless discussions over what might have been? "Of all sad words of tongue or pen, the saddest are these 'it might have been'".

Beyond the inevitable period of grief, one might best then aim to get free of the endless agony of futile ruminations. The impact of his death upon the emotions especially of the next of kin would have been less, perhaps, had that outcome been inevitable or truly random. But contingency enters into the equation because we mere mortals are the agents (as well as the objects) of our own historical fate. As entities of that agency, we are the embodiment of contingency. Which is to say that what Tom thought, said, and did obviously effected the evolution and outcome of his own problems--for "the child, too, is father of the man". To a lesser degree, those of us more closely involved with him in his life, might possibly have spoken, written, or acted to greater effectiveness. Thus are we emotionally drawn in, to become involved--to share the pain of triumph or tragedy. Human life exhibits a pattern obedient to the principles of human psychology; and those laws of nature are in the background, but there is contingency in the details (says Jay Gould), and contingency matters where it counts most.

I was up early on the 20th, to have a little breakfast and then head out for Spokane. I stop at the funeral to view the body and join the small gathering of family there. There lay Tom, so large and still. I nudged him on the shoulder and felt the cool of death upon the brow line. He would not stir. It was my last view and final adieu. I mingled with the folks in the anteroom amid the others with hushed unsteady voices, and was soon ready to retreat to the sunshine of the out-or-doors.

Duane and Georgia were to stay over for a few days with Doby and

114

Karen in Spokane. I drove out to the farm to spend a couple of days alone in the bunkhouse, and returned to Spokane for the funeral on the 23rd. I got a late start that day and came into the service twenty minutes late. I am told that they asked for comments from the floor. I missed hearing what Vic had to say as he led off that segment of the funeral service. After the service we made our exit and as I walked out was greeted enthusiastically and cheerfully by the six year old Michaelia--Tom's oldest daughter. Bright and bouncy, she apparently didn't grasp the full meaning of all this business of the permanency of death. We of the Brasseur side of the family repaired to a nearby city park on this mild sunny day. There we spent 3 or 4 hours together over some eatables with Duane and Georgia's people. Others of us present were Jauhn and Massy's family, and the families of brother Gene's children, Michelle and Adrienne. From there I drove to Yakima to spend a few day's at Vic's place

As we walk atop the mansion-strewn ridge overlooking Yakima behind Vic's place, the local signs of affluence recalled to mind the national wealth which I have seen to accumulate from coast to coast across this country. It recalls to mind the relative modesty of life as I remember it back in the immediate post-WW-II years. Undoubtedly there is still a degree of relative poverty scattered about the land, but compared to the mass of the lot of mankind even in our own times--what is that?

I returned to the farm on the 26th of April to see how Duane and Georgia were adjusting to their loss, with only vague plans for how I might kill some time before ending up in Hardin for the wedding of niece, Roxy Davis on 21 May. I figured I might hang about the farm 2 or 3 days before moving on and not wishing to remain under foot overly long while they were in the process of grieving. Louis and Wanda Rapp came over to visit one evening. I planned to leave the 28th, but Duane and Georgia encouraged me to stay around longer, and as I was developing a rather troublesome sinus problem, it seemed best to settle into a quiet life in the bunkhouse for a spell to treat my sinus problem with some antibiotics, a heating pad, and rest. I ended up staying through the 9th of May, making almost daily excursions into Ephrata to use the library and supply myself with some snacks. And after sending in my annual fee for medical licensure to the state of Washington, I stopped in to the Ephrata Wal-Mart to enquire for possible work doing eye exams. In fact, they were looking for someone. But their management people in charge of the vision center were off at some seminar meetings and there was nobody about with the authority to hire until they got back. I keep that possibility in the back of my mind, for it might be good for me to get back into that part of the country to settle in where I would be a little closer to family, while also possibly finding some part time work. Meanwhile, Duane and Georgia are again keeping themselves preoccupied with the chores of the farmstead and getting through what seems to have been the darkest phase of their grieving. Both Ray Tippens (from the west bank Indians of the Okanogan near Kelowna) and Doby stopped by the farm to talk a while over lunch, before I departed for Spokane in the early afternoon. I stay 2 nights with Phil and Dot, and enter into the trials of life which fate has in store for me beyond that present birthday, in now my 73rd year. Who would have thought that a fellow could live so long and still be enabled to get around fairly well? Its an encouragement, as I have yet a good many projects to work out. I do my laundry at Phil's place on my birthday and head east over Lookout Pass into Montana on the morning of the 12th after Phil and I get in a 30 minute walking exercise. I spent that rather cold night with extra clothing in the Wal-Mart parking lot in Helena. In the morning I had a donut and a can of pop before heading out to Townsend. I stopped in at the home of nephew Gordon Huft, but both are apparently off at work. I drive Hwy 12 and make a 45 minute stop in Harlowton to look over the old electric locomotive that used to operate over this section westward upon the Milwaukee Railroad, which went out of business somewhere in the early to mid 60's. Even the track and ties have all been pulled up. Perhaps 3,000 people still live there as the town continues to decline. I stop briefly at Melstone and Ingomar to drive through their muddy streets. Only a few people yet live in these places. Dying towns where the communities are already many miles apart. Only a few buildings yet stand in Vananda, where the deserted but yet sturdy brick structure of the two story school stands empty since, I guess, the late 1930's. When I arrive in Forsyth in the late afternoon, I wondered as to what was the white line upon the eastern horizon. Arriving in Miles City, I see piles of snow at the curbs and the edges of parking lots. I am told that they had a foot of fresh snow here last night.

I planned now to stop over here in Miles City about a week to bide my time until I head for Hardin and the wedding of Roxy and Kevin Cain. I arranged for $107.00 to get a room for six nights at the Olive Hotel in their Motel addition across the street. They informed me I must be out by next weekend as the rooms would all be taken by those to be attending the annual bucking horse sale. I am told that rodeo people attend this event in search of wild stock to use in their various rodeo shows out here in the west.

Each day I spend an hour or more walking through the various sections of Miles City. I am quite familiar with the north side of town, as we always lived in the north and I had newspaper delivery routes there. There, I can readily discern the changes that have evolved. But I am only moderately acquainted with the south side of town where I rarely ever had cause to venture. It appears to me that the south side is generally much more nicely maintained, while on the far north side many buildings are beginning to stand empty and the overall maintenance is being neglected. I had an easy life here for a few days with time to read and to cogitate. I do some history research at the city library and used their equipment to do some e-mail correspondence. I stopped briefly to visit Harold and Steve Kransky. I also looked up a few high school classmates who still live here. I visited Frank Samuelson whose wife died a few years back. He is active and looks well, and is retired from a lifetime of painting buildings for a living. His house and grounds are well maintained, and the inside of the house is clean and tidy. Even the beds are all made. Quite a contrast for example to the way Harold neglects cleaning and maintenance of his place.

Frank told me an interesting story about his mother who a hundred years ago came west from Wisconsin to Rosebud and Custer County area to grub out a livelihood. She married and they tried to carve out a homestead near the community of Angel, but found it a very marginal existence. Her husband was desperate enough to try to make up a bit of their financial deficit with the handling of a few shipments of bootlegged hooch. The husband was pointlessly murdered by an agent of the underworld, and she gave up the homestead attempt to go back to Wisconsin. Remarried again, she came back once more to give the homestead another try. A desperate life--the hardships of marginal existence on the frontier. They finally again left the homestead and moved into Miles City where Frank's father then began painting for a living. Interestingly, Frank's mother sat down in about 1930 to write up the details of the various desperations that constituted her life. When the mother died some 15 or 20 years ago, they found her interesting handwritten manuscript among her belongings. It has since been published in a Montana historical journal. What a nice legacy for Frank, this manuscript.

Dennis Blunt became paraplegic several years ago subsequent to complications of surgery for abdominal aortic aneurysm. I was able to visit him--propped up in his wheel chair--for about an hour before his wife hauled him back to bed. For, being unable to squirm in his perch, he is predisposed to the development of pressure sores if he sits upon his backside too long at a time. Another day I visited Bernard Riley out tending his front yard in his motorized wheel chair. He tells me that 10 or 20 years back he worked at a stockyard in Billings. They were using chemical pesticides to keep the area sanitized. In retrospect, he recalls that there were not even any birds such as one would expect to frequent such an area. He wonders if the exposure to those toxins might have had something to do with the osteosarcoma he developed in his thigh bone. He first had to have his leg removed. Later, they had to go even further and removed half his pelvis. Considering that he has now to get around in his wheel cart, perched on his one remaining haunch, he seems to be in pretty good spirits. So are we all, "inheritors of some few years and sorrows".

On May 20th, I drove to Harden to be on hand for Roxy's wedding on the following day. I spent a little time with Phil and Dot, and that evening we attended a nice pre-wedding dinner provided by Roxy and Kent. And I spent that night and the following at Jody"s place. During the day of the wedding, Phil, Dot, and I toured the nearby Custer Battlefield Historical Monument, and then attended the wedding ceremony in the early evening. After the wedding there was a light buffet supper and a wedding dance at the fairgrounds. Mike Kransky and Jan were there, and Ed Ban and Skippy's daughter Nicki and granddaughter Christie.

The morning of May 22nd, I had breakfast of cold cereal with Phil and Dot, in Jody's kitchen before I headed south at 10:00 AM, to do the 1000 miles of continuous driving through Wyoming and Colorado in 14 ½ hours and arrive home at 12:30 AM. There, I have a bite to eat and work on a crossword puzzle before getting to bed at a customary hour of 2:30 AM. I called Tina and made arrangements with her to take Cui and Beaux out with me on a summer jaunt through the Northwest, June 12 through 18. She tells me that Real has proposed that the two of them finally come to agree to give up their futile legal wrangling through expensive lawyers. And so once again the moral influence of economic reality exerts its benevolent influence upon the hearts of mankind.

Our foster daughter, Heidi Begay was to graduate from high school, and some of her people from the Navajo country stopped by to eat with us and spend the night sleeping on a mattress on the floor before we had breakfast and then off to the graduation exercise the following day. In anticipation of my upcoming trip, I am working on an essay to include into my manuscript. Meanwhile, I am also still exploring the possibility of locating some part time employment through Wal-Mart or a Sam's Club here in northern New Mexico, but their managerial team appears to be so excessively dominated by committee influence, that their progress evolves at a geologically slow pace.

Bayloo flew out to Missoula on the 1ˢᵗ of July, and I headed north on the 2ⁿᵈ. Up through Chama, Pagosa Springs, Cortez, Moab, Salt Lake City, and Pocatello to reach Missoula. I pulled into a rest area near Dubois, Idaho about 3:00 AM on the chilly night of the 3ʳᵈ, and pull on an extra layer of clothing before getting 7 great hours of quiet sleep and then continuing the beautiful drive northward to reach Missoula about 2:30 PM with a red gage light informing me that I was about out of fuel. I can make about 450 miles on a full tank of gas. I stopped a bit at Annie's place to drop off the bag of clothing Bayloo had sent with me. I hung around there about 20 minutes awaiting a sign from Bayloo as to the agenda for the evening and the night, but no sign came, so I went out to the pickup to get my nap, followed by a 2½ mile hike, and then rapped again upon the door to gain readmission to the kitchen at 6:20--to sort of estimate the social temperature to my presence there. That was beginning to seem cool, for some reason that I was unable to fathom. They had just eaten, and I stood there quietly about five minutes with no invitation to have a bite to eat, nor any indication as to what were "our" arrangements and schedule for this family get together; which was centered upon the graduation of one of Bayloo's grandchildren. Having not eaten since oatmeal time of yesterday morning, at that point I just picked up my pride and headed out upon my own devices to await some new turn of events. One must always have a private agenda to supplement any joint agenda that goes into default. The natural history of a more or less useless and unemployed old man of our species is that of a retreat to the solitude of his own company, to await the pleasure of the benignly indifferent grim reaper who pays us each a call, eventually. Meanwhile, I am not destitute and I head out to get a bite of junk food; and then philosophize in soliloquy, as I prepare to spend the night in the pickup at the local Wal-Mart to await the events of the morrow. It is not as though these folks had no idea as to where to find me--if they had some inclination to visit with me, or were curious as to what had become of me. I did have a little trouble getting to sleep finally perhaps about 3:30 AM, but then slept soundly until about 8:30 AM. I had a soda pop and a pastry for breakfast in the pickup, and then used the Wal-Mart facility to shave, brush my teeth, wash up, comb, and change clothes before I drove over to the Adams Field House facility for the graduation exercise. The campus has changed a great deal since I graduated from college here in 1958. As long as I was here anyway, I just as well watch Nathan's graduation ceremony before continuing out upon my private journey westward. The crowd was large and I thought to mingle in anomalously with it. Suddenly, I seem to have acquired visibility once more to the eyes of Bayloo, who caught my attention and waved me over to where she was sitting. Some of her other grandchildren soon came along to join us. Nothing was said about yesterday. Was my being ignored and slighted a mere figment of my imagination?

From this point on, I seem suddenly to have been included into the events of the times. A couple of big festive feedings and genial group gatherings hosted by Dean and Cindy. And in the late evening, four of us had an interesting three or four hour long philosophical conversation, and I eventually retired to a bedroom for the night. The next couple days pass comfortably and on 7th, I head west over Outlook Pass after dropping off Bayloo at the airport for her return flight home to Santa Fe. I spend some time at the library in Cheney before Phil, Dot, and I go out to the casino with the intent of having a bigger meal than what I had need of. But for some inexplicable reason, the price per plate had been upped from about $11.00 to $18.00--on account of it being "fish day". As though the fish menu were not available on the other days. And who can eat eighteen dollars worth of food in one sitting? In the spirit of good fellowship, I was (grudgingly) about to spring for the tab but was relieved by the sudden outburst of indignation from Phil. And why should we--after all--voluntarily submit to this robbery? As the potential payee, I had felt sort of socially trapped into the indignity of this fleecing. So we left our place now at the front of the long line of fleecees to exit the casino and stop for a meal at "The Prospector". There too the price seemed a bit exorbitant, but Phil and I divided one meal between us--and still had more than enough to eat. These expensive restaurants surely know full well that they are selling two meals on one plate--and very few individuals can ever get around the mountain of food.

I depart Spokane the 9th and stop over one night at the farm, where Duane and Georgia seem to be maintaining their stability in the face of their recent tragedy. On the 10th I head over Steven's Pass to visit a couple hours with Jean Buchanan before continuing north to Everett to stop over at Andre's place. Laura Lee and the three little girls were at home. Laura Lee served me some stew and then we two talked a couple of hours. She tells me of her work and her plans, and we listen to some of her own harp recordings--a disc copy of which she gives me. She then departs to her house-setting job when Andre and Gretchen arrive home at 10:30 PM. But Andre is soon off to a second job (of minimum time requirement) as they put me into a spare bedroom for the night. It seems to me that he is also involved in some course work for a degree in management. One wonders how he is able to generate so much energy.

I was up at 8:30 in the morning and talk a bit with Gretchen while she is preparing what seems to be a rather elaborate breakfast. To my surprise there soon arrives Gene's wife, Betty, and his daughter, Michelle. And so, we visit pleasantly a while. Then there comes the taking of photographs, before I toss my gear into the pickup and head south. I arrive in Medford about 10:00 PM and talk a bit with Tina before Beaux and I drive out to order up some tacos through Poco Uno who is working there at Taco Bell. One of the boys gives me his bed for the night, and in the late morning, Cui, Beaux, and I head out for a tour of the Northwest. We head out over Hwy 140 to Lakeview and then north at the foot of Albert Rim to arrive at Jordan Valley in southeast Oregon about sunset to set up our tent, have sandwiches, and then I take my 45 minute hike about the camp on this cool evening before retiring. The next day we head through Nampa and Boise to take the Gooddale Cutoff road and arrive at Craters of the Moon National Monument. There we take a camp site and set up our tent before spending the remaining half day viewing the displays, climbing a couple of the crater mounds, and taking a hike before retiring to the tent.

The following day we head over the Sawtooth Range to Stanley and then to the Bonneville camp area where we stop a couple hours to bath in the natural and unimproved hot springs that empties into the creek there. From there we head through New Meadows, Cambridge, and then into Hells Canyon at dusk to take a tent site for the night. The following morning we head north to drive up to view the Seven Devils but the top part of the road up to Heaven's Gate was still closed with snow drifts. We drive up to Lewiston and then along the beautiful Grand Rhond River formation to Enterprise, Oregon where we set up our tent at a campground before I take my evening hike, read a bit, and then retire. On the 16th we then take breakfast at a café in Enterprise, before driving to Walla Walla, where we stop at Wal-Mart to get an oil change. From there we drive up to visit Dry Falls to view the exhibits and the formations; and then on to Ephrata where we stop to have hamburgers before stopping at the farm about 7:00 PM. The 3 year old Sophie is visiting there with Duane and Georgia, and we are invited to put ourselves up in the bunkhouse.

The next morning Georgia serves us breakfast before we depart. We stop to visit the Ginko State Park museum before continuing on to Vic's place in Yakima. There they serve us some ice cream and then Vic gives the boys some information about the mosaics he is creating before we continue our journey. We stop at Chamberlain Rest Area 45 minutes before we reach the Portland area where we stop to have tacos and then stop at Pierre's place about 9:30 PM. In the morning Pierre's bunch were busy making preparations to head out on a vacation trip as the boys and I head south at midmorning to arrive in Medford about 4:00 PM, where I drop the fellows off at Tina's place. I stop at the library a bit before they close at 5:00; and then I have a fine deep 1½ hour nap in the pickup in the midst of a wonderfully cooling rainfall. I exercise and read before spending the night in the Wal-Mart parking lot. The next morning I drive over to the rest area near Talent to spend the day reading and working on my manuscript. I saw Poco Uno briefly again as I stopped at Taco Bell to have my evening tacos, and then back to Wal-Mart. There, by chance, I ran into Real. We shook hands and exchanged a few words, but we are not actually on talking terms and we parted without exacerbating our differences. In the morning I have some pastry and soda pop, and then stop by at Tina's place as previously arranged to pick up Mijita and Nombres for a trip to the coast. We got to Coos Bay about 3:00 PM, but had no idea as where to find Bart and Miette, as they had only within the past couple of weeks moved here to North Bend (adjoining Coos Bay). I finally located the church to which they are connected, but no one was there to provide us any information. We went to the city library and could not find them in the phone directory. Nor could we locate them even through the undertaker. It finally dawned upon me that Bart's father lives in the area and I did get an address from him. Miette and Bart, however, were not home when we located the place. It was getting late in the afternoon, so we stopped to get our evening dose of beans at the Taco Bell before again trying--without effect--to locate them at home. Of course, I do have my tent and sleeping bags along and I was about to find us a camp site near the beach, but as we drove down one of the main thoroughfares, one of the youngsters spotted their van at a park were some kids were playing baseball. The father had called to inform Bart and Miette that we were looking for them; and so they in turn were looking for us. At their new home, I park the kids with them as they were preparing to eat, while I got my 2½ mile hike before sundown. Mijita, Nombres, Josh, and Izzey play well together as we trot out the baby for inspection and catch up on the news before they are all retired by shortly after 11:00. We spend the next day at the beach and head back to Medford the following day and arrive there about 2:30 PM. There, I took a nap and hoped then to get in contact with grandson Cowboy, but discovered that he was working out of town, and so I head out over Hwy 140 (Winnemucca to the Sea Highway) about 5:30. For I was anxious to get back to Santa Fe, in order to explore the employment opportunity that seemed to be presenting itself.

Always a beautiful drive over the mountains, and across the face of Albert Rim into the lava and wastelands of northern Nevada: enjoying my donuts and soda pop as the day is cooling down, and listening to the worlds finest music. I stop at 2:30 AM at a rest area east of Winnemucca to retire into the camper for the night. More donuts and soda pop in the morning at 8:00 before I continue on Hwy 80 across northern Nevada, into Salt lake City, across Soldier Pass to Price and as far as Cortez, Colorado, were at 2:30 AM, I stop to overnight in the Wal-Mart parking lot in anonymous company with a dozen other traveling vehicles. Onward on the morning of 24 June after some pastries and soda pop; through Durango to Chama and then home by 1:00 PM. After a nap, supper, and a 2½ mile hike, I work a few hours on manuscript and get to bed at 3:00 AM.

The first of the week, I pursued the possibility of some part time work with Wal-Mart and finally spoke with their area manager on the 29th, and that evening attended a dinner and educational program on contact lenses which they hosted in Albuquerque. There I met a few of the local optometrists in the area. Prospects for some work were looking fairly good, for the area manager had already two or three times tried earlier to get in touch with me, and from our conversations I could read between the lines that his immediate prospects for filling the openings in either Santa Fe or Espanola were not brisk. In addition, there seemed the possibility of his needing someone to work a day or more in Las Vegas. Jarvis seemed determined to get me to commit to work in Espanola, though that site was being remodeled and was not yet ready for a practitioner. He talked of three days in Espanola, and one in Santa Fe. Apparently he had an uncommitted local on the string as a possibility for Santa Fe? And at that point, I preferred the Espanola location which is an easy 30 mile drive.

Meanwhile, I had to go through the cumbersome formality of making a formal work application, trying to remember the myriad details of a work career that spanned some 55 years. That, and my awareness of the many direct and indirect pathways by which the insurance entanglements can obstruct the possibilities of an old geezer in returning to work after five years of being retired: that, to my mind, seemed to weigh against the possibilities of this thing working out for me. There are other problems as well. Even as of this very day, I am not aware of any Ophthalmologist that practices out of any Wal-Mart store. The Wal-Mart seems to have no experience with that. Be that as it may, I went through the application ordeal and handed in copies of my various credentials, and then must wait to see what would come of it.

Concerning the opening in Espanola, it turned out as I had told Jarvis it would--the remodeling of the Espanola Vision center would not be finished on time, and so Jarvis indicated that there could be no starting till near the end of the month. That left me with a couple weeks to burn in pursuit of a couple other travel projects that had interested me. So I made plans to travel. But first, I had to get myself fingerprinted as a requirement for being licensed to be a foster parent. And then, I wanted to get rid of a polyp on my leg that had begun to chaff and bother me. Having no anesthetic on hand, I injected its base with a solution of B-12 that gave me just enough numbness to enable me to excise it myself--and it subsequently healed very nicely. After Bayloo gave me a free haircut, I was ready to depart. Heading out on 9 July at 12:30 PM, I stopped at the Wal-Mart in Espanola to inspect their equipment and facility; and then proceeded up through Cortez, Moab, Price, Salt Lake City, and pulled into a rest area east of Wendover about 4:00 AM. A mercifully cool breeze was blowing to facilitate my four hour nap, before continuing on to Winnemucca. There I stop at a casino for an omelet breakfast, and then stop at the local hospital in an attempt (without success) to locate Bob Brown, with whom I attended medical school. I arrive in Medford about 8:30 PM, and take my 2½ mile hike; then stopped to talk a bit with Tina, before I retired to the Wal-Mart parking lot to spend the night in the pickup. In the morning I was first in line to get an oil change and then stopped by Tina's place, where I had a bowl of cold cereal while waiting for Rousseaux, Rabeaux, and Beaux to ready themselves for our trip north. Rousseaux preferred to lounge on the bedding in the camper shell--we were to drop him off at Jauhn's place. Just 3 days ago ,Jauhn's family have returned from a 6 week trip to Europe. We arrived there at mid-afternoon. There I get my walk and Massy serves us all supper before Jauhn and I with the half dozen kids play basketball for an hour or two - and they then off to bed relatively early.

In the morning we have breakfast and talk a bit before Rabeaux, Beaux, and I toss our gear into the pickup and head east to attend the German Convention in Pierre, South Dakota. Cui will stay on at Jauhn's place until our return. He always has a great time there with these cousins, and always looks forward to the opportunity of spending some time with them. About 1:30 PM we travelers stop in Yakima to visit Vic and Marg. Long enough for me to get a bit of a nap: and Marg served us some refreshments. Again, the boys were interested in Vic's mosaics, and he explained to them some of the details of their production. We arrived in Ephrata about supper time and stopped at the A & W to make an evening meal on hamburgers, fries, and milkshakes, before stopping at the farm, where Duane and Georgia give us the use of their bunk house. I talk a bit with them before I take my 2½ mile hike about the perimeter of the farm, settle in, read a while and turn in early.

At 6:45 AM, we awake to the alarm, put the bunkhouse in order, and gather our gear into the pickup. Georgia feeds us some breakfast and there is then again a little time for talk before we head out on a long day of travel eastward. About 7:00 PM we stop in Billings to have tacos for supper. And then proceed south to Hardin. I didn't tell the boys that my nieces, Jody and Roxy lived there, and instead implied that we might find a camping place there for the night. The situation didn't lend itself to my intended ruse, as we knocked at Jody's door to inquire if we might pitch our tent in her large back yard. They were immediately skeptical of the unrealistic nature of the situation and it soon was necessary to present them the real details of the situation; and introduce the boys to their father's cousin. Jody told us she had plenty of room and invited us sleep indoors. And I was up at 6:45 in the morning. Then to roust the boy, I sang, "Oh, its up away at the break of day, at the peep of early morning/ Staff in hand, and eager band, our hearts as light as air/ In a drum and fife there is joy and life as our feet the earth are scorning/ Off we start with boy and heart with never a thought or care . . . ." Jody was making us some breakfast. She seemed a little touched by my song, and told me that her mother often used to sing to them when they were at home as children.

We left Hardin about eight, through Ashland and Broadus--an interesting route I had never before traveled. En route to Pierre, we stopped at the Wall Drug to have each a milkshake and give the boys a chance to wander about their extensive premises filled with interesting novelty items. At supper time we arrive in Pierre and took a room at the Governor Motel for the next 3 nights. Walking back from the Burger King, I found a ten dollar bill in the gutter--quite an uncommon thing, as people generally keep close tabs on their larger bills. The motel had a nice swimming pool for the use of the boys in the next few day, and we generally get a swim together in the evening--besides all the swimming they do when I am at the convention meetings. The boys eat fast foods in the day, but we all have tickets to each of the big evening banquet meals. And on Saturday they attend the German music dance with me, after which we walk back to the motel together.

Late morning, Sunday the 17th, we head back west, stopping again at the Wall Drug, and then to spend a couple hours at Mt. Rushmore, before continuing on through Deadwood, and to Sturgis were we stop to have some pizza for supper. We reached and explored Devil's Tower, and then at dusk we pitched our tent in the campgrounds at the foot of the basaltic lava plug whose mountain has long since eroded away. In the morning we broke camp and stopped in Gillett for breakfast. From there we passed through Buffalo and drove through the spectacular Ten Sleep and Wind River Canyons to get as far as the Craters of The Moon where we took care to pitch our tent in what we calculated should be the shade of a tree, come morning. Our tent was thus undisturbed by the heat of the early morning sun, and we slept comfortably until 8:15 AM. We quickly broke camp and continued westward to stop for breakfast at the first little town (Cary) we entered. Being short of time, we drove steadily all day, stopping only at magnificent Chamberlain Rest Area late in the day to refresh in the cooling wind and have a little picnic lunch. From there to Hillsboro where as arranged by Tina, I drop off my two fellow travelers and talk a bit with Rochelle, Jessica, Bam-bam, and Beans. I then drive to Jauhn's place to spend the night, and there I run into Belle who is spending a couple days with Stan. She has been helping Jauhn's kids clean up the garage, the yard, and the bunkhouse. Stan has finished her first year or two of Junior College and has been accepted into the Architecture School at Portland State. I gather she has some design for making the bunkhouse her work studio.

In the morning of the 20th after talking a bit with Jauhn, Massy, their kids, and Belle; Cui and I take leave and head south, arriving at Medford about 4:00 PM. I was anxious now to keep moving, for I was on short time--expecting to start work promptly on the 22nd; and I was expecting the arrival of Vic and Marg from Yakima enroute to Florida. It was a warm day, but we had the luxury of air-conditioning in the pickup. I stretched out on one of the boy's beds in Medford to try for a bit of a nap, but it was far too warm to be comfortable, and I soon gave up the idea and headed eastward over the mountain towards Winnemucca about 5:00 PM to drive on through the night and finally stop about 4:30 AM to get a four hour snooze in the cool of the early morning at a rest area west of Wendover,

Nevada. I arrived home at 10:00 PM that day, having traveled this 1330 miles from Portland in about 36 hours. Bayloo informs me that I am to call Jarvis Mixon in the morning, for the plans for my starting day of work have changed. The remodeling of the Espanola facility had still not been completed, and I was rather, now, to begin work in the Santa Fe facility next week on the 26th

I now had the time to send out an e-mail note to Pierre and to Jessica, concerning the summary of my findings of eligibility for scholarships and grants-in-aid to persons of native American Indians. Vic and Marg arrived in the late afternoon of the 23rd, en route to visit daughter, Yvette, who works in Florida. The four of us drive out to pick up Heidi from work and then drive out to look at some local public mosaic work, in which Vic is interested. The next morning, Vic and Marg continue their journey and I continue to prepare myself for opening day of work after having been retired for six years or more. I still had grave doubts that this was actually going to happen. But I did finally get my foot in the door and showed up promptly at 10:00 AM the 26th, for my first day of work. In my handicapped situation of working in a new routine, with new people untested to my experience, and with equipment new to me, I was pushed to keep up, but struggled through it. That evening, Heidi's mother and aunt showed up to spend a couple nights with us.

Though I haven't fit contact lenses in twenty years, I was suddenly in the thick of it. But the process hasn't much changed in all those years, except that now we keep on hand a large inventory of lenses that enables us to fit most patients at time of the primary eye examination. Tim Neumann was in charge of managing the vision center and has been aching to have a practitioner on the premises so as to get the department into full scale economic production, for he is anxious to demonstrate a positive record to facilitate his climb towards the top of the managerial personnel with the Wal-Mart organization. He is a big extroverted fellow who buzzes about to greet and glad-hand all of the drop-in shoppers to the department as courteously and continuously as though he were a fundamentalist preacher. And not without effect--for he signs up 2 or 3 drop-in exams daily to fill out the eye exam schedule. Though he is a little bit heavier, he otherwise reminds me very much of Pierre. He and I are natural allies. Now that I was situated comfortably in the Santa Fe facility, I was comfortable with it; and preferred this short drive, to that of each day driving the 35 miles to Espanola. He and I were both pushing Jarvis to figure on keeping me in this Santa Fe facility rather than putting me out to Espanola. And, by degree, it finally came to this. We were soon busy enough to go from a three-day to a 4-day work schedule.

I had not been employed directly by Wal-Mart, but rather, they have been paying me on a day-by-day. They wanted me take on the clinical facility as an independent contractor, though I am reluctant to be in a situation where I must take over the business aspects of dealing with employees, patients, insurance companies, and government; and finding my own replacement sub-contractor for days I wish to be off to post-graduate education and vacation. Even so, if they are not willing eventually to take me on as an employee, I will be in a situation in which I must consider that possibility--and provide my own medical malpractice insurance. And I have already seen that the insurance companies--on just general principles--are highly reluctant to go through the complexities of researching the "background of scattered records" of the 50 year career of a physician who has practiced no medicine whatever in the past six years. And so, I did contact a couple of insurance companies in the attempt to get insurance. They were polite enough, but one of them just could not seem to find a way to get me an application blank--though I contacted them three or four times. The other, had a stonewalling gauntlet of procedure that I must follow before they would consider my application. I must first join the local and state medical societies (at a cost of quite a tidy sum of dollars). To do that, I must attend the monthly local medical society to become known to these strangers. And then I might make my application to that local society--once I am well enough acquainted to get a couple of members to recommend my membership. After those months of bowing, and scraping, and prevailing upon strangers, I can then submit my application for membership into an organization for which I have no actual enthusiasm. What have I in common with these hospital based physicians all silently scrapping to preserve their individual territories in a myriad of distant specialties and subspecialties all quite remote from what I propose for the earning of my living? Once submitted, my application would then have its first reading at a subsequent monthly meeting. And then a second reading in a subsequent month. At the third reading (now several months down the road from where I initiated the process), they very well may approve my acceptance into the membership. And then I must come up with the big bucks before it is all finalized. Am I home yet? No. Now I may make my application to the insurance company and submit to them copies of a long professional career spanning fifty years. They are then at liberty to track down all of my past credentials and my reference to former medical acquaintances, etc. But I have outlived most of my former associates, and even some of the institutions where I have had my training and practice experience have long since withered away. The stage is set you see, for another long delay while they pretend to research my past and credentials. Such is the nature of my skepticism regarding the possibility of acquiring malpractice insurance. Even if my application eventually were approved, they still have the prerogative of making the insurance prohibitively expensive to me.

Thus it happened that month by month, I have been employed on only a day by day basis. Meanwhile--apparently--there seems not to have been a viable alternative candidate to put into either the Santa Fe or the Espanola vision center facility. Or into one of several other openings that are available in New Mexico or Washington states. And since I have actually proven myself an experienced, dependable, and capable practitioner, it finally appeared that before the year's end, Wal-Mart was giving reconsideration to the possibility of taking me on as "associate practitioner". (It finally happened in mid-February).

Regardless of all of the above, I continued to have an income and was quite pleased that now I was almost in a position to have my manuscript published into book form. Beginning 17 August, it was all systems go, on that project. The next day Bayloo and I ordered up a new computer for her work projects and I was then to have her previous unit set up at my own exclusive and private work desk in the bedroom. On August 27th, I wrote to Vantage Press to try and get them to take up my project under the terms they had proposed 3 years earlier. Economic circumstance had prevented my acceptance of the terms originally. I received from them a letter of acceptance on 12 September, and the project was then officially kicked off when I mailed off my first payment for the work the following day. On the 19th I put the finishing touches on the manuscript and mailed it into the publisher with a great sense of relief to be out from under all the work of it and expecting that the completion of the project was imminent. And by October 22nd I had earned enough to be able to make the final payment to the publisher as soon as that was required. They had been editing the manuscript and I--alas--was not yet done, for on the 24th, they sent me notice that I was to write to the writers of each of the reference sources that I had used in the manuscript--to obtain their consent for each of the longer quotations above 500 words. With heavy heart at all the obstructions, I made the effort and wrote about for said permission. My letters came back unopened. Just where should I guess I might have to write in order to find the person, estate, or company who held the copywrite authority to give me the release? Seeing the futility in such a paper chase, I gave up the idea and decided to get around the obstructions by simply citing the sources and rewriting in paraphrase the essence of what they were saying. It meant more work for me, of course, but the prospects for completing the task were now back into my own dependable hands. And I was finally finished with the rewriting and mailed back the edited manuscript to the publisher of December 7th.

About five years previously I had heard an excellent sermon by Rev. Archibald at a Unitarian service in Albuquerque, and had spoken with him after the service to tell him I was writing an essay on just that very subject, and that my impressions of the matters of concern--based on my own observations and experience in the field of Psychiatry--were in exact accordance with his own. At my request, he gave me a copy of his sermon so that I might use it in my own evolving manuscript; for my own writing seemed to me not destined to be a whit different, nor better written than what he had accomplished. I should have gotten him, right then, to give me his written authorization for its use--but I overlooked that now obvious detail. In mid-January of 2006, the Vantage editors wrote to inform me that I must now have his authorization, if I wished to use it in my manuscript. I finally did manage to get his address in Durango, Colorado, and finally got over that obstacle. In so far as I know, I am now finished with all that I must perform, and was then awaiting news of how Vantage is progressing with the final stage of publication.

Meanwhile, in mid-September, having completed our civilizing projects with Heather and Val, they had departed to attend college, and we got the first of our two new foster-girls. The second came in early November. The work of the hormones in the breast of the undisciplined teen-ager produces a sometimes unimaginable variety or mischief. Three of four of the several foster girls that that have been with us, occasionally call or drop by to visit us. Another wrinkle in the fabric of bureaucratic thinking is that next I must attend a series of educational courses pertaining to the various types of mischief into which the wayward foster child may indulge. And so, I must spend a couple of 3-hour sessions weekly, being lectured pedantically by high school and college graduates with psychology and social work degrees over a course of 6 weeks.

Vic and Marg stopped through again for a couple days on their way back home, and we toured some of the attractions of the area together. And towards the end of September Bayloo's sister, Carla, and some of their family stopped in with us for a day. Bayloo flew to Missoula to spend a week with the families of three of her children who live there. In that time, brother Phil flew down to spend a few days with me and I took a little time off from work so we could take in some of the points of local interest.

Thus ends the summary of my years 2004 and 2005.

R. Garner Brasseur, MD

Year 2006 Summary
R. Garner Brasseur, M D
Written 25 December 2006

From time to time I sit me down to organize my thoughts and ponder as to what project I should now enter upon to occupy my spare time. it's sort of dilemma to me. On the one hand, any of the several projects I contemplate requires of me to strain, think, and exert myself. And I (like other mortals) find myself reluctant to want to put forth a full effort. On the other hand, neither am I at all content loitering and wasting away the hours. Only work and accomplishment seem to give one a sense of purpose. Meanwhile, above and beyond all of that, the greater reality is that this world can get along as it does without the necessity of my being, or of having existed at all.

All of that aside, I need now to get on with what the title of what this essay suggests.

Now into my 74th year I have continued to work full time doing eye examinations and fitting contact lenses at the Wal-Mart, here in Santa Fe--a job that I had begun in August of the previous year. Until early February I had been working upon a day by day basis and finally then officially became a Wal-Mart employee. I work Monday, Tuesday, Thursday, and Friday from 10:00 am to 6:00 pm. Plenty of irritations and annoyances with the work and the untrained 'help' which is intended to be of some assistance to me. But the hope is that the various problems will eventually be ironed out. Meanwhile, merely being employed does help me to sustain, onto myself, the comforting delusion that I am still of some use in this world. And I do believe that the income somehow improves my status in the home--a wage earner and all that. Besides working four days a week in Santa Fe, I was also working a fifth day each week at the Wal-Mart in Espanola--about 35 miles north of Santa Fe.

In the previous two or three years we were accustomed to having a couple of native American Indian girls living with us while attending school and working at part time jobs. But this year, the treatment plan of IYC did not include any remedial consequences to the girls for their episodes of misbehavior or for being AWOL--sort of unreal expectations from the supposed principle of 'positive reinforcement techniques'. Needless to say it didn't work. "No pain, no gain". And with this new 'enlightened' program the girls became so unmanageable that Bayloo opted out from the arrangement, and we no longer continued to do foster parent care for IYC. We still hear occasionally and are occasionally dropped in upon by some of the girls who stayed with us previously.

It was sometime in May when at last I completed the final draft of my manuscript and sent it in to Vantage Publishers in New York for printing. I was finally out from under that (longer than expected) task and now had time for other things. Next, I had to get caught up with my post-graduate education courses so that I could get my medical license renewed at the end of June, which required me to spend a few days in Albuquerque.

I was making preparations for a trip into the Northwest in mid-July to visit my people and friends, but just a few days before my departure, while at work, I began to experience some chest and left arm pain which I immediately recognized to be the beginnings of a myocardial infarction, so I immediately left work and headed for the hospital, where I was admitted. On 12 July I underwent a surgical coronary artery bypass graft procedure requiring five grafts. As I had gotten into the hospital in an early stage of symptoms, I apparently had only minimal--if any--damage to the heart muscle. I was released home on the fifth hospital day. The day by day progress in my recuperation seemed to me a rather slow and trying business, but after seven weeks off of work, I was finally able to start back to work full-time just before September. Though I still worked four full days weekly in Santa Fe, I had not yet again returned to do any work in Espanola. Perhaps I ought not press my luck. I sure didn't mind getting three full day off work each week.

In December, I flew to Dallas for a three day convention of Wal-Mart eye doctors. All optometrists except myself, as best I could discern. And more focused on the politics of optometric practice than on postgraduate education.

While I was hospitalized, Real, Catheryn, and daughter Claire came by to look in on me, and stayed a couple of days. Perhaps the rebuilding of bridges between us, since I had not seen nor heard much from him since our falling out a few years earlier. Bayloo went to Montana for the Saur reunion towards the end of July and brother Phil came down to watch over my recovery and visit while she was gone. And in October, Vic and Marge stopped in to visit with us a couple of days.

I occasionally stop in to see Dr. Tomlin here in Santa Fe. He and I worked together at the state hospital a few years ago. I also visited with Dr. Cuykendal in Albuquerque--we worked together in Hobbs some twenty years ago. And I occasionally saw Dr. Ghosh who still worked at the state hospital. I was still in touch with old schoolmates Lynn Fitz, Raymond Horton, Bernard Chase, and Grant Mosby. I heard some stirrings suggesting the possibility that there was to be a reunion of the old high school class of 1952 in Miles City the coming summer? Once every two or three weeks I stopped by to visit a couple of hours with Paul Lewis and Jackie (Phalen)--old acquaintances from Miles City--who retired here from Brazil about twenty years ago. Jim Phalen comes through to see them occasionally and I visited a couple hours with him a few months ago.

My book, "*A Studied Impression of That Which Is*", finally came off the press in September, and they sent me 50 copies to do with as I wished. In early October I mailed copies out to various relatives and friends. It was a project I had worked on from time to time, for more than twenty years. I count myself fortunate to have had the time to study, ponder, and write up the conclusions I have come to regarding the nature of reality. And very fortunate to finally have found the means of getting the book published. A project that had been dear to my heart for so many years. My whole life seems to have been centered around that subject. I had gradually come to regard that investigation as 'a calling'--my primary mission in life. Having then had my say on the subject and rendered my honest and well considered testimony on the matter, I was then content at last to give up the ghost to the next life-or-death crisis that confronts me. These mile-stones of misery seem to have been coming around at about ten year intervals, but the aging frame is loosing its resilience. ("By my troth, I care not. We owe the deity one death. Let it come which way it will! He that dies this year, is quit for the next", says Hotspur.) As for myself though, I can assure you that I am aspiring toward an exit that is quick and easy, rather than one of those long and tortuous finales that I have seen all too much of. I have no fear whatever of the state of non-being that we call by the name of death. By way of first-hand experience on that subject, I am at times blessed with a night of deep and dreamless slumber "like unto death"--a blissful sort of oblivion towards which I regularly aspire and from which I arise to a sense of well-being and fulfillment. And I have also on several occasions been taken down to the gates of death anesthetically for surgical purposes and have learned that the agonies of living come home to roost in one's consciousness only when one (if one) recovers from the anesthetic.

But I am not in any hurry to go, for the long habit of living is too much with me. And there are yet many curiosities that continue to elude my poor powers of comprehension as I follow along with Dawkins in the unweaving of the rainbow. Meanwhile, I hoped I might yet be able to work for yet another year or two, so as to be a bit more economically settled into a final retirement. Beyond that, there is of course always the endlessly uncompleted project of genealogy at which I might fritter away some endless weeks and months of organizing. What I more hoped for, however, was to find the inspiration I need for some literary project. And if the fates be with me, I may yet find myself in a position to take a few summer trips with some of my grandchildren while they are yet young and free enough to be interested in 'roughing it' with a frugal old geezer in the wide open spaces of the glorious west.

And I am still curious about this life, this world, and this universe of which we are a part, and of which we are all partakers. Here in Santa Fe, we have access to some several hundred TV channels, of which some five or six have some occasional excellent educational programs. The Nature programs are among them, along with some occasional history programs. But the very best programs that I had seen in the past few months was a series narrated by Carl Sagan, entitled "Cosmos". Curiously, the best programs seem often to be available in the late evening hours when perhaps most of the youngsters are off to bed just for those very programs that are of best educational value.

RGB

Summary of year 2007
R. Garner Brasseur, MD

Nothing to do but work
Nothing to eat but food
Nothing to wear but clothes
To keep one from going nude

Nothing to breath but air
Quick as a flash 'tis gone
Nowhere to fall but off
Nowhere to stand but on

Nothing to comb but hair
Nowhere to sleep but in bed
Nothing to weep but tears
No one to bury but dead

Nothing to sing but a song
Ah well, alas and alack
Nowhere to go but out
Nowhere to come but back

Nothing to see but sights
Northing to quench but thirst
Nothing to have but what we've got
Thus through life we are cursed

Nothing to strike but a gait
Everything moves that goes

Nothing at all but common sense
Can ever resolve these woes

Ben King

What is life if full or care,
We have no time to stand and stare.
No time to stand beneath the boughs,
And stare as long as sheep and cows.
No time to see when woods we pass,
Where squirrels hide their nuts in grass.
No time to see in broad daylight,
Streams full of stars, like skies at night.
No time to turn at beauties glance,
And watch her feet, how they can dance.
No time to wait till her mouth can
Enrich that smile her eyes began.
A poor life this if, full of care
We have no time to stand and stare

Author ??

THE CONDITION OF MORTALITY

In scattering end collections all.
High towers at length must fall.
In parting every meeting ends.
To death all lives of creatures tends.

The early fall to earth is sure,
Of fruits on trees that hang mature.
Of mortals here behold a type,
They too succumb for death when ripe.

As houses fall when long decay,
Has worn the posts that formed their stay,
So sink men's frames when age's course,
Has undermined their force.

The nights which once have passed away
To mingle with the morning ray
Return no more, as streams which blend
With oceans, there forever end.

Revolving ceaseless night and day,
The lives of mortals wear away
As summer's torrid solar beams
Dry up the ever lessening streams.

In hours when men at home abide,
Death too reposes by their side.
When forth they issue day by day,
Death walks companion of their way.
Death with them goes when far they roam,
Death with them stays; Death brings them home.

Men hail the rising sun with glee.
They love its setting glow to see.
But fail to note each passing day,
In fragments bears their lives away.

All, natures face delight to view
As changing seasons come anew.
Few see how each evolving year
Abridges swiftly life's career.

As logs which on ocean float
By chance are into contact brought
But tossed about by wind and tide
Together cannot long abide.

So wives, sons, kinsmen, riches . . . all
What'er our own we fondly call,

Obtained, possessed, enjoyed today,
Tomorrow all are snatched away.

As standing on the road a man
Who sees a passing caravan
Winding slowly o'er the plain
Cries, "I will follow in your train"

So we the beaten path must tread
On which our sires of yore have led.
Since none can natures course elude,
Why? o'er their doom, in sorrow brood.

On May 11th of this year, I entered into my 75th year. As a youngster I sometimes wondered what it would be like to be an old man. And now I have about forgotten what it was like to be a youngster. I don't recall it being especially easy. Nor is being old. What is this stuff we call time? Perhaps it was invented to keep everything from happening at once, and we mere mortals would not be likely to handle that well. What is this stuff we call space? Perhaps it was invented to keep everything from occurring in the same place, which would also be a confusion. Einstein supposed that time and space were sort of woven together into a single fabric. There could be no time without space, for time is perhaps only the measurement of the interval required to move from one point to another in space. Without time there could be no space, for no movement from one point to another would be possible except that there were time to accomplish that. With neither time nor space, there could be no existence.

And what is the nature of light?

Perhaps you were wondering how it is that I go about trying to keep up with what is happening in this world and universe? The constraints of both time and space make that exceedingly difficult. The best that I can do does very little towards even keeping up to speed from my assigned watch-post, let along giving me access to the other vast quadrants of the universe beside the vastness of the quadrant in which I am standing watch. Never-the-less, I make my time-consuming efforts to observe and comprehend;

and then make my puny report back to those who might perchance be interested to hear of it. And this little annual essay is about the best that I can muster. Hello? . . . . Is anybody out there listening? Perhaps not. I continue, never-the-less. And I continue to make my effort to become aware of what others might likewise be reporting back. Through the years I have roamed about the countryside tracking down friends and distant relatives in order to gather what they might have to report. Additionally, I read some magazines such as Scientific American, The Week, Discover, and Chronicles . . . in attempt to stay in tune with current events. And I listen to news commentators such as Rush Limbaugh, and Sean Hannidy, since my own personal skepticism concerning what I hear seems inadequate to the task of ciphering the mass of misinformation with which we are inundated. And each weekday night at 11:00 PM, Charley Rose does in-depth interviews into the ideas and thoughts of various politicos, writers, and gurus for our contemplations. I also read some books in my spare time in order to discover what historians and philosophers have had to say on the eternal questions. In truth though, I have done but very little of book reading in the past year or two as I have been preoccupied with a full time job to earn my livelihood and in attempt to prepare for the retirement which the passing of years is apt soon to enforce upon me. And besides the troubles of my family and of our species in this world of crises, I keep finding myself confronted with my own personal problems; and am occasionally called upon to be of assistance to various friends and relatives.

During the previous year I had to wrangle with the manager of the Vision Center where I was employed over a host of issues pertaining to personnel, equipment, and supplies; and policies pertaining to our dealing with patients. Though he has been given authority, he does not have the training or experience to enable him to perform up to expectations. Talking to him was rather like talking to a post, as nothing ever comes of it. I was thus forced to get problems settled by going over his head to two or three tiers of personnel above him in the hope of getting action. It required of me to analyze and study out the issues, and then compose extensive reports to support my views. These reports must be in written form and with cc: designations, so as to leave a 'paper trail', if there is to be any hope of action. Otherwise they also have no incentive to respond to merely local situations when they are persons with corporation sized territories and responsibilities. Though they never deign to write me a response, problems are slowly beginning to be resolved.

I worked the wards of the state Psychiatric Hospital in Las Vegas several years with Dr. Ghosh before I retired from that job seven years earlier. Dr Ghosh had recently contacted me concerning his recent firing from LVMC and made me aware of some of the allegations against him, upon which his dismissal had been predicated. It is a matter of record that I myself had tangled with LVMC administration concerning their bogus allegations to be rid of me back in 1999. It is also a matter or record that I was absolved of those allegations. I was given a letter from the LVMC medical staff which indicated that the medical staff investigation of allegations proved those allegations to be without substance.

Various allegations against the hospital and the staff come to the attention of hospital administration intermittently from other members of staff, from patient allegations, patient guardian representatives, patient advocates of their legal rights, and political issues originating within LVMS and in Santa Fe, and about the state from private citizens with complaints. In response to such things there are administrative 'investigations' of a sort, wherein it becomes expedient to fasten some blame upon some one or another staff member, in order to give the impression that some 'remedial action' has been taken and thus to satisfy the blood lust at the heart of the complainant. I recall some twenty or more various medical doctors and psychiatrists, as well as some psychologists and social workers that have been dismissed or placed under enough pressures as to have encouraged them to resign. Shall we suppose that all of these now dismissed and pressured-departed professionals are to be considered incompetent or involved in grievous misbehavior? Or might we not well suspect that some sort of politics is here involved? Scapegoats, of a sort, in my view. Not a new or unique solution of convenience to the politics of LVMC: and widely resorted to in all bureaucratic structure of political and economic organizations.

It was my impression that Dr. Ghosh had been subjected to more than his share of adverse actions from the investigation of various allegations over the years. He is an obvious and easy target. A foreigner of East India origins, and owning a foreign accent that easily identifies him as an 'outsider'. And it is my impression that the Chief of the General Medicine Department of LVMC seemed to harbor a special animosity towards him. I recall several of those situations where charges were laid at his doorstep, and I had taken the part of Dr. Ghosh in some of those confrontations. Anybody who has lived and worked in Las Vegas, NM would probably agree that it seems a tight community of Hispanic peoples and somewhat centered on their own racial self interests with a certain animosity even towards we Anglos. This seems no less true concerning those of them employed by LVMC.

Some ten years before, a group of we LVMC professionals agreed to attempt to establish a union, in order to secure ourselves against the secretive and high-handed dictates of the LVMC administration through the state mandated rules pertaining to the abridged rules Public Employees. Dr. Ghosh and I were both a part of that effort to establish a union. We did succeed in that effort. Again, our involvement in that effort did seem to precipitate upon us some additional animosity from administration. The union's existence was short lived, as the governor of the state absolved the union about a year after its birth. I expect that Dr. Ghosh was now probably one of the last of those union members to have systematically and finally at this time expelled from employment at LVMC.

In my view, the recent charges against Dr. Ghosh were irresponsible allegations, as they seemed not well substantiated. And more especially, they were irresponsible in that they threatened his livelihood, threatened his medical licensure, and threatened his reputation. Those things, in addition to subjecting him to personal unnecessary mental anguish. In short, the whole business seemed to have something of the quality of malicious mischief.

Polybius reminds us that it is well to keep in mind a firm distinction between a cause and a pretext. It is my impression that the slate of charges against Dr. Ghosh seems to have been drummed up against him as part of a specific concerted action during the period of time that he was absent on a prolonged leave to visit his family abroad. In his absence they seem first to have decided upon a conclusion concerning Dr. Ghosh; and then proceeded to manufactured the 'cause' by a superficial search through some fragmented charts. The perpetrators of this injustice seem also to have specifically marched about among the line staff to solicit vague and incomplete 'supportive' statements of innuendo and partial truth by force of their gravitas upon the lesser beings of various ward line staff.

Dr Ghosh had been unable to summon up any show of support from his fellow employees towards his self-defense. They were not wanting "to get involved". For they might be next in line, if they incur the wrath of administration. Thus it was that Dr. Ghosh asked me to be of assistance to him in this matter. Though I too am reluctant to involve myself in such time-consuming adventures, one must do what one can for a good physician in the interests of justice. And so I studied the bogus allegations against him, and wrote a lengthy defense on his behalf. And he and I were both relieved when this railroading job came to an abrupt halt. He was then reinstated to his employment and given back-pay for the many months that his case went awaiting arbitration.

I was getting three days off each week in which to contemplate how swiftly that time flies. One must walk an hour of each day, and make the occasional visitation to the homes of elderly old friends; Dr. Tomlin and Paul and Jackie Lewis. There is information and forms to be brought together in preparation for a meeting with the CPA and the submitting of form work to the IRS and state tax agency. There are medical and dental appointments to be kept. There are appointments for the servicing of one's automobile and the necessity for getting in line for renewal of one's driver's license. There are forms and fees to be filed for medical license and DEA annual registration. There are post-graduate education courses to be attended. All of this in addition to one's domestic correspondence leaves one with but little time for contemplation in quietude.

I only rarely hear anything from my children, for they too seem to live overly busy lives. Though I missed the opportunity to visit them and other friends in the previous year, I did take three weeks to visit about this past summer. I do hear occasionally from Tina, and she sends me some information about her children, but they are now moved to Florida since early summer. Vic and I drove up to Burlington WA to visit sister Ookie, who seemed to be weak and ailing, and we raised a little stir about her condition so as to encourage her children to see to it that she got some medical attention. I have not yet heard how that turned out, but I presume something came of it, since she yet remains among the living.

I took three or four days off in September to attend the 55th reunion of my high school graduating class in Miles City. About three fourths of the class seem yet to endure well into our seventies. In mid-December I received word from Raymond Horton's family that he had passed away subsequent to surgery for a hip fracture. He was about as close a friend as I have ever had, and I will greatly miss him. We were closest of friends at ages 12 and 13, and I never saw nor heard from him again for 50 years, though in my late 50's I did make a couple unsuccessful attempts to locate him. And then, suddenly, in September of 2000, I received from him an E-Mail note. I stopped by to visit with him in Redding a month or two later; and I stopped by as often as two or three times yearly--for two or three days at a time--to visit with him and his family. It was astonishing how much we seemed yet to have in common. Perhaps a lad's character becomes fairly well set in about those tender years of age 12 or 13. In any case, our perceptions and general outlook seem always to have been fairly congruous. In the course of our many hours of subsequent conversation I expect that we fairly completely filled one another in on the course of our lives through the hiatus of our friendship from 1946 through those years to Y2K. Besides the reciting of our personal and family experiences, our conversations then ranged widely through subjects such as Geology, Astronomy, History, Natural History, and Philosophy--in which we had common interests. In point of fact, I don't believe that I ever had the opportunity to share more extensive and far ranging discussions with anyone else of my personal acquaintance. But of course, we were already then a couple of old geezers, and such openness of discussion is one of the few benisons that those of our age are apt to fall into--in those declining years. A sort of natural inclination to arriving at a kind of summing up of our seasoned conclusions. Yes, a sort of debriefing before moving on. Betty and Jim were also about at times to enter into our conversations, and I was astonished at how closely they kept in touch with Kelley by phone. And so, I am grateful for the hospitality and good fellowship I so much enjoyed in the home of Betty and Raymond in these past seven years.

This year's annual summary is mercifully short because of the fact that in the mid year, I took the time to put together a manuscript to summarize my pilgrim progress in the interval since I completed my Personal and Family biographical experience (Inheritors of a Few Years) in 1996. This recent manuscript I entitled *"Life Continues--Trouble Follows"*. I also updated the master copies of my manuscripts of both the Brasseur and the Boepple genealogies; and made a couple of copies of each to assure survival of the information should something happen to my copy. Also, now in the past couple of months, I am making an attempt to write a novel.

I was now informed that current Wal-Mart policy requires that us fellows in the trenches must now agree to accept patients who are covered by insurance. Our fees are already the lowest in the area, and under insurance rules they would be even a bit lower than our standard rates, so I have not enthusiasm for dealing with insurance companies. In addition to the fee problem, there is all of the red tape of their rules; and of forms to be submitted. And since the current customer base of cash-on-the-barrelhead self paying patients seems already adequate and growing, I see no point of my trying to make arrangements for dealing with insurance companies. So, unless the Wal-Mart were agreeable to excluding me from their one-size-fits-all policy, my job seemed likely to come to an end in at the end of February.

Though it was not absolutely necessary for me to continue to be a wage earner, the work does give an old geezer something to do, and I am therefore casting about in search yet of some part time work. If it didn't materialize, I must then content myself with again traveling about intermittently to visit some friends and family, doing some additional genealogy, and working at some writing projects.

RGB

2007
2008

I scanned my Journal of the year 2008 and came up with the following train of thought:

Mind is the epiphenomenon of the neuronal machinery of the brain. And, as Albert Schweitzer puts it, thinking is a harmony within us (the mind).

Speech is conveniently located somewhere between thought and action, where it often substitutes for both. Writing may sometimes achieve somewhat more than speech--something closer to action. May at times stimulate will (which might be defined as: desire of sufficient intensity that it is translated into action). We mere mortals are strongly influenced by our emotions--which derive from the subconscious. Emotions in turn, produce in us a tendency toward action. But emotions are not tools of cognition, and cannot or ought not be tools for the making of decisions. The rational aspect of one's being must then determine whether or not an action is justifiable; for to be guided by raw emotions is to court disaster. The responsibility of one's emotional apparatus ends with the registering of the emotion and its action potential. It is then a matter of concern as to whether the powers of one's reason are sufficiently informed by valid experience, accurate information, and good judgment, so as to produce a plan of action that has some probability of producing effects and reactions to serve one's purpose. But what, after all, is one's purpose in the contemplation of any specific action?

Each species seems not to have any purpose beyond the imperatives created by it's own genetic history. A struggle for existence and a drive to procreate in accordance with its own biological nature. The affection for offspring appears to be the noblest sentiment in all biology, says Huxley. That sentiment appears to be the rudimentary basis for a primitive cultural influence that is manifest in the protection of the young and the instruction to the patterns of behavior and skills of hunt in search for sustenance and self-defense, and the survival of youth into maturity. The successful completion of yet one more cycle in the repetitive sequence of the species. Is it a cycle? Or is it an upward spiral? No species has become more advanced in the progression of its cultural evolution than has Homo sapiens. A consequence--seemingly--related to the necessity of caring for progeny which are uniquely naked and helpless among all species of creatures. A cerebral species with cerebral progeny; and who as individuals are destined and required to cerebrate in their highly social and ever evolving give-and-take society. A society which aspires to grasp the nature of truth and reality which hides behind illusion and the infinity of highly elusive inter-related fact, detail, and possibility.

The immensity of that reality is such as to be beyond the poor powers of comprehension of any one individual; and in part--probably--unknowable by mere mortals.

Despite a vague aspiration to grasp reality and truth, it is yet obvious that human beings are still largely in homage to myths. And moving only slowly and reluctantly towards a gradual connection with truth and awareness of nature's realities.

I conceive that, like myself, each individual is well advised to acknowledge that there is no certainty in this life except the reality of uncertainty. And, no security except in one's own ability to adapt. Thoughts compete in the mind, just as organisms compete in the wilds of nature. And individual intellectual brilliance is no guarantee against being dead wrong. There sometimes seems to be more acquired ignorance than acquired knowledge. The intellectual potential of each individual needs must be prepared by a dedication to honest inquiry, and seeded with valid fact and principles--to the extent that such a thing can be achieved in the ever evolving state of one's consciousness. **Common sense** (the superficial acquaintance one acquires from the day-by-day experience of one's daily life) is admirable in the background of the mind, but unless it be watched by a lofty disquiet ever ready to remind one's self, it dwindles into the mere routine of the baser lethargic side of intellect. And education isn't how much you have committed to memory, or even how much you know. It's being able to differentiate between what you do know; and what you don't.

Each individual is confronted with the existential reality of his own being--in the immensity of the universe. Stare up at the night sky a while if you wish to gather a sense of this. Ponder that reality and make an effort to grasp the extent of intellectual effort it will require to grasp the vast unknown. Quite a task. But one can choose (and most do) completely to ignore a consideration of that matter day after day as . . . "the lives of mortals wear away--as summer's torrid solar beams dry up the ever lessening streams". And yet, mankind--as a whole--is launched out upon just that very quest. Actively seeking and acquiring valid new knowledge, experience, and information. And you there . . . what intellectual effort have you yet put forth? Is it required of you? Are you in hot pursuit of what is real? Or just frittering away your mortal existence in daydreams and homage to vague mythology?

The adult mayfly lives one day. The lifespan of we mere mortals is not all that much more, when considered in relationship to the scale of geologic time. A third of our time is spent upon the necessity of sleep. Half of our waking hours is spent in earning and in preparing to earn a living. The interests of those of us from un-moneyed families is necessarily centered upon the work required to earn our food, clothing, and shelter. But little of our time is allotted to the cultivation of our personal interests. Those interests are primarily the inescapable reality of our sexuality and some few personal pleasures. Ten or twenty years is required in the acquiring the skill and information needed to support ourselves. Of the hundreds or thousands of occupations to which one might aspire, there is time and energy enough for usually mainly one. We remain generally ignorant concerning what is knowable to those pursuing other career choices.

There is some little time potentially available to one for the pursuit and contemplation of esoteric subjects and accomplishment. Most perhaps would like to have accomplished some such thing. But thought is taxing . . . and inspiration is elusive. So too, have passed my years and I must face the fact that my personal accomplishments have not been significant.

At the end of May I took off 6 days to attend the graduation events of grandson Michah from Loma Linda Medical School. He was the youngest student in the graduating class. Jauhn and Massy were down there for the event; and to help Michah gather his gear and move out of his apartment. He was next to relocate to Milwaukee, Wisconsin to begin a seven year Neurosurgical training program in July. Jauhn and Massy took a motel room while I hung around Michah's apartment a few days while all these matters wound down. One afternoon, Jauhn and I made an outing to Joshua National Park, about 75 miles to the east. Traffic was all jammed up for many continuous miles as we head out over the San Jacinto pass on this weekend. That seemed strange. Why would we not soon come upon the site of the causative incident and then get into a normal flow once more? Then, far away--perhaps five or ten miles distant and beyond Indio--I noticed a tall tower out on the open desert. Another oddity. What would that be? Surely not a tall grain elevator out here on the desert? And traffic continued to be in grid-lock. Approaching slowly nearer, it soon became evident that the tower was a huge gambling casino, surrounded by acres of black-top parking space. The two right lanes were then seen to be traffic awaiting the opportunity to trickle into the casino area creating thereby a monumental traffic bottle-neck. An astonishing thing to contemplate. We did finally reach Joshua Park about mid-afternoon and spend a few hours touring the sights before darkness settled in about us and we headed back to Loma Linda. I was up at 8:00 the next morning to prepare for graduation. Jauhn and Massey came by, and she went on ahead by foot to find us a place to sit under the awnings of the outdoor graduation proceedings. Jauhn and I got there just before the march of the graduates and sat in a couple of vacant seats adjoining her, her mother, and Ali. There was a little rowe about this, as the guy next to me claimed that he was saving the seats for an uncle of one of the graduates. Massey rebutted the claim and we held fast to our seats in silence. There followed a few minutes of silent animosity that hovered about us before the proceedings, but the alleged uncle never showed up. "All's well that ends well." There were about 170 graduates and the thing seemed to go on forever before it ended and before the morning became overly hot, and we then escaped to a café for a snack.

The night before departure from Loma Linda, Massy drove out to San Diego to spend the night with her mother and catch a plane back to Portland, while Jauhn and I encamped on a mattress in his dining room in order to arise next morning to help get Michah and his gear extricated from the apartment. There were several identical student apartment quarters in a row, and I drove my pickup up close to the apartment entry ways, to haul in the half-thickness mattress which furnished the pickup camper. But I had mistakenly parked behind the wrong apartment unit as I shouldered the load and entered into the apartment without first knocking. But it was the wrong apt unit. I presume that the astonishment I saw upon this stranger's face was much like what he saw on mine as I quickly excused myself to turn upon my heal and beat a hasty retreat.

Later that evening as we three talked, Jauhn and Michah seemed determined to discuss religious philosophy. I struggled to make an end to the topic, as it had no hope of going anywhere. I then drove on down to El Centro to take a room at the Motel 6, and spend some time with an old classmate, Lynn Fitz, who is still working full time as a pharmacist. We exchanged information of old mutual acquaintances and made yet another effort to fathom the metaphysical questions and issues of the universe. But soon it was time for me to return home and back to work at the end of May--splitting my work days between the Santa Fe and the Bernallilo Wal-Mart offices. I was now having to pay 4.86 per gallon for gasoline. By the end of January 2009 the price had fallen dramatically to just over 1.50 per gallon. I am puzzled as to the economic reasons behind such radical price changes. It has been suggested that commodity "speculators" have been gaming the system. And by year's end the national economy--indeed, the world economy--was threatening to collapse as major banks and the giant auto industry corporations were petitioning the federal government for bailout money, claiming that they were on the verge of actual bankruptcy. These "fat-cat" high rollers are the very entities that are the root cause of the impending economic collapse as they bleed the monetary system of millions of dollars to CEOs and management bonuses. This, while hiding their losses and misrepresenting to the authorities the reality of their losses; and while "leveraging" their bloated "earnings" up to 30 to 1 with "margin" financing that ultimately leaves them without enough cash reserve to stay afloat when public confidence begins to perceive the immensity of the "sub-prime" housing loan "bubble" and making their rush to withdraw their deposits to the safety of their personal hiding places in the walls and mattresses of their homes. In the stampede, the mass of ordinary citizens are losing their retirement benefits and many are losing their jobs, as well. No one seems to know where all this financial chaos is heading, and there seems no consensus of what can be done to resolve the situation. It all reminds us of what Thoreau says in his "*Celestial Railroad*", to whit: "and when the smoke has cleared and the train has left the station, it shall appear that only some few are riding--and that most have been run over".

In mid-June, Bayloo's oldest daughter, Kim and Wes Mikes dropped by to visit a couple days with us. And then, towards the end of June, Bayloo developed a worrisomely slow pulse, for which she was hospitalized a few days. Both the cause and the subsequent resolution of the problem remain a mystery.

In early July, brother Vic and his daughter, Yvette stopped by to visit with us a couple of days. He had gone to Florida to help her get her gear packed and shipped out Hawaii, where she is taking on a new job with the court system. Vic's son, Guy, also lives in Hawaii. The other son, Jay, lives in New York. A few weeks earlier, Vic sent me a thick notebook concerning the history of a Brasseur family that had settled in the Virginia and Maryland area in the mid 1600's. That, and an interesting collection of reprint information about life there in the colonial times. I hadn't yet gotten around to reading that and he now left with me a very interesting book on the life of Sir Henry Stanley and his several trips into darkest Africa which began with his search for the missing Dr. Livingston.

I resigned as an employee from Wal-Mart at the end of February 2008, but I continued to work there as a private contractor until the end of September. Having had very little time off from work in the previous 2½ years, I decided to take the month of October for my personal use. Being in good health and possessing a set of good wheels and new tires, that meant a journey to the Northwest.

Brother Phil and Dot at that point came out to spend a few days with us in Santa Fe and visit some of the local attractions and points of interest before I headed out upon my vacations trip the first of October. The autumn season is certainly my favorite for this sort of extended travel.

I was up into the Northwest in October and stopped by see my sister, DeMaris (Ookie), in Burlington. She has been holed up in her apartment there feeling weak and ill for the past two or three years. She says she is anemic and not able to eat anything, and complaining of stomach pain etc. Yet, she looked much the same to me as when I last saw her a couple years ago. In fact, had recently been to the ER where they treated her for hyperventilation and gave her a diagnosis of anxiety. She seemed not to have needed hospitalization. I gather that she has not been an easy patient to deal with over the years, and that the doctors in the area are not anxious to be involved with her. Possibly not overly anxious to take on any new Medicaid patients at all. She has lived apart and isolated for so many years that she seems to have lost her perspective. It commonly happens to people in solitary confinement etc, whether that confinement be voluntary or enforced. Anyhow, just as I tried two or three years ago to get her sons to get her to the hospital for diagnosis and referral to a better living situation, so did I again hope to get her into a situation where she has some supervised living and other people to mingle with. I now have word that she fell and was hospitalized, and that the social workers have had to put her into first a convalescent home, and that from there, they will have to get her into a managed care facility. My brother Phil and his wife Dot in Spokane are in more regular contact with her than am I. As I supposed, she does seem to be getting along more contentedly with the managed care situation. I am told that her sons are cleaning out her apartment and getting her belongings taken care of. I don't know where she will be when her placement is finalized.

I awoke at 9:30 AM having slept well about 7 hours in the cabin on the farm. I read a while, and then went over to the house to talk a bit with Duane and Georgia. Shortly after 11:00 I decided to take my exercise. I talked Duane into taking the two mile hike with me on this fine clear day with temperature hovering to almost 60 degrees. I discover that he has not been on any exercise at all. I don't know if he still does his yoga as he used to do. About a quarter mile around the perimeter of the farm I noticed that his gait became a little clumsy. I suggested that perhaps we ought to head back rather than attempting to climb the little knoll directly ahead, but he wanted to get on up past the bee pasture, and so we proceeded. At the northeast corner I convinced him that we should head back rather than proceed about the whole perimeter. His coordination declined progressively. Soon he was stumbling about and began to stoop forward as one sometimes sees in persons with advanced Parkinson's Disease. I took his arm to keep him from falling and a few stumbling steps further I suggest we sit a spell. We were still conversing superficially about old times even as his steps were flagging. He was quite aware, and commented that his sense of balance was failing. Several times after continuing for a dozen steps we paused a few seconds as he then partially recovered before he once again was on the verge of falling on his face. I found myself having to lend him ever more support as we thus haltingly proceeded. Soon I had almost to face him to support him both on the right and the left arm. His sensorium seemed to cloud a bit, but he replied that he was in no pain. What was going on with him? Was he in the early phase a stoke? I helped him down to his hands and knees and even there he seemed to need some help. I got him to lay down on his side on a grassy spot at the edge of the field and placed a downy vest under his head for a pillow. Through the haze of his awareness, he agreed to stay put right there while I jogged back to the house to get a vehicle for transport. Georgia was in the kitchen and we hurriedly gathered the keys to the pickup and started back to pick him up. She reminded me that he was a mild diabetic and on oral hypoglycemic medications--but not on insulin. Just as we started out, we could see that he had once more gotten up and was staggering forward; and then he fell upon his face. And by the time we reached him he was again up and stumbling forward. He had scrapped up the bridge of his nose and face somewhat; and had hold of his now broken glasses. I leaped out of the cab and grabbed him by the arm to guide him into the pickup cab, closing the door and indicating to Georgia that I would ride in the pickup bed. In the excitement, she was immediately headed homeward without realizing that I had not yet climbed aboard. I grabbed the gunnel of the pickup bed and managed to toss one leg over the edge as we gathered speed; and managed then to haul myself in as the pickup bounced along. When we reached the walkway to the house, I grabbed Duane by the arm and walked him into the kitchen to sit him down on a chair while Georgia got him some sweetened fruit juice to drink. He was still dazed, but drank it down without difficulty. Within a few minutes the fog of his perceptions seemed to clear as Georgia doctored the blood and dirt from the scrapes of his face. It was now shortly after noon and Georgia prepared us a lunch of eggs and toast; and then found him an old pair of spectacles for his use as Duane and I continued our conversation.

I conclude from this episode that a diabetic can indeed become hypoglycemic from oral hypoglycemic medications. Dr. Winters in Miles City says it can happen. The effect as Duane was haltingly staggering along was much the same as that of a battery that is at the edge of reserve of it's energy. The slight demand of the skeletal muscles for blood sugar drew the glycogen level down to the point that the CNS was insufficiently supplied and the sensorium and the motor cortex became erratic at that point. Then, to desist from physical activity for a few moments, is enough to permit the glycogen level once more to rise sufficiently to partially restore the functions of the CNS.

The next morning I called brother Vic. We had talked about driving out to Grand Forks, ND to attend a homecoming event and inspect the med school facility where we completed the first two years of our medical education in 1960. After all these elapsed years, I don't suppose it likely that we would have encountered there many even among the oldest alumni with whom we might have been acquainted, but we like to launch out occasionally upon these journeys into the past. There was some confusion between Vic and I as to just when we intended to arrive there; and how long the trip might take. He likes to drive along at a somewhat slower pace than that to which I am accustomed. The upshot of it was that it seemed to him now too late for us to make our start; and so he decided against taking the trip this year. Well then, perhaps next year? And so I proceeded eastward alone into an alternate plan of travel. I stopped over that night at Phil's place in Spokane, and left there the next morning after attending to a bank transaction. That evening I managed to locate Norval Fandrich in Belgrade, Montana, where we visited a couple hours about our high school days and experiences before I took my leave from him to drive to Bozeman, to spend the chilly night snuggled comfortably in the pickup camper. I arose the 16th, to breakfast on an apple turnover and a can of soda pop. There was fresh snow covering the mountains all about, and I arrived in Miles City about 4:00 PM to take a $43.00 room at the Olive Hotel where I napped a bit before dining on a nice Mexican meal; and then hiked about town for an hour before returning to my room to read a few hours before tuning in. The following day I spent some time at the library and stopped over to visit an hour with Dr. Malcomb and Beth Winters--he was one of Gene's best friends through high school and medical school. In his early eighties, he still works part time a couple days a week at the clinic. That night I attended a dance function at the senior citizen center, where I encountered a few people of my acquaintance. Lucille, the sister of Ted Heiss was there, as was Frank Samuleson. And I ran into one of Ookie's friends--Sharon McKinzie, as well as Myrna Bealer, the widow of Bob Martelle. Bob was a friend and neighbor of mine in grade school--as was his brother, Jim. She tells me that Bob died of colon cancer in 1998; and that Jim died in 1978 in Walnut Grove, Calif.

On the 18th I continued on Hwy 94, then up north from Dickenson to follow Hwy 200. I stopped at a Saturday market in Dodge--from whence my mother's cousins, the Almendingers and the Wolffs have issued forth. I snooped about there and finally settled for a piece of homemade kuchen before continuing on first to Beulah (where Phil was born in 1940--I still recall that day); and then to Hazen (where Gene and I were born) looking for cousin Elmer Neuberger. I didn't actually find him, but I stopped to pick up a copy of the Hazen Star to see if there were perhaps a dance this weekend at which I might locate him. Interestingly, there in the newspaper is a picture of Elmer with wishes to him for a happy 80th birthday. Later that day I drove on to Washburn (where Ookie was born in 1934) and spent the night there in the parking lot of the Interpretive Center at the edge of town. I arose the following morning to have a caramel roll and a cup of coffee at a café and then drove a few miles further north to visit a couple hours with Dick Morgan (a 7ᵗʰ and 8ᵗʰ grade classmate from Dunseith) at the tiny hamlet of Falkirk. Then south to Bismarck and down Hwy 83, to Linton, where I stopped for two or three hours to take in a Polka Festival. I enjoy the music and watching them dance--wishing I knew how to cut so fine a caper as the "dutch hop". I got as far as Aberdeen, SD that evening, where I stopped to call Massy for the address of Michah in Milwaukee, and then I crashed out in the Wal-Mart parking lot for the night. I arose in the morning at 8:30 to breakfast on an apple turnover and soda pop before driving through Minnesota and Wisconsin to arrive in Milwaukee twelve hours later. Within a half hour the grandchildren, Michah and Tristan, arrived from their outing in Chicago with their cousin Sarah Krahn (who is attending Wheaton College there--it was my understanding that brother Gene had attended college there 60 years ago). We went out for a bite to eat and then returned to Michah's apartment. Michah and I each slept on one the two couches in his nice little apartment. He and Tristan had to arise at 6:00 in the morning to get her on her flight back to Portland, and he continued on to work from the airport. Ah, all these youngsters of Jauhn and Massey are so astonishingly accomplished and well rounded in their education and promise of achievement as to leave me with regrets at how little I have ever accomplished. I spent the day putting some order into the clutter of Michah's apartment and then reading a tourist's book of information on what to see and do in Wisconsin. And then hiked about the neighborhood an hour for my exercise. He and I went out for supper of pizza and talked a bit before turning in. Next time I am up there, I will shall take some time to investigate some of the geological features of the state. Michah was out early to work the following day, while I slept in until 9:30 before heading out just ahead of storm conditions that were setting in. I have my music and talk radio to occupy my thoughts as I journey through the day to end up stopping at a rest area just east of Valley City, ND for the night. The next day I stopped in Bismarck to look up my cousin, the Rev Gordon Neuberger, who must now be about 82 or 83. His wife answered the door when I called about 2:00 PM. She tells me Gordon is still in bed; never invites me in or even offers to tell Gordon of my arrival. Just shrugs me off as a sort of poor cousin. I first met her in 1948 when Gordon was courting her there in rural Beulah. I spent that summer working on the Neuberger farm south of Beulah. She has never at any time through the years been cordial, though they at one time spent a night at my home in the Tri-cities. Perhaps she is just socially inept? Well, anyhow, I know that when I caught Gordon a few years ago, he told me that he had undergone treatment for leukemia. For all I know, he is perhaps ill and nearing his end at this time?

I stopped there in Bismarck at the GRHS genealogy library an hour to do a little Boepple research before heading west at mid-afternoon. About 6:00 PM I arrived in Terry Montana, were I stopped in to visit with Ed Ban (Skippy's husband). Both Kate and Skippy lived in Terry the last 15 or 20 years of their lives. Ed is well into his eighties at this time and though the age shows in his features, he is still good-natured, vital, alert and active. He keeps himself preoccupied doing lawn and yard jobs about town. He made a mess of eggs for our supper and we then talked a few hours before he opened the spare bedroom to me and then headed off to bed a little before 11:00 PM. I read a couple hours before turning in; and arose about 9:45 in the morning to shower off some of the livestock I have accumulated. Ed served me eggs, bacon, toast, and coffee. One of his granddaughters had written an article about Ed and Skippy's life and the history of the Ban family who came out of Gospic, Yugoslavia to settle up north of Terry about a hundred years ago. The article was printed in the local newspaper. He gave me copy for my genealogy archives before I took my leave from him and headed west a little before noon.

In Miles City I drove up to the home of my high school classmate, Bernard Riley, about 1:30 PM, just as he was arriving in from his doctor's appointment in Billings. In addition to having had have surgery for colon cancer, he also lost his right leg and even part of his pelvis to bone cancer several years ago, he has crutches and gets about mostly in a motorized wheel chair. And so in the space of a couple hours I became acquainted with his interesting life story and I wonder at how such folks seem to tolerate so easily these barbs of fate and their disabilities. Us older models of course have an increasing susceptibility to all forms of cancer as we continue to advance in age. I supposed that after a couple hours he might benefit from a bit of a nap, and so I took my leave and drove out to the Wal-Mart parking lot to get my own restful two hours. After then walking about streets with the ghosts of times past, I stopped by to visit with the Kransky's. I was wondering how it was that I had failed to catch sight of Aloha's son, Steve at the Montana Theatre as I circled by it a few time both on this and on my previous few days in town. Harold is now into his early nineties, has been losing some weight and needing a little supervision and encouragement in his food intake. Rather than pay someone to come in and be with Harold, Steve has recently just quit his job and hangs about the house with him. Says he wasn't making that much on the job anyway. I had a sandwich with them and spent the night there. Harold likes to watch "Walker, Texas Ranger" on TV. Next to watching a children's T-Ball game, those episodes are the most tedious and improbable of all pastimes. They served me eggs, toast, and coffee the next morning before I headed west to Harden, to visit with sister Kate's Daughters. Jody just got married last year to Cory Metcalf, who has two sons, about nine and twelve, and she still teaches the 4th or 5th grade in school. The two girls live right next door to one another. Roxy came over with her two year old daughter, and she was anticipating the arrival of a second infant just any day soon. Roxy still works full time doing accounting at the local hospital. After that brief visitation, I headed west again and stopped by in Fishtail to visit an hour with a high school classmate--Janet (Fiechtner) and Ray Potter. I stopped to nap an hour in Bozeman before I continued on to Missoula, where I camped out to read a couple of hours before retiring to the sleeping bag. Finding no answer to the door at Cindy and Dean's place the next morning, I continued west. At Alberton, a large billboard reminded me that here was a large collection of used books that I had long intended to peruse, and so I spent two or three hours there and found a dozen books I intend to read. I arrived in Spokane about 3:30 PM to stop over with Phil and Dot. It was deep into autumn; Phil and I took a two mile hike through the streets there on the south hill near Manitou Park. Above, below, and all about, we were surrounded by a plethora of vivid colors.

The following morning Phil and I drove up to the hot springs at Ainsworth, Canada. We took a ferry boat ride to the other side of Kootenai Lake before returning to our hotel room to fashion ourselves a meal of bologna sandwiches; and then we soaked a few hours in the hot pool. We returned to Spokane the following day, and the next day I headed out for the farm. I took a wrong turn out of Moses Lake and soon found myself bumping along a rabbit trail that ended in a gravel pit somewhere out deep in the desert. As I tried to retrace my errant course I finally came out on a paved Farm-to-market road at the edge of Moses Lake where there was a good stream of traffic. Having found a sign pointing me off toward Ephrata, I was just congratulating myself; but I hadn't gone half a mile before I was confronted with flashing blue lights. "Do you know what the speed limit is here?", says the officer. I didn't, and I said so. He says I was doing 51 mph in a 35 mph zone, but I had not yet encountered a sign indicating that. I told him my little story about the rabbit trail and the gravel pit and he let me off the hook. I stopped at the Wal-Mart in Ephrata to snatch a batch of apple turnovers under a sign that said $2.50. But the check out clerk didn't believe the 2 cent scanner reading and the delay caused by her uncertainty was holding up my progress, so I told just to accept my $2.50 and let it go at that. I got to the farm and Duane thought he might take a bit of a walk with me. But I only took him out about 300 yards into the field, and then back to the house. I think it best to only gradually build up the length of his walks, if he intends to continue with an exercise program. I then got a short nap in the cabin before Georgia served us a salmon supper. We watched a history program before I left them to retire early while I went to the cabin to read a few hours.

My vacation days were growing short, so I left the farm the next morning and drove to Yakima, arriving about 1:00 PM. Vic and I took a two mile hike and I then laid down on a cushion on the floor in the basement for an hour, before Marge served us an Italian supper. They went to bed early and I read until 1:30 AM. The next day I drove to Jauhn's place in Portland where I found him and the boys cutting wood on his 10 acre plot of land, and loading it into the pickup to be stacked for sale up near the house. Miette's boys, Josh and Izzy were lending a hand with the work. Besides Miette and the boys, I knew that Jauhn's mother was also in town, so I had a quick bite to eat and then drove to Liberty High School to watch Bam-bam's football game. After the game, I ran into Pierre and Bam-bam near the parking lot. They were engaged in a contest of will as to whether Bam-bam ought or ought not be allowed to attend an after game get together with other high-school students. Bam-bam hadn't done well in his Physics class and the consequence was this silent stand-off out there in the chill of the evening. It being none of my business, I left them in their stand-off and drove out to their hilltop acres, expecting Jackie would soon arrive and let us in the house. When she did arrive, she stopped near the barn to check the animals, and managed to leave the car engine on and lock herself out of the car. By-and-by, we all got into the house and the boys off to bed while I was left with Pierre and Jackie in a conversation about what is happening to who, and why. More of the detail came out in the morning when we again discussed the various little crises in the family. We agreed that Bam-bam is going to have to take upon himself the solution to his scholastic problems if is going to have any hope a achieving his goal-- possible admission to the air force academy and his hope of becoming an airplane pilot.

And there is now also a new problem concerning Jessica, who is now about 23 and who has had very little contact with Pierre--or indeed with any of her extended family in the past couple years. She and her sister, Belle, have moved out of their mother's place into an apartment of their own.

I returned to Jauhn's place in the early afternoon of the following day after his relatives had departed. I spend a couple hours talking with Massey, telling her about my trip and getting her slant on where and with what my various twenty grandchildren are preoccupied. She seems to keep pretty good tabs on all of them; and by talking over with her the various family problems and situations, we try to form some estimates of where things are going and what--if anything--might be said or done of possible beneficial influence without over-reaching into that which is improbable and beyond our limited spheres of influence. I prevailed upon her to find out for me when the coast might be clear for me to make a brief visit at Miette and Bart's place in North Bend--as Miette's mother seems to be hanging out there not infrequently. Massey is a great cook and served us a fine supper, after which Jauhn showed me his collection of fossils. He, Jojo, Norg, and I played some card games before they all turned in. After breakfast of waffles the next morning I gathered my gear for departure. I dropped Stan by to her Portland State College Architectural laboratory. She showed me her model projects and introduced me to some of her classmates before I headed south on Hwy 5. South of Goshen, I took Hwy 46 west to the coast and then south on 101 to North Bend. There I napped an hour or more in the Wal-Mart Parking lot before I drove over to Miette's place. A high school exchange student, Rachel, had just moved in with them. Josh and Izzy are very friendly, and the two year old Moriah is very talkative and hyperactive--all of which eases the strain of the cool and awkward relationship between Bart and I, who are so philosophically remote from one another as to electrify the air. After a light supper and hot fudge sundaes, Miette, the boys, and I play cards a while before they are all off early to bed. Josh let me use his room for the night and I was up at 7:45 in the morning. I knew Bart had left early to take the girl to high school, and the house was quiet as I gathered my gear into the pickup, thinking to depart without disturbing anyone, but when I came in for the second load, suddenly Miette and the kids were up. And so, we sat down together to a bowl of cold cereal; and I had a bit of a conversation with Miette. I asked her about this thing between Jessica and the married colored fellow with the two or more kids. Everybody seems to know about it, but no one seems to want to discuss the problem. A taboo subject? Maybe everybody in the family thinks it is all hunky dorry? Am I the only one that sees this as trouble in the wind? Why does none of her family corner Jessica to moderate this insipient disaster? Miette knew fewer of the details than what I had already discerned. What she tells me implies that Jessica has pulled away from everyone in the family, so that no one can get close enough to her to bring this up. I told her that if no one else had the guts to approach the thing, that I might have to do it myself. Somebody has to lift a finger to make at least an effort. I left it that way for Miette to ponder as I ended my little sermon without an amen, and changed the subject to a lighter content. I gave Miette her birthday present, bid them all adieu, and departed. It was now my intention to get in contact with Jessica by e-mail. Certainly not a correspondence such as might please her. So? what difference if Jessica becomes upset with her grandfather about what he has to say of the thing? Perhaps I might have written Tom, to poke my nose into the troubles of his personal business. Troubles that were a portend to his subsequent disaster a few years ago. Sometimes--perhaps--a disaster can be averted by an ill received human intervention.

To granddaughter, Jessica--December 2008

People want to be happy. To achieve this, they must do two things. They must predict how they will feel in a variety of possible futures, and they must act to bring about the best of these and avoid the worst. Although it may seem that "getting what we want" is more difficult than "knowing what to want", research in psychology and behavioral economics tells a different story. People not only have trouble predicting the future, they have trouble predicting how much they will like it when they get there.

The lives of we mere mortals are generally tragic in one sense or another. And generally the more tragic because we, ourselves, are largely to blame for the problems we bring upon ourselves. It is easy enough for one to justify one's personal poverties (of life and being) upon the circumstances of his family and upbringing, but the reality is that "the child, too, is parent of the adult".

It has been said that every person, in the end, is either trying to make up for the mistakes of a parent or two; or is struggling to live up to expectations. One or the other--or both--can give one something to aim for. But, if one aims at nothing in particular, that is generally what one is most apt to attain. As for myself, though I was born and reared in poverty; and though my parents seemed engaged in endless antipathy to one another: yet it seems to me that I was generally struggling to live up to the vague hopes and expectations of my family. I certainly never blamed my parents for their inability to be of much help to me beyond their struggles to keep me an my brothers and my sisters fed, housed, and clothed.

It is possible that you may have seen or even read some of what I have written through the years. There are two books, Inheritors of a Few Years and A Studied Impression of That Which Is. In addition to these, I have compiled two genealogy manuscripts, one on the Brasseur family and one on the Boepple family--the result of 15 or 20 years of research: and miles of travel to make inquiry of many distant relatives and other sources. I have also written some shorter manuscripts and about thirty poems (a few of which have been published). It is not, of course, for me to pass judgment on the quality of any of this. I only cite these things as evidence that I have made my efforts in this life to understand, to accomplish, and to achieve. It seems not unreasonable for me to hope that some of my descendants might similarly make some effort to accomplish something in their lives. But hope is not promise; and even promise does not inevitably come to fruition.

In general, my life has been easy in that I have generally enjoyed good health--which is the best of good fortune that can befall one. That, and the freedom I have enjoyed in consequence of my ancestors having had the wit and courage to try for better lives in this great nation. But the climb from poverty, to obtain an education, and earn a living has been a struggle--as it is for most of us common folk. Two or three miracles of modern surgery have prolonged my years. Now, into my 76th year, I have again been back to work for the past three years.

Having had almost no vacation the past 3 years, I decided finally to take off the month of October to visit friends and family about the country. As I travel about, I generally catch word of the various problems that people are facing and getting themselves involved in. I not infrequently get caught up into the middle of some of these problems as though there were something I might do to be of assistance. I don't know that my aid or advice has ever been of much help to anybody, or that I have ever been able to defuse any potential explosions. More often perhaps, I merely make a nuisance of myself. Perhaps the best that one can generally even hope to achieve is to give the poor suffering souls another point of view which might possibly give them cause to rethink some of their problems; and in consequence, help to work themselves out of some problem or another.

It is my impression that most of your extended family seems not overly thrilled that you are "dating" an African-American fellow. That alone is significantly unconventional. Oriental, Mexican, Native American, East Indian, Pacific Islander . . . anything at all rather than a negro of the American slave tradition culture would seem reasonably acceptable. It is almost as though you were going out of your way to offend your relatives. The reality is that the negro men who come out of the black slave tradition of this nation continue to harbor a vast animosity towards any and all of us "whites".

As you know, the business of "political correctness" has precipitated upon us the notion of "hate crimes". The idea that white crimes against negroes are precipitated by the hate that whites have for negroes. Crimes that thus entail much stiffer penalties than ordinary crimes. In reality there **IS** some prejudice of whites against blacks. Prejudice, after all, is ubiquitous among all peoples. But . . . a far greater reality is that of a far greater quantity of prejudice and hatred that emanates from the black soul to those of us they consider to be white.

Having grown up and been schooled in the Northwest, I have had relatively little occasion to interact with many negroes, but that limited experience leaves me with the definite impression that they tend to go about with "a chip on the shoulder". Hypersensitive and difficult to get along with. A corresponding reality is that a large proportion of negro men in this country are either in jail or on probation. And there are far more crimes of negro males against whites than the other way around--even though the negroes constitute only about ten percent of the population. THOSE, are your hate crimes.

There are a certain proportion of domestic pairings that are troubled with violence between mates. The more their differences (color, culture, religion, and substance abuse) the more likely the violence. What would you think are the probabilities for violence between persons of such diverse difference as exist between such extremes as black and white? For generations now, these people of the black slave tradition have been unable to get over the injustice of their slave history. They continue knitting their brows into a storm and nursing their wrath to keep it warm, as the expression goes.

Most of us folks of white European background have also come from slave ancestors. Peasant stock and serfs who were bound to the land and compelled by the lord of the castle. But having gotten free of that a few generations ago, we cease to dwell on those things. Content enough only to be free, or at least only to be bound now to some degree in economic slavery.

Neither did my parents (or ancestors either--so far as I know) ever get along famously well in their version of domestic tranquility. But I (and we siblings) manage to get over these disruptions and disagreements between them and among ourselves without harboring deep animosities or cutting ourselves off from them; or from one another. They, after all have been our main benefactors through the thick and thin of times past. And in the final analysis, when the certain but unforeseen difficulties of one's life begin to seem hopeless, one's main hope for sympathy or relief from these--is generally among one's own people.

The natural course of each life proceeds always towards that which is tragic. And it is invariably the more tragic because we, ourselves, are commonly the agency of a large part of our own problems.

I occasionally get back to Oregon to look up some of my people and inquire into the lives of those who are reluctant to present themselves for renewed acquaintance. The three or four times I have attempted to catch you at work have met with no success. I have heard that you are now working only a couple days per week. Seemingly with no intention of working more than that and not casting about for a better job, nor with intention of getting an education?

The fragments of information which have come to my notice suggest to me the following:

- It would appear that you are living (in sin--as the expression goes) with a man of black color.
- That this fellow is or has been married, OR that he has had a common-law spouse.
- That this fellow has at least two children.
- Perhaps he even has a regular job?
- That besides living with him, you are acting the part of a nanny or mother to these children.
- That the example of your folly is of the nature of an example of waywardness to your own sister.

Is it likely that this very troubled and improbable arrangement is destined for any ennobling fulfillment to you? I am sorry, (and I must presume that all of your extended family are concerned) at the obvious difficulty into which you have precipitated yourself. But you must surely be aware of that! And that would seem to be the reason you have cut yourself off from your own people. If you lay down with dogs, you are much apt to wake up with fleas. How then to rid yourself from the plague? I wouldn't think it is likely that you are bringing this fellow around to introduce to many of your adult relatives. Excuse me for wondering if this fellow is not intending to be more of a pimp than an intended spouse for you. Having worked many years with disturbed people on the psychiatric wards, I have seen enough of this world and that sort of thing to know that it is not uncommon for girls to get themselves into these situations which are then often imposed and continued by fear and brutality.

Well, you are, as they say--free, white, and 21. So what you do with your life is up to you. Nor does it require the blessings of your family. But, since no one else in your family seems to have cautioned you about the statistically probable difficulties you are bringing upon yourself, I feel obligated to bring the matter to your attention. Yes, of course, not all of black color are of the same mould, but this one that you are 'dating' seems already to have several strikes against him at his young age.

Should it happen that you need a secret quiet and unknown hiding place in which to escape the unforeseen difficulties that are apt to arise, you are welcome to come down here to Santa Fe and put up with us for a spell while you rearrange your life and options.

But--obviously--such a secret would not be a secret if you were to tell anyone. A train ticket would bring you right to Lamy, NM--where I could arrange to have you picked up and brought to our home. The spare bedroom is now available as we no longer have any of the troubled native American Indian foster girls living with us. My phone number is under the name of my spouse, Betty Scott. (505) 473-7324

Best wishes and kind regards, Jessica.

Sincerely,
Gramps.
R. Garner Brasseur
year 2008

And the remainder of my year 2008 passed away without significant deviation from my routine of work and pattern of domestic tranquility. The years of one's endless toil and endeavor do seem inevitably to weigh upon one, so that we often long for rest. Oh, yes, there still are multitudes that anticipate with dread the notion of reincarnation. But I am not intimidated by these threats, for I see no reason to believe them. One must suppose, in fact, that these treats are conjured up the more easily to induce one to comply with the social controls which the political systems wish to impose upon one. My belief is more optimistic. That eternal rest is exactly that--an escape both from mortality, and from immortal existence. And the endless wheel of reincarnation--a mere rhetoric. And I am far too tired to go through all of this again.

"May the menace of the years yet find us yet unafraid."

R. Garner Brasseur, MD
Finished in March of 2009

Summary of year 2009
R. Garner Brasseur, MD

January 1st of 2010, and I have just killed a tiny flying critter as I sit here about to watch the second half of the Rose Bowl football game. Oregon versus Ohio. The insects don't quit. Can't quit . . . for their natural lives are far too brief to ponder anything so troublesome as a reciprocity of civil decency, or a duty, or a thought. And my intervention in its brief moment of being is nothing more sinister than an expression of my right to be left alone. In the scheme of eternity, what matter one insect more or less? And its end was mercifully more swift and painless than mine is ever apt to be.

THE FLY

Little fly
Thy summer's play
My thoughtless hand
Has brushed away

Am not I
A fly like thee
Or art not thou
A man like me

For I dance
And drink and sing
Till some blind hand

166

Shall brush my wing

If thought is life
And strength and breath
And the want of
Thought is death

Then am I
A happy fly
If I live
Or if I die
Blake

Well into my 77th year, my declining residual of health, energy, wit, and
good fortune permits me yet to earn a living. I am currently working at
three different sites in and about Albuquerque. It is a one hour drive of fifty
to sixty miles so that I must head out at nine AM, and am usually home
about seven PM. I have a bowl of oatmeal for breakfast after taking my
morning medications; and do not eat again until I return in the evening.
After supper I nap an hour or more, and then arise to do my weight lifts,
in order to maintain my upper body strength. Then, I read or write an
hour or two before I sit me down to watch TV for two or three hours and
then get to bed about 1:30 or 2:00 AM. I generally work three to five days
per week, depending on the schedule work-load. On my off-days, I take
a hike of two plus miles; and on work days, I often have some intervals
between patients to permit me to hike about the aisles of the store. Bayloo,
too, often works two or three days a week, but is generally home to prepare
us a little supper in the evening. If not, I bake up a prefab Totino's pizza
or a Banquet turkey pot pie. The place is always stocked with all sorts of
good things to munch upon, so that I needs must forever restrain myself in
order to keep my weight down to below 175 pounds. I drink only water--no
soft drinks, coffee, or tea as the sugars required to make them palatable,
add to the threat of weight accumulation. Oh, yes, I would like to drink
root-beer, and pink lemonade, and O.J., but allow myself that latitude only
when I take my three or four week vacation each year. Root-beer floats?,
oh yes, I miss them; but, again, only succumb to that temptation when
visiting about on my vacation. And we generally keep some chocolate
about. A regular cornucopia of many assorted other tasty temptations;
apple, oranges, bananas, pineapple, cheddar cheese, ice cream, popcorn,

carmel-corn, Oreos and milk, pistachios, cashews; and, two or three nights a week, a wee aliquot of liqueur. I have to discourage Bayloo from heaping up my dinner plate so that I can continue my relentless pursuit of the tasty and calorie laden dessert pleasantries.

In the past year and a half, I have had no personal health problems, nor found myself entangled in any family crisis. And so I am free to continue to work two to four days per week. Being thus occupied, and with a bit of a stream of income, I am able to nurture the comforting delusion of being yet useful; and even in some sense of value in these advancing years. But one can never be totally unaware that:

> "As houses fall when long decay
> Has worn the posts that formed their stay,
> So sink men's frames when age's course
> Has undermined their force."

We manage to live comfortably sheltered in our little house and home in an agreeable climate here in Santa Fe. BL works a day or two per week; and sees to it that I get an occasional warm meal; and that our diggings and the old war-horse are kept clean and tidy. She puts a lot of effort into populating the yard with plants, and keeping it from then becoming a jungle. And she was determined the past summer to spend a tidy chunk of change in tearing out some carpets--to be replaced with shinny wooden floors--which, of course, she then again protects with loose scattered carpets. And I have come to prefer the wooden floors over the carpets. She was determined next to drop anther chunk of cash into having the house re-stuccoed--she says it is a periodic necessity. It is all somewhat more extravagant than what my frugal nature is wont heartily to endorse, but still, we live within our means, and she doesn't prevail upon me to personally provide the time and labor to her self-appointed ongoing changes and 'improvements'. And so, in my spare time I am free to read and write; and worry unnecessarily about whatsoever I choose. She has even gone out of her way to outfit me into one of the spare bedrooms to be used now as a 'den'. There, I can be out from under foot, when on my off-days and leisure hours. To paraphrase a poem:

> 'Tis a merry thing to see
> At our tasks how glad are we,
> When at home we sit and find

Entertainment to the mind.

So in peace our tasks we ply
She finds make-work as do I.
In these arts we find our bliss,
Mine . . . and whatsoever she may wish

Better far than praise of men
'Tis to sit with book and pen,
With spouse that bears me no ill will
As she plies her art and skill.

Practice every day has made
For us, contentment at this trade,
Where I seek wisdom day and night
To turn my darkness into light.

In my youth I owned but the scantiest interest in matters intellectual and literary. But through the years I have been so rocked and tossed about by the winds and tides of troublesome reality, that I find myself forever crowded into the complexities of laborious thought and analysis. I wish that I were proficient at it. Like Xeneophon, in his <u>March Up Country</u>--I too am consumed with the necessity for the ubiquitousness of the-sleepless-night-of-thought; in order to guess at, perceive, and confront the inevitable troubles of each new morrow. Then, each new day, into the breech with ought more than a forlorn hope for yet another escape into yet another new evening's encampment, "by the rivers of Babylon", as it were. There, repeatedly to morn one's fresh injuries and losses; and alone to heal one's wounds. There, to remind one's self of the existential reality of one's aloneness and personal responsibility in this populous world.

"Born but to die
Reasoning but to err
Sole judge of truth
(yet) in endless error hurled.

The glory'

The jest,
And the riddle of the world"

(from Pope).

"Thus, at the flaming forge of life
Our fortunes must be wrought.
Thus, at the sounding anvil shaped
Each burning deed and thought."

(Longfellow)

Where then, amid the din and clamor of mortal being shall we repair for respite in the confinement of advancing years--that we might discover such *"Consolations of Philosophy"*, as recommended by Boetheus some fifteen or sixteen hundred years ago?

Obama's 'hope and change' does not seem to be working out well for our nation under the administration imported from the Chicago corruption system into the already polluted Washington D.C. political cesspool of scandal and intrigue. Where is 'progressivism' progressing us towards? Seemingly progressing us away from the founding principals of our Constitution and our Bill of Rights, and moving us step by step under the label of 'Progressivism' towards Socialism . . . and ultimately towards Marxism and/or Fascism. Towards systems that we know to have caused the brutal deaths of many millions under such tyrants as Stalin, Mao, Hitler, Hirohito, Pot Pol, Comenesque, Castro, "Che", and Hugo Chavez. "And when the smoke has cleared and the train has left the station, it shall (**ONCE MORE**) be seen that . . . "but few are riding; and that most have been run over".

Why would any <u>private citizen</u> wish to kill the goose that lays his own golden eggs? It might easily happen--accidentally, or unknowingly. But it surely seems counterproductive to one's own best interests. Why would anyone want a golden egg, except that it <u>represents</u> wealth . . . portable wealth. For it, nor a dozen of such, is wealth-in-itself. Now, in a world devoid of food, drink, shelter, and clothing; a mere golden egg would then seem to be a thing of very little utility to one's needs or comfort. But, in a world of merely limited supply, we can readily perceive why men are wont to fill their barns with ever more larder, or the imperishable but indigestible gold.

But if this "fundamental transformation of America" bodes ill for the individual citizen, then why would the president, his cronies, and the wide assortment of political elite (both self-proclaimed and non-self-proclaimed) "PROGRESSIVES" be willing to kill the goose that lays the government's golden eggs? Presumably because they anticipate being the dictatorial masters of the 'new state'. Once arrived into the splendid 'purple', they will no longer have to put up with any further criticism from 'the masses'. The masses will then be required ever to be in awe--of "The Dear Leaders". As in ancient Rome, they may then intend to become, and be deferred to as living Deities.

History, and a man's intuitive perceptions of human nature well inform one that the prospects of communism (advanced socialism) do bode ill tidings for those who have not squirreled away some little nest egg against the inevitable shortages of the political short-sightedness of progressive socialism. Even the well informed philosophical layman must forever be striving against the gathering storm. My own near relatives (and yours) out of Russia have already recently reaped the whirlwind . . . only two generations past. Thousands of our ethnically related Germans in Russia were intentionally disinherited from their lands and intentionally--and literally--starved to death by Stalin in consequence of his New Economic Policy beginning about 1923. Their grain crops which they had planted and reaped were seized and exported as a source of income to the revolutionary government. Those who were discovered (or even merely accused) of having squirreled away enough of their crop for their just bare survival, were shot, or sent to death in labor camps in Siberia.

From "Song to the Men of England":
Sew seed--but let no tyrant reap;
Find wealth--let no imposter heap;
Weave robes--let not the idle wear;
Forge arms--in your defense to bear.

Shelley

In our own country, the dust-bowl generation of our American nation was not necessarily unaware of the ever present lurking menace of troubled times, but more likely just short of time and opportunity to make an adequate preparation before the 'dust bowl' drought settled in about them. The recollections of a people tend somehow to linger in the memories and DNA across even generations of a people.

FOR WANT OF A NAIL

For Want of a nail, a shoe was lost.
For Want of a shoe, a horse was lost.
For Want of a horse, a rider was lost.
For Want of a rider, a message was lost.

For Want of a message, a battle was lost.
For loss of a battle, a victory was lost.
For Want of a victory, a war was lost.
For the loss of war a kingdom was lost.

And all because of horse-shoe nail.

Todd Rungrin

Men have had cause to fear and entertain thoughts of economic death not infrequently in the history of this world. For there have always been big 'big bubble schemes' that have burst; and many a man has found himself in something like the situation of the parson in "The Deacon's Masterpiece" when he found himself suddenly "sitting upon a rock, at half past nine by the meeting-house clock." He "had sworn that he would build one chaise to beat the town, and the county, and the country round." Yet, "what do you s'pose the parson found when he got up and stared around/ the poor old chaise in a heap and a mound/ as though it had been to the mill and ground./ Well, you can see of course, if you'r not a dunce/ how it went to pieces all at once./ All at once, and nothing first/ just like bubbles do when they burst."

The nature of reality seems perpetually to 'set-up' we-mere-mortals into life situations in which we are forever confronted by the probability of yet another great crash or a bursting of our bubble of economic reserve against the ever then grim future. We have seen it now again in the past few years in America. It hardly seems likely that this idealistic delusion of equality of men in a benevolent society will ever come to pass. The reality is that men forever have been, are, and forever shall be unequal as to: talent, wit, health, wealth, opportunity, luck, hope, will, determination . . . .

What I saw, read, and heard some five years or more past, was that the "housing bubble" of our nation was inevitably destined to burst--and that it would have sweeping economic consequences. Even those with only meager assets felt some urgency to invest, even while they were leery of it; and hoped to get in--**and out**--before the crash. Long before the most recent 'crash', Rush Limbaugh, Glenn Beck, my private conversations with Vic and Phil and other 'grapevine' sources concurred with me that I was fortunate in not being (of necessity) desperate enough to play the game at that time. And so I only suffered 'collateral damage', in common with the average citizen. But that collateral damage may yet progress even deeper into my personal economic solvency, as "the fundamental changing of America" (as enounced by the current president of the nation) continues in relentless effort to saddle "we, the people" with its programs of redistributive largess--at the taxpayer's expense--to the super-citizen 'too-big-to-fail' corporations, industries, overly 'progressive' unions, and independently wealthy multi-millionaires.

No, I did not vote for the pie-in-the-sky vagaries of 'the anointed one'. I actually doubted that the man-on-the-street would sweep him into office. "Predictions are always difficult, especially about the future." But, on the other hand, there was not much to be said for the alternative that was left to the voters. And fads and 'crazes', along with 'bubbles' seem an ever recurring theme among we mere mortals.

The one hopeful gesture by the president was the original rhetoric of indignation at the banks and commercial houses concerning their fiscal irresponsibility at leveraging their investing instruments at 30 or 40 to one as that swindle eventually jeopardized their own solvency and financial health--along with the invested holdings of many individual fortunes and the retirement funds of unions. And we were cheered to have him admonish exorbitant bonus money paid to these irresponsible CEOs and their other executives despite their fiscal failures. And there were harsh words and castigations concerning Federal Securities officials who failed in their regulatory duties to protect the private investors. But, nothing came of that. "Just words--just speeches". And since then, the president has apparently now established a somewhat cozier relationship with the big money interests.

Would that the recent housing, 'derivatives', and 'toxic assets' bubble had continued still unrecognized, for then our imaginary wealth could have continued to be a welcome and pleasing <u>delusion of comfort</u> to us into our smug declining years. But, in fact, Fanny Mae and Freddy Mac are continuing to create toxic assets for which our taxpayer's dollars are being spent into oblivion. Losses that we the taxpayers will not even be permitted to deduct as business expenses and losses, nor used as deductions into their tax reports.

The Bernie Madoff thing was only a trite symbol of what the 'progressive' agenda is perpetrating upon the American Public even-as-we-speak (as the expression goes). Even after the great bursting and revelation of a new fiscal reality, there are still many of the ever evolving Ponzi schemes to lure one into an ever greater degree of fiscal oblivion.

The 20/20 news program recently treated us to the details of yet another meteoric fireball that flashed across the political horizon in the person of Edwards of North Carolina and the saga of his mighty demise just as he recently (Jan 2010) cringed for shelter into the darkness of Voodoo among the po' folk of Haiti. You will remember that he wanted to restore 'moral dignity' to the presidency of the United States. Ha! Pity him. Pity us. Feet of clay. All!

But many of our disappointed American citizens have come to ponder another great omen. "What is wealth?", as the king did say, "for even this shall pass away." The po' folk, from among your fellow citizens are to be commended for their capacity to reach down into their spiritual reserves to find their solace. Have perhaps come to realize that every person has many facets to his individual being. Have perhaps begun to reorganize the living of their lives upon a new ethic. Have begun to taste the rougher satisfactions of plain living. May have begun to reestablished their connection to old friends and to long forgotten poor relatives. May have come to discover that humor (the capacity to laugh at oneself) is less injurious than wit (the tendency to laugh at the foibles of others).

Among our species known as Homo sapiens; infants and children are by nature dependent upon parents for food, shelter, clothing, and care. In reciprocity, parents undertake to prepare the children for eventual attainment of their majority and passage into a self-sustaining 'adult' independence. Children tend to be focused preponderantly on short term goals and satisfactions--and tend more to focus on long term goals and objectives <u>only</u> as they mature. Adults too, continue to focus on short term satisfactions, goals, and objectives. But, as adults, they are socially, morally, and economically responsible for their own choices; and in their relationships among their fellow full citizens, to maintain a reciprocity of civil decency and to provide support for the community. To be overly remiss in their civil duty and responsibilities puts them at risk of social and economic penalty. And responsible for the economic support, supervision, care, education, and training of their own children until aged into adulthood.

Our species is, by nature, a social and emotional race. And the human family is the fundamental social unit of our society. The ongoing intimacies, sharing, and caring within the family can generally be expected to result in strong social bonds between and among the members of the family. A concern for the emotional, and physical well-being of one another. Similar but generally lesser binding attachments develop--to some variable degree--to and among the closer relatives and friends of the family. Spheres of relative lessening affinities and attachments extend out diminishingly to the outer reaches of the community, across national borders, and around the world.

Available resources to supply the need, wants, and desires of the community are always limited so that there is always some strain and tensions that tend to disrupt the coherence of a community. And the straining of social bonds can become a bit adversarial between fellow citizens and friends. Where the natural resources to supply communities are plentiful, they may co-exist amicably. Where and when resources are scarce, communities tend to find cause for conflict and war.

Individuals are born free, beholden to none except their parents. It is almost invariably the case that the parents have never any intention of enslaving the child, though the child is disciplined and encouraged to put forth efforts to various accomplishments--physical, social, and mental. Having once attained adult size, mental, and physical ability, the child is free; yet might often need to be encouraged to take his own life and liberty into his own hands to make his individual way into the world.

Since time immemorial, there have been and still are, places where children or adults have been sold into various forms of slavery, and forced to remain in slavery. Some slavery exists even in current times, and often nearer to home than one might well imagine. But, through the ages, it seems to have become less common and in our times, there are persons and institutions actively engaged in rhetoric and efforts at ending slavery.

Every person--slave or freeman--must always have believed that he has a natural right to freedom, and had always at least desired to be free. Freedom to decide for oneself, the care, management, and generous support of oneself. Freedom to decide when and where he might roam, and to self-realization of his multi-faceted potential. Freedom to decide with whom he might associate. Freedom to believe what he perceives to be true or false; worthy of unworthy; possible or impossible; profitable of unprofitable. Freedom to succeed or fail. Freedom to indenture himself as a private contractor as is necessary to his own support and the support of his family and free to associate with those of his own choosing. Freedom to bargain with his own life and the fruits of his own labor to achieve and acquire that which he needs and desires. A freedom of person and action that both limits and constrains him in a spirit of civil decency and in constant reciprocity with all with whom he would associate; recognizing always such similar rights and prerogatives among those with whom he likewise had dealing. And never himself to enslave--either by force or by the purchase of slaves.

In the history of the world, some few only, of governments have gradually evolved, by revolution and bloodshed, towards an ideal of universal emancipation of all persons within their borders. Freedom, founded on the recognition of some several natural rights, guaranteed by a bill of rights, and a constitutional form of government "of the people, by the people, and for the people"--so as to have blessed the people of this nation with perception and the strength of character to once more rise and make the effort to vanquish the threat of even this new challenge of 'progressive' socialism. Will the people arise from the lethargy of overabundance to extend that guarantee of freedom to our subsequent generations?

A guarantee that among a free people, none shall be allowed to infringe upon the reciprocal rights of one another. A form of government that permits private dealings and contracts between its equally free citizens to permit and encourage commerce and production, such as to sustain and enrich the lives of its free citizens in free reciprocity with one another, and the always encouragement to civil decency among them. A freedom that recognized the always imminent potential danger from unconstrained governmental meddling in the private affairs of commerce and in the ordering of the lives of its always free citizens. A freedom from unwanted and unnecessary authority and from over-reaching government, taxation, and excessive legalities. A freedom such as might encourage men to struggle and risk their lives and fortunes to remain a nation of free men of equal rights.

I doff my hat to Rush Limbaugh, whom I first heard on public radio in the late 1980's. It may be that I had accidentally happened onto the very first of his ongoing talk shows from the Excellence in Broadcasting

(EIB) daily news analysis programs. I continue to be impressed with his opinions, analysis, and his exposure of fraud and deceit in the public area. I get the impression that his gruff mannerisms and to-the-point approach irritates his liberal opponents and a good many women, who tend to take offence at the same things that strike me as being humor. And now, in the past year or so this Glenn Beck Fox-TV program has enlightened us continuously with ever new revelations of specific details of governmental misbehavior and exposes to our view much of the rascally troublesome shenanigans of various political persons. It finally becomes apparent that most of 'the mainstream media' may have been generally more involved in pandering to politicians and in trying to keep the public <u>un</u>informed with bitty snippets of half-truths; and with their unwillingness to do any hard investigative reporting. And the ratings seem to indicate that the Fox Channel viewing has gotten far far ahead of it several competitors (CBS, ABC, and NBC).

Fox News programs so informative, analytical, and dedicated to informing and educating the public, that a groundswell of grass-roots protest has begun to rise among we proletariat. There appears now the hope that something reformative could evolve in consequence or it all.

Our nation was founded on a capitalist basis which too is gradually being subverted with socialistic programs. None-the-less, before that erosion has been completed, the nation has prospered and gradually become the most successful, influential, and powerful nation in the world. And around the world, socialism has failed repeatedly. **"The unsustainable reality of socialism is that eventually the ruling tyrants run out of other people's money."**

Obama's Chicago machine has taken over the administrative branch of our government, and has demonstrated the socialistic agenda behind his policies. The thrust of the Obama policy seems to be, as Dick Armey has put it, an aggressive dislike for our nation's heritage, history, freedom, and constitution; and the re-distribution of wealth through big government economic management--though no such policy has ever in this world been successful. Here are some of 'the **signs of the times**':

- 'Progressivism' proving itself to be creeping socialism.
- These 'Progressive' politicians have infiltrated both the Democrat and the Republican parties.
- Negro or white? The president seems highly to regard that he is part negro; but seems never willing to 'fess-up' to the fact that he also had white ancestors. Ashamed of white roots, perhaps?

He is in fact a 10th cousin to the recent newly elected Senator Brown. Some question of where the president was born. Who knows? Found floating among the reeds in a wicker basket, perhaps?

- A reckless president. Notice even how he disembarks from his endless airplane trips--'The Ego Has Landed'. Narcissism on parade. Clumsily bouncing his flexed arms in front of himself as he jogs down the tall stairway and onto the tarmac as though he considered himself immortal and immune from the consequences of a nasty spill. Against which inevitable fall, the handrail is always available. And he, tall enough that you might think he could be aware that "the bigger they come, the harder they fall".

- Reckless in his seeming determination to the "transforming of America"--into what? A socialist welfare state?

- Presidential association with criminals and Marxists: van Jones, Cass Sunstein, Andy Stearn, Mark Lloyd (diversity czar). . . . I am unable to comprehend how it comes about that Ayers and other agents of the weathermen (who are known to have bombed federal buildings) are to be found as professors in universities, in their advancing years, rather than as inmates of a prison. Or how Creamer (who is known to have stolen millions of dollars) ends up as an advisor to the president after luxuriating only a year in a 'White Collar' security suite of the Bureau of Prisons.

- A president apologizing around the world for America. Does he perhaps believe along with 'The Axis of Evil' nations, that America is 'The Great Satan' as he journeys about scrapping and bowing to foreign royalty and despots.

- War on terrorism? Undecided Commander-in-Chief dithers and hamstrings his own troops with incomprehensible rules of engagement.

- Delayed and begrudging Military support.

- Homeland security mess; Ft Hood; Flight 253; the Arkansas recruiter shooting.

- KSM NYC trial

- Reckless determination to close Guantanamo and release its enemy militants back into the ranks of the terrorists to further their suicidal missions against this nation.

- Failure to prosecute black panthers thugs who threaten the voting public.
- Cap'n trade scandal still looming on the near economic horizon
- Loss of sovereignty to "cap'n trade" interests. In Copenhagen, the Third world and Second world nations of the world enthusiastically gather to 'rip-off' some vague alleged 'carbon-tax' 'debts' from the wealth of America. And the UN is forever scheming for the hope of being able to level taxes on this nation and its citizens.
- Interpol foreign police recently being 'given' immunity from restraint against American citizens.
- A reckless president, blatantly reneging on his election promises. C-span promise, no new taxes promise, bipartisan cooperation promises,
- 'Obama-care' evil dealings with 20% of American economy.
- The threat of even more national 'entitlements' to a nation that is already drowning in entitlements.
- Taxpayers required to pay years of charges for Obama-care before delivery of services.
- On immigration--will we have Rule of Law(?), or are going to be inundated with the Ruse of racism?
- Smoke filled back room deals where bribery is being paid with taxpayers money. Millions in taxpayers money used to bribe senators of Nebraska, Louisiana, Connecticut, Florida, Vermont.
- SEIU / Acorn given preferential low cost health care federal insurance premium costs.
- Acorn fraud has been mounting ever more significantly through the twenty years of it existence, and has been given access to millions of federal funds (taxpayer dollars) that they find useful in perpetrating voter fraud and intimidating funds from financial institutions.
- Fanny Mae and Freddy Mac (government agencies) into the federal pocket for billions of dollars of ongoing free money; even as their immune executive get million dollar bonuses in the mishandling of funds in the production of the very 'derivatives' ('toxic assets') that produced the 'housing bubble'. Senators Dodd and Barney Frank own a large share of the

responsibility in the creating of this mess. The housing bubble, 'derivatives', and toxic assets have their origins in Fanny and Freddy. And now that the 'toxic assets' have been bundled and sold off into 'derivatives', these 'scrambled eggs' are not now easily unscrambled. No one seems now willing or able to place a valid value on them ('mark to value')--as against what the holders of these 'toxic assets' insist that value to be. The only certainty is that they are worth a great deal less than what was paid for them. And in all probability, worth much less than the price the American taxpayer is eventually to end up paying for them. "And all the king's horses, and all the kings men, will not put Humpty Dumpty together again."

- AIG and big banks "too big to fail?" get bail out cash at zero percent and lend it out at 3%. Even we ordinary citizens, without a degree in Economics, might possibly thrive if the powers-that-be would extend to us a similar arrangement.

- Global warming deceit as a ruse to vastly increase our taxes.

- Government 'green jobs' farce. Jobs that are heavily subsidized by federal funding because what little they produce is at such inefficiency or of so little value that the cost of production far exceeds the value of what is produced. The federal subsidy they receive is, in fact, just another tax upon the long suffering American taxpayer.

- Fraudulent job package 'stimulus'.

- Cash for Clunkers give-away.

- Bail-out funds being converted to 'slush funds' for covert Democrat purposes.

- Million-dollar CEO's Getting million dollar bonuses from taxpayers money. How many millions of dollars is enough for each individual banker? Is there not such a thing as indecent wealth?

- The swindle of private investors by super-corporations, unions, and big business. Andy Stearn and SEIU favored over actual bond holders and 'given' partial ownership of automobile industry.

- Failure of mainstream media to seek out and inform the voting public of continuous political scandal. Thomas Payne has returned from the times of the American Revolution and the American public has been forced to rely on Glenn Beck of Fox News channel to bring to our attention the muck and scandal of the culture of corruption that is subverting the Constitution of our once great nation. "The last and best hope for humanity."

- The looming possibility of a "Fairness doctrine" that threatens our freedom of speech and our access to information concerning the infamy in which we are submersed.

- The ilk of Bernie Madoff--one, among who knows how many more, who remain yet protected, undiscovered, and unsuspected.

- The spirit of Boss Tweed lives on. The two party system of government has eluded our grasp. Loyalty to party and party leaders has come to supersede loyalty to constituents.

- Politicians held in the grip of their party bosses, rather than representing the citizens who elected them. Would a 'tea-bagger' third party remain loyal to its roots? How and when shall the nation solve this problem of the ongoing election of politicians; instead of electing representatives of the citizens?

- I was disturbed to learn from Fox TV sources that there had been an effort and the early beginnings of an attempt to get 'the dear leader', Obama, into the classrooms of our public schools. Fortunately there was a backlash of discontent among the parents about this matter, and so far as I know this subversive effort has been at least toned down. We definitely do not want the equivalent of a "Hitler Youth" movement among the school children of this nation. We prefer **an education that teaches a student HOW to think; Not WHAT to think**. This is already too much of a problem even in our college and postgraduate schools.

- Cloward and Pliven have already for a couple score of years been launching programs of instruction on how to subvert our system of government with intent of replacing it with "Advanced Socialism" akin to Marxism.

- Some thirty of forty Czars have been appointed by the president to oversee and influence various aspects of the administration of our government. Who elected them? I think Americans should fear this business of doing "shadow governing" which hints at the possibility of a power grab by the White House. They seem to be advising and bringing leverage to bear concerning various aspects of the administration of government. They are appointed directly by the president, paid for by our government, and have their loyalties directly to Obama. Something that recalls to mind how Hitler organized the brown shirts, and then the SS with sworn loyalty directly to him. And eventually the entire Wiermacht was required to swear allegiance to Hitler--rather than to the nation.

- Monetizing the debt by the printing and additional greenbacks, (the new volume of which are not backed by any additional assets). The effect of that is that each newly printed bill diminishes the real value of each and every bill that is in circulation. Though one might thus be enabled to pay off the entire domestic and international debt obligations with now these large new volumes of greenbacks; yet each lender is getting progressively less value with each new printing of each additional "fiat" greenback. In essence, being cheated of the value he has loaned. And each wage earner being paid in dollars, is likewise being given less purchasing power with each of his newly earned paychecks.

- Bernanke and Guitner of the Federal Reserve (and Paulson before Guitner) along with our government and the Federal Reserve monetary manipulations; and in cahoots with Big Banking interests, are being protected against scrutiny. The effect of which is to preserve the banking industry from the folly of their own overreaching mismanagement; and passing their toxic assets and business losses onto the back of the taxpayers who have now bailed them out with government financial backing.

And before I sign off on these matters of political concern, there is yet one more matter that comes to my attention from Millie Wright and Bernard Chase--a couple of my high school classmates.

"For too long we have been complacent about the workings of Congress. Many citizens had no idea that (1) Congress members could retire with the same pay after only one term; (2) that they didn't pay into Social Security; and (3) that they specifically exempted themselves from many of the laws they have passed (such as being exempt from fear of prosecution for sexual harassment. Congress's latest game is to exempt themselves from the Healthcare Reform Bill that is being considered. Somehow, this doesn't seem logical. We do not have an elite that is above the law."

"I truly don't care if members of Congress are Democrat, Republican, independent, liberal, conservative, progressive or whatever. The self-serving must stop. The below listed proposed 28th Amendment to the U.S. Constitution would do that. This is an idea whose time has come."

Proposed 28th Amendment to the United States Constitution:

"Congress shall make no law that applies to the citizens of the United States that does not apply equally to the Senators and Representatives; and Congress shall make no law that applies to the Senators and Representatives that does not apply equally to the citizens of the United States. Nor shall any such past nor current law continue to be valid."

This is fair, to the point, and non-partisan. Who could be against it? Congress, that's who.

Reflecting back on matters, you and I might perceive that in the past 18 to 24 months I have been unusually much given over to following the political goings-on of the nation. Since about 1989 I have often availed myself of the opportunity to tune in to Rush Limbaugh for his analysis and commentary. Not only does he seem to me to have keen insights as to <u>what</u> is going on in political circles, but his analyses of these matters is much more profound than any such as I might personally arrive upon. For I simply do not have any first hand experience of mechanisms of even honest Washington Politics; let alone the subtleties of its subterfuges. The business is so complex and what-goes-on in smoke-filled back rooms of the capitol is so opaque that it seems to me as though one might have regularly to spend a daily large proportion of one's time to have any hope of keeping up with the details and complexity of political intrigues. I might well suppose that even were I suddenly to find myself enmeshed in the process (as for example were I suddenly to be elected to congressional representation), it might take me months and years to get into synchronization with its murky details and procedural requirements.

The citizens of this nation are caught between the several great evil forces of the world that make it difficult for we ordinary citizens to live our lives of simple pleasures and satisfactions without the threats from these various evils. The Federal Reserve, Wall Street, and the big banking and financial interests regulate the legal tender which is the medium of exchange that enables the commerce necessary for the day-to-day transactions of we ordinary citizens with our everyday needs of food, shelter, clothing, utilities, services, and the infrastructure of our communities. There are various levels of prosperity which we might enjoy; and there is competition among the citizens of the community and nation as to who shall live at mere basic subsistence levels and who shall--somehow--acquire the highest standard of living. Additionally, because of uncertainty and fluctuations in the supply and demand of what we need and desire, there is an ongoing competition in our efforts to lay up a store of wealth against the inevitability of periods of want, such as may arise from crop failure, destructions by war, natural calamity, and periodic disease. Always then, the additional ongoing competition ever for MORE MORE MORE to put into reserve for a rainy day. "There can never be enough", perhaps, "unless there is too much". Thus does simple greed and excessive greed become a problem to our several societies where there is never quite ENOUGH. Those whose occupations place them into financial circles seem certainly the most likely to attain the greatest wealth. And among the wealthy, there is always the competition to possess the MOST. An extra cushion of comfort. And with wealth, comes power--a natural concomitant benison.

There is no doubt that Wall Street and the big banking industry have long preoccupied themselves with financial self-aggrandizement at the expense of the man-on-the-street and in his prairie "soddy". Would that our government had the will and made some serious effort to rein-them-in on behalf of the common man. But alas, our professional politicians preoccupy themselves with gaining; and then with holding on to the reins of their power. And become wealthy in cutting personal deals with insurance, big business, and banking interests. And so, the man on the street is caught between the complexity of the common interests shared between politicians, banking, the federal reserve, major corporations, over-reaching union bosses; and the ever present reality of the simple thieveries we lump together under the term of mafia. Can the voting public find yet some way to make meaningful changes against the major current inequities of vested interests? Can such changes yet come about in an orderly manner? **Or will social chaos continue to the breaking point that will once again require a stirring up of the old dung-heap? . . . and the possibility of "blood in the streets".**

The federal government was already plagued with mounting national debt and the regular necessity of raising the ceiling of our debt. So much increasing debt that it has begun to appear the debt will never be payable. And then we come now to the Obama administration that is recklessly and pointlessly doubling that debt in a single year. We rapidly have approached the point where the nation may soon find no source from which to borrow. Potential lenders from afar begin to see that we will never be able to repay what they have lent us.

11-08-09

Grant,

Despite what seems to me as a tremendous voicing of grass roots opposition from the American public for the quashing of Pelosie's health care bill, these arrogant so called congressional 'representatives' have lifted their tunics and farted in the face of the voting public. It may well be that they were not worried about the insult because what they have done is not yet law, and because they know that the senate will be charged with the ultimate responsibility of the finalizing of this monstrosity upon John Q. Public. It is already being said that there is very little chance of their bill being ratified in senate.

The voting public seems to have so little direct say-so in what is happening, that only some drastic and immediate action is possible to catch the attention of the senatorial legislators--now that the monstrosity has passed some several hurdles.

As to what could be done peacefully, I suspect that nothing would have so much effect as this. Immediately to discover and make public the names of each congressman who voted for the measure. And immediately then to initiate impeachment and recall petitions against each and every one of them. They have already proven themselves as complicit in congressional disregard and irresponsibility for what is in the best interests of the American public to whom they ought to be responsible. If that could be brought about, the senate would then be exposed to "clear and present danger" in their support for monstrous legislation. The whole system needs a jolt and a sweeping overhauling. It would have to be a strenuous proceeding. I do <u>not</u>, however, believe there is even yet enough political will of the voting public to put forth that much effort at this time.

It seems to me that the party leaders have acquired far too much power and influence over their own congressional and senatorial cohorts. Their definitely needs to be term limits to lessen the 'need' of legislators to worry about each their own individual re-election. And to encourage the representatives to make their mark with a short and honorable term of service to their constituents.

As to the two party system, they both appear to be under the sway of overly liberal and socialistic ideation. There is need for the influence of a strongly conservative party to share in governance and to preserve some semblance of balance.

Yes, with no current family crisis to compete for my attention I have in the past year or two begun to take notice of the political and economic problems of this nation. Power and money. Both have always been at play, and subject to corrupt dealings among men. As in the ancient Roman Republic. As in England's prelude to the Magna Carta. As in the outcome of the French Revolution. As with the fall of Germany's Weimar Republic. As with the Russian and the Chinese revolutions. So also with events subsequent to the newly established American Constitution and its Bill of Rights. A new order of business and governing is being set into motion. A sort of overturning of the old dung-heap, as it has been described. The evils of previous systems had brought about the demise and the downfall of its rulers. And the new system is now <u>hoped to evolve</u> into something more equitable, more just, more useful, and more sustainable. **But hope is not promise: nor is it common for promise to come into fruition.** The question being mainly, how sustainable and how useful will hope and promises prove to be? Immediately begins the contest for power and wealth. Winners, losers, and animosities evolve even in this renewed effort to move in a direction such as to encourage some minimum of justice and stability that will at least permit (and hopefully encourage) commerce and production. The congressional malfunction and corruption that Glenn Beck and Rush Limbaugh are bringing to light may yet progress to notions of impeachment. Even more likely is that 'the progressive element' within both political parties shall be threatened with expungement in the coming mid-term elections. One wonders even but that "the tea party" movement may yet give birth to a new political party. The stakes are becoming high, and we must hope that political sanity can yet be restored to the republic without resort to bloodshed.

But returning now to what I had intended, let me say something more about my own experience, discoveries, and travels of the past year. Day by day, and week by week, I continue to work and earn a regular income as I think of the day--that's coming fast--when the advancing years shall inevitably render me incapable of earning my salt. Meanwhile, with all of the current economic and social uncertainties of the times, it seems like a good time yet to have a job. Thus it is that I continue to maintain a regular daily routine of living. "Moving easy in the harness" as Robert Frost has put it. And in my off hours, there is yet time enough to pursue some of my personal projects, interests, and passions. Time enough occasionally to repair to my 'den' or lair,

> "Where I seek wisdom day and night
> To turn my darkness into light."

And the wheels of my little red wagon still accommodate me in those "miles to go before I sleep". So, in September I took a little over three weeks to once more enjoy being able to hit the open roads in another autumn of my life. Harkening to, and reveling in the wander lust that ever calls from somewhere deep within my being. Accompanied by EIB, fine music, and the pleasant recollections of time past. Renewing my acquaintance with the western landscape and halting at the occasional whim to enjoy a frugal snack, or settle in to an occasional roadside nap in the quiet comfort and solitude of the pickup camper shell.

I stopped a few days in Miles City to attend a conjoined high school class reunion of those graduated 1950-1959. It was too ambitious--not many people with whom I was acquainted. But I still managed to have several isolated small conversations with the ever diminishing few of my familiars--Grant Mosby, Ed Neuhardt, and his sister Lynn, Bernard Riley, Janet Potter, the Smith girl, Joann Dolan, Art McCrae, Joe Harbaugh . .

. . And I visited briefly with Gene's old buddy, Dr. Mal Winters. I drove to Terry but was unable to find Ed Ban, who seem to have sold his trailer house and now occupies the Catholic Church parsonage--subsequent to the death of the priest. He seems to be the custodian of the property.

I stopped to visit the Custer Battlefield National Monument. But I was unable to locate Jody and Roxey--sister Katie's daughters--the evening I made my pass through Harden. I had to keep moving along, as a mere three weeks is very little time to travel the many miles and visit the various parts of my scattered family ties. I stopped over to spend a couple days with Phil and Dot in Spokane. In recent years Phil has taken to walking for fitness and seems now to keep very little chocolate about to tempt him (and me) as he has a touch of Diabetes that puts some constraint upon his diet. My experience is that walking is also one of the best paths of easy conversation. He showed me a cozy little building site he is working on, out near Cheney. Says he drilled a well that produces 300 gallon a minute. I presume that he is once more thinking of building a home out there if he can pry Dot out of Spokane when she retires.

I stopped over a couple of nights on the farm to visit with Duane and Georgia. Duane is retired the past couple of years after having sold the farm, and I have heard rumors to the effect that he is in a bit of a decline. Aren't we all? I must acknowledge that he does seem to have difficulty maintaining focus. What else do I see to suggest he is having problems? He still shuffles about his shop and about the house easily enough but I am not aware that he has ever taken up the useful habit of regular daily walks. Involved in farming most of his life, he has always of necessity been somewhat isolated out there, and through the years he has been forever disinclined to travel; though several years ago I did talk him into taking a trip with me back into North Dakota. But Georgia says she can hardly even get him to go into town anymore. And I am given to understand that she has even become a bit wary of leaving him alone out there for any length of time (I didn't ask her for the particulars of why). I notice that in the course of our conversations there are a half-dozen repetitious word-for-word vignettes that he interjects and recites repeatedly--I have to try to steer past these carefully. He keeps saying that he is 85 years of age, even though I have reminded him a couple of times he is only 80; and he seems not to recall that I reminded him. Repeatedly he says that Aloha is buried in Coeur d'Alene (she is not), that Tom has been buried there (he was re-entered there a couple years ago), that Tom was a wonderful and talented fellow (certainly Tom was a sort of hero to Duane--and Tom is greatly missed), that mom was a wonderful mother (she was), that he held her hand as she was dying (not so), that he lived with her in an apartment once for six months (not true), that he never liked dad (an element of truth in that). He narrates how he once encountered a fence on the Mexican border, and he had to dig a hole to tunnel under it and then walk ten miles up an incline (there is no reason to believe he has ever had such an experience; and he gives no reason as to why or for what purpose; nor does the story come to any conclusion). I gather that he has read my own writing a few times (*"Inheritors of a Few Years"*) and seems to have incorporated some of my information into his own memory, as though they had been his own personal experiences. I cite some of these things as evidence to myself of a reality that I am reluctance to have to accept. I have no reason to suppose that there is anything I can do to reverse this unhappy process.

"A feeling of sadness comes o'er me
That is not akin to pain
And resembles sorrow only
As the mist resembles rain"

I originally intended to stop over a day or two with Vic and Marge, but by the time I contacted them, they already had plans to be gone to Cape Cod to visit with Jay and his wife; and the two grandchildren.

Shy, socially retiring, and always short of time, I never get around to visiting all with whom I might wish. And my travels being whimsical from day to day, I am unable to predict any such thing as a definite day or hour of arrival. My length of stay and times to departure are necessarily influenced by what I perceive to be within the comfort range of all parties involved. For like myself, I presume them too, to be constrained by the obligations and necessities of their day-by-day lives. And as I travel and visit about, always too there is a certain reluctance and hesitation that inevitably precedes my each such encounter. Concerned, lest my arrival end up being nothing more than an unnecessary intrusion into their domestic tranquility; or if it might somehow come to be regarded by them in some sense as a bit of enrichment. And I oft times wonder at why I make so many visitations, and yet receive so few myself. Still, the day may yet come, as I bumble and metastasize about, that I will again get in a visit with Michelle, young Garner, Dolly, Stephanie, Malcomb, Dobie,

Jay, Guy, Yvette, Mark, Greg, Mike, Jeff, my many grandchildren etc. I stopped in Everett to visit with Andre and Gretchen, and the three youngest girls still at home; Anna, Clair, and Emma. Andre's mother, Betty, was also there visiting. A fine meal and a little time for conversation before the evening was soon spent. Of course they offered me a bed, but I preferred the cool of the night in my bedroll in the camper. And Andre, anticipating the possible needs of the an old fellow's night, assured me that it was acceptable to take a whiz just anywhere near the back of their big back lot. I had coffee with them in the morning before I headed north to locate my sister, Ookie, in Sedro Wolley, just north of Burlington.

Ookie was (as Duane puts it) "being warehoused" in a fine spacious nursing home. I knocked upon the door to her room, but got a feeble response only after several tries. A thin voice to inquire who it was. I didn't sense any great enthusiasm for my unannounced arrival, but she recognized my voice and eventually let me in. At mid-morning, she had just now gotten out of bed. She was weak and unsteady as I helped her into her bathrobe--came close to losing her balance. She was alert but with a sad expression on her face, and a sort of far away look in her eye. She moves with but only a few small uncertain steps to sit and talk with me a bit. I gather that she spends most of her time abed. She used the phone to call for a breakfast tray to be sent up. Seems rarely if ever now, up to be dragging herself down to the communal dining room for her meals. Is it illness and malaise, of rather just a progressive reclusiveness? That seems to be part of a new problem she must now face, for to remain here, they expect the residents to come usually down to the dining hall for their meals. She called her oldest son, Brent, who lives only a mile distant--seemingly needing him to fill me in on what was happening. As though she didn't fully comprehend the details of her situation. Sort of resigning herself to his guidance. Nephew Brent Krahn arrived this Saturday morning within about fifteen minutes. A handsome tall, trim and husky fellow. He displays a sort of take-charge positivism as he tells me what new plan has been arranged concerning his mother. He seems definitely convinced that this is the right course to pursue, and I concur. Though her enfeebled helplessness is manifest in every word she speaks and in her every act and uncertain movement, he keeps his distance from her, and avoids pandering to her. Talks directly to me in laying out the details, and with no input whatever from Ookie, as she sits meekly at hand, but only slightly attentive to this discussion between Brent and me.

Brent indicates that unless they can manage to get Ookie more active and involved in the community aspect of this nursing home facility, that she will indeed have to give up her residence here. I am left to suppose that alternative living arrangements would necessarily be less attractive. The formulation of Ookie's social work team is that Ookie has become progressively overly medicated. Maybe hooked. A suspicion that I have long considered. I am left to suppose that Brent too, may long have entertained something to that effect. Though she has long and continuously referred to her ongoing pains, one sees little evidence of it. Among other things, she is using Vicoden regularly four times per day. And so the plan now is that she is to be admitted to a geriatric psychiatric ward in Seattle for a few weeks of observation and an attempt to get her off of some of her many medications. Brent seems definitely convinced that this is the right course to pursue, and I concur. A sort of last ditch effort to return and keep her into a functional state of existence.

A few weeks later, we get word from Dot that Ookie is now doing better and has returned to participate more actively in the rest home community life.

"Toiling, rejoicing, sorrowing
onward through life we go.
Each morning finds some task begun.
Each evening sees it close."

Having again poked my nose into someone else's business and after my discussion with Brent, I headed south on Hwy 5 to find a rest area where I got in a pleasant little nap late in the afternoon. And I arrived at the home of Jauhn and Massey in Portland about 9:00 PM. No one was about. I drove over to a nearby mall. I know they are expecting my arrival, so I intend to look them up a little later this evening. There at the mal, I dug some crackers, sardines, and a can of Root Beer out of my grocery reserves; and found a public bench nearby. I sat me down to enjoy my snack, and reflect upon the events of the day. As I got up to dispose of my garbage, up yonder across the parking lot arrives an SUV that looks much like Jauhn's. And it looked like Massey, getting out from behind the steering wheel and entering the video rental shop, as three tall lads headed the other direction to a grocery store. I approached the entrance of the video store and peeked in the window to confirm my impression. It was Massey. I thought I might sneak up on her to startle her good-naturedly. Just as I pulled my face from the window, she turned and seemed to catch a momentary glimpse of me.

Just enough to faintly register in her mind's eye, yet it seemed to leave her uncertain. As I peeked out again from behind the pillar, I saw her turn on her heel and head to the exit. Once out on the public walkway, she stood there a moment, looking this way and that before she saw me as I again peeked out from behind the pillar. We exchanged a few words, and I then walked over to the nearby grocery store where the three boys were perusing some junk food snacks. What might I do to give them a slight start?, without risking a reflexive shot to the jaw?

Then, returned to Jauhn's place, we resort to the usual little celebration with Root Beer Floats etc. I located an empty nest in the attic where I got my sleep before a breakfast of waffles in the morning, and then, off with Jauhn to attend his soccer game on Sunday morning. That evening there was one of the seemingly not infrequent religious-social get-togethers here a Jauhn's place--perhaps 20 people more or less. A large part of them seeming to be of Russian Jewish extraction? Plenty of food; much of it ethnically unfamiliar to me. I had a bit of light conversation with a few of the folks. One says she had lived in Fallon, Nevada; and indicated she was a nurse--her husband a doctor. I haven't been able to get in touch with my old friend (Dr. Robert L. Brown) in the past few years. By chance, she knew of him. He had worked in the Fallon hospital emergency room for a number of years. She says that he was beginning to display some deterioration of his mental powers. And that her husband had the unpleasant task of then informing him he was no longer to be employed there. It seems that his dementia progressed, and that he died a couple years ago. So that is the story of a good friend of many years, whom I had known since we were Medical School classmates at the University of North Dakota 1958-1960.

And so: "Since none can Nature's course elude, why, o'er their doom in sorrow brood?"

I spent four nights in the Portland area. Bam-Bam and Beans were over to Jauhn's place a couple of evenings. Still some intermittent contact of Jauhn,s family with those two youngest of Pierre's children. Georgia told me that Jauhn had stopped over to spend a night at the farm in the past summer, and that Bam-Bam and Beans, as well as JoJo and Norge were along on that several day outing of geological exploration. And just a few days ago, I heard from Jauhn, and that he is still coaching some of the youth teams. Says that both Bam-Bam and Beans are on his basketball team, along with Norge. And these two youngest boys of Pierre still spend alternate weeks at Pierre's place--a split custody arrangement. But Francois, and Pierre's two girls Belle and Bah seem to have hardly any contact with either Pierre or with Jauhn's family.

I spent one night at Pierre's place. Both Sam and Chris seem now to be out on their own. The afternoon before I departed the Portland area, Jauhn and I spent a couple hours looking for fossils in a road cut up near Veronia--a place where my dad spent a year grading lumber as a young man.

I ended up next at Miette's place, in North Bend (at the northern edge of Coos Bay). Izzy, Josh, and Moriah are energetic little rascals and all caught up in their various interests and projects. The two boys slept on the living room floor that night and let me sleep in their room. Somewhere in the middle of the night, Josh came bumping around in the dark-- apparently sleep-walking. I awakened him and put him back on course to his bedroll on the living room floor. Of course there remains this large social desert of distance between Bart and I. Not his fault, nor mine. Its just that his apparently total immersion in fundamentalist religiosity (and my having escaped from it) seems destined to remain an unbridgeable span. In the morning I had some cold cereal with Miette and the kids before I gave Miette her birthday gift and headed eastward through the Siskiyou Mountains. I stopped a bit in Grants Pass to visit with Dr. Larry and Nancy Otis. In Medford I contacted Real and met with him and Sheri (his recent spouse) to dine on fine pizza. Granddaughter Clair was there too, along with Cowboy and the young woman (K'la Davis) he is soon to marry. After we parted, I took my hour long hike in the Wal-Mart parking lot, read a bit, and then turned into the comfort of my sleeping bag for the night.

I arose in the morning and drove to near by Central Point to have breakfast and talk a while with my distant cousin, Dorothy (nee Boepple) LaValle, her husband, Joe and their grown daughter, Nancy. We then had a morning walk together before I headed south on Hwy 5, intending to locate granddaughter Tristan in L.A. it's a long drive and it turned dark before I even reached The Grapevine. I had some reservations about trying to navigate the murk of downtown L.A. in the dark of night, so I took a motel room, ate my sardines, and awaited the new day before continuing on into L.A. in the morning. Once there, I was still unable to reach Tristan by phone, and I didn't have her apartment number. I called Massey and discovered that the phone number I had thoughtfully obtained in advance, was off by one digit. Thus did I finally manage to contact Tristan. She had been expecting me the evening before. She occupies a one room high-rise apartment there in the Japanese section of central L.A. I got a little nap there while she got some of her school chores done--she is doing graduate school work for an advanced degree in Architecture. She is a lively and enthusiastic young woman, and easy to talk with.

I had planned to take Tristan out to dinner, but she was determined that she was going to treat me. And then she became a little ill that evening, so I advised her to get off early to sleep. She insisted on crashing out on the floor, so that I could sleep in her bed, after I finished my reading. I knew she would need to get to her class-work in the morning, so we got up early enough for me to make my departure without bothering her school schedule.

I drove on down Hwy 101 to San Diego and then eastward on Hwy 8 to reach El Centro. I looked up my high school classmate, Lynn Fitz at his pharmacy job and arranged to get together with him that evening. It had been a hot day. We went out for dinner and then talked a while at his place. Knowing that he had to work on the morrow, I took my leave about 11:00 PM and headed east on Hwy 8 into Arizona. About 3:00 AM it had become cool enough that I could stop at a rest area near Gila Bend and get a bit of sleep atop the sleeping bag.

After six hours of sleep, I continued on through Phoenix, up Hwy 17 to Flagstaff and eastward onto Hwy 40. Arrived home about 9:00 PM, where I had a bowl of Campbells soup, watched news etc, got to bed by 1:00 AM, and was back at work in Rio Rancho in the morning.

It had been a long and busy trip but a pleasant and refreshing change of pace.

R. Garner Brasseur
Completed 3/8/10

Summary of year 2010
by R. Garner Brasseur

ere mortal that I am, and having been born into one of the vast majority of impoverished families of this nation, it has been my lot in life to have to expend my life's time and life's energy in often desperate struggle to hold body and soul together, and to need to struggle competitively for the economic wherewithal such as to enable me slowly to acquire sufficient education; in turn to allow me to earn enough of intermittent income such as to permit me to raise a family while yet providing me with enough of inadvertent free time to pique my interest in History and Literature; and pursue a few of the answers to some of life's persistent questions. And fate had ordained to me enough of an occasional 'good hand' in the game of life, to enable me and encourage me (against the odds of mere personhood), to achieve somewhat more than what was otherwise likely. No achievement of any great significance, surely, but enough to make a stand against an occasional injustice and to permit me to shed an occasional ignorance or misunderstanding. I am indebted to the founders of this nation, and to my own ancestors whose fortuitous good judgment resulted in my being born and raised is this land of opportunity. I am indebted to fate and family for a reasonably healthy body and an average intelligence as well as for siblings who have borne me no ill will, and who have been encouraging and of a some assistance to me in my progress through life and against life's obstacles. Grateful too, for some few friends who have shared with me the pleasure of their company and have been to me of some assistance.

This world and universe remains to me a great mystery, and my slow progress in penetrating through my ignorance towards its source, has (after all these years) now left me convinced that I shall never have succeeded in making much progress at it. But, says the poet, "The ways of shining heaven are far. Turn thou. Ah! Turn to things yet near. Turn to thy earthly home, O friend. And try to do thy duty here."

And thus it is that in the past two years I have been drawn into a deeper interest and concern in the political affairs of this nation, whose Socialistic and Communistic advocates--and their minions--seem to be dragging the nation towards its ruination. The prospect of it is unpalatable to me. For America seems to me to be (as has been said) the best, and last great hope in this world for individual freedom, individual justice, and for the survival of the possibility to individual citizens--of a right to the pursuit of our personal interests and happiness.

A QUESTION RE: RICHARD W. WETHERILL (1906-1989)

There is a one-page routine advertisement in *Discover* and *Scientific American* that I have seen so often and regularly over the years, that I pay it no attention whatsoever. It becomes finally a curiosity to me. What is it all about? Who has so much "expendable" cash on hand that they can afford the regular expense of it? What exactly is their purpose? And so I finally scan a couple of these full page advertisements to attempt to glean some clue as to what it is all about.

The script says that the law of absolute right was discovered by him (Wetherill) and "requires mankind's behavior to be rational and honest, according to natural law--not according to man-made law".

"Whoever or whatever created natural laws had to wait centuries on end for people to identify natural laws by studying the environment and nature's phenomena."

"Introduction to the law of absolute right and its influence on behavior is vital information desperately needed by every member of society."

"It could be said that the only choice people have is whether they will live in accord with the requirements of natural laws or die for ignoring them."

"This public-service message is from a self-financed nonprofit group of former students of the late Richard W. Wetherill."

? So, can anyone fill me in on what I seem to be missing here? Is it a lead-in to Marxism: or some self-styled new prophet with yet another new message from yet another cult or religion, from some distant realm of the universe . . . or what?

RGB

ODD, AIN'T IT

On Saturday in August 2010 as I was working at the word processor, I noted a couple leafs on the table and carpet. Odd, ain't it? Within the next hour I several times caught just a glimpse of some faint movement off to my left. Was it a fly buzzing about, perhaps? As this continued, I later noticed that there were now 3 or 4 times more leafs lying loosely about than previously. I looked up towards the ceiling just as another leaf began its tumble from a basketed plant hanging there in the corner, 4 feet above the printer. The plant had not been there the previous day. Is she going eventually to inundate me with her growing collection of plants?

The next day (Sunday) as we had taken our 2 mile hike, I mentioned to BL that I had seen the leafs of her plant all about my work station. How is it that it is shedding all these leafs about me? Later that day, I saw then that she had replaced the plant with one that was not casting off its leafs.

On this day (Monday) I decided to print off some various items to place them into hard-copy manuscript. The first page printed off without a hitch, but the second page hung up at about 4 inches into the printer. Nothing I tried resolved the problem. So I called in the local expert--Bayloo--to look at the problem for me. First thing she did was turn the printer upside down while she rattled and shook it. Nothing. How does one's ancient mechanistic suspicions square up with gizmos which are basically concerned with electronic connections? Yet, how does the electrical micro circuitry of the human brain relate to one's physical acts in this world? Frustrated and disgusted, I left her with the enigma, and wandered off to read for an hour or more before I lay me down to a fairly satisfying little siesta of a couple hours. BL had just finally managed to solve the printer problem, and now served me up a mighty tasty supper of left-overs. She tells me that a leaf from her domesticated plant had fallen into the base of the paper feed mechanism; and that now the thing was once again operational. Odd, ain't it? Her, then, having precipitated this little conundrum upon us, had now had to pay an unanticipated price for a seemingly insignificant rash, but unnecessary change--it had taken her two or three hours to figure it out.

In retrospect, one can see that both she and myself ought to have tumbled to the cause of the problem much sooner, subsequent to my having mentioned to her the fallen leafs thing. It all brings to mind the current economic political mess our government is precipitating upon our nation. "Fundamental transformation", "hope and change" . . . . Is change destined inevitably to be improvement? It might as easily be counterproductive. Unanticipated consequences, you know. And the pied piper (and his minions) might intentionally be leading one astray.

A previous similar incident that ought to have been instructive: A couple years ago there was a cork-board behind and above the printer. Some little plastic-headed pins affixed some notes to the cork-board. One day I prepared my document for printing, but immediately ran into a problem. The printed page came out wrinkled, skewed, and torn. It was a new enigma, and left me quite frustrated. Obviously something mechanical. But what did I know of the workings of these magical little printing boxes? I pondered as I peered some while into the innards of the paper track of the machine: I saw no clue to enlighten me. I happened then to look up at the cork board, and there my attention was attracted to the plastic-headed pins. Bingo! I got a flashlight and some magnification to look a little closer, and there was a plastic-headed push-pin, now that I knew what I was looking for. A little fishing with a light and a hemostat--and a few nasty words--and the printer was back in working order. Odd, ain't it?

RGB 8/31/10

FROM PAGE 9 OF "*THE WEEK*"; 3 DEC 2010

New York 9/11 settlement; More than 10,000 New York City construction workers, police officers, and firefighters who claim their health was damaged from clearing the World Trade Center site after 9/11 reached a compensation agreement with New York City last week. The city will pay at least $625 million to the workers in payments ranging from $3,250 to $1.8 million. The deal ended seven years of legal wrangling. Kenny

Specht, a retired firefighter battling thyroid cancer, originally opposed the settlement — which allots him between $127,000 and $158,000—-but changed his mind. "I am not sure that holding out for a better offer will ever be something that is attainable," he wrote in a letter. The U.S. House of Representatives has approved more than $7.4 billion in compensation and medical payments for the workers, but the legislation's fate in the Senate was finally trimmed down to 4.2 billion.

Related to and a part of the above issue is my impression that the recent 'lame duck' session of congress just recently did vote that trainload of freshly printed paper dollars to this cause as a sort of bleeding heart donation, though it beggars the imagination as to how we the taxpayers are responsible for "the cloud of toxic dust particles that the 'responders' (construction workers, mainly) <u>stirred up afresh onto themselves each new day</u>, and against which hazard, they were not required to wear protective breathing apparatus to give themselves a measure of protection."

What is certain is that there were deaths and injuries sustained by 'the first responders' in the 9/11 incident. Deaths and injuries "in the line of duty", to those whose chosen occupation does leave them vulnerable to such hazards. By virtue of their service in such hazardous occupations, they are remunerated with generous pay, insurance benefits, and other perks.

But that matter aside, there is no mention of the fact that the firefighters and police of New York City are already well endowed with insurance and retirement funds to be paid out subsequent to such calamity.

The initial great cloud raised by the collapse of the twin towers was largely an innocuous haze of gypsum along with some shards of fractured concrete particles which soon settled and was wafted away by the winds. But every daily new cloud which arose in consequence of 'clean up' operations contained the more toxic ultra-fine metallic particles which did progressive damage to the respiratory and cardiovascular systems of the clean-up construction crew members as it accumulated to their systems day by day. These too, were presumably union employees whose insurance benefits and disability benefits were covered by their contractual arrangements. The nature of their labor was not 'heroic', though in retrospect it has come to be recognized that the work was hazardous. And I would not be surprised to learn that the above mentioned "$625 million to the workers" by NYC is yet an additional 'gift' from the unknowing taxpayers of NYC.

Additionally, as I recall, there was yet again another source of booty for distribution to the dead and the survivors of the dead in consequence of whatever they suffered in 9/11 incident--moneys paid in to a charitable fund from generous citizens all across this nation. And the generous voluntary contributions of the citizens across the nation is commendable. But how is it, that the taxpayers of New York are then having to pay out this additional (involuntary) $625 million?

And how is it that our congressional legislators are so freely handing out an (involuntary) $4.2 billion in compensation and medical payments for the workers from federal tax funds--and seeking to placate us 'stingy' taxpayers by cooingly and flatteringly suggesting to us tax-paying citizens how generous we are?

Is it likely that the (above mentioned) man with thyroid cancer had acquired that cancer in consequence of the 9/11 disaster? And we can be sure that there are a great many "hangers-on" zeroing in on the windfall of greenbacks that are to be so lavishly applied to their individual marginal, imaginary, and pre-existing "conditions".

In pondering this matter, we might harken back to Page 18 *"THE WEEK"* June 4, 2010, for some few specific examples concerning public pensions, as follows:

> The coming crisis In New York, retired public hospital executive Edward A. Stolzenberg collects a $222,143 annual pension. Hugo Tassone, a retired police officer, receives $101,333 a year--at age 44. In California, more than 9,000 retired public workers collect annual pensions in excess of $100,000 (in addition to SS benefits, IRAs etc.). Because of lavish benefits like these, public pension systems are going bust, said Mary Williams Walsh and Amy Schoenfeld in *The New York Times.* State and local pension plans already face a collective deficit of $1 trillion or more, and it's likely to get much worse in coming years. Politicians are worried that the "outsize retirement pay" will cause a public backlash, at a time when state and municipal budgets are strained and "everything from poison-control centers to Alzheimer's day care is being cut". Yet mayors, governors, and legislators say their hands are tied: cutting pensions, or even "reducing benefits for

their existing employees, is considered impossible under the current laws of most states."

How did we get into this mess? asked Laura Cohn in *The Washington Post.* "Simply put, the states didn't make big enough payments to their pension plans, they failed to squirrel away enough money to pay retiree health benefits, and, perhaps most egregious, they later even increased benefits to recipients without figuring out how to pay for them."

How is it that after governmental and industrial representatives have done their collective bargaining agreements with union workers, that they then simply fail to deliver on the terms of what they have agreed to?? Next then, the financial crisis of recent years badly eroded the dollars that pension funds invested in stocks and bonds. Now politicians are threatening to scapegoat public workers by eliminating guaranteed pensions, says Raymond Edmondson, CEO of the Florida Public Pension Trustees Association, in the South Florida *Sun-Sentinel.* "But people who faithfully served the public for decades shouldn't be penalized for politicians' mistakes."

But "the politicians and public employees have been partners in this scam all along", says Mortimer B. Zuckerman in *USNews.com.* Public-sector unions deliver campaign workers and votes to politicians. "Once elected, the politicians approve obscene benefits with 'gold-plated perks' for the unions, taking taxpayers along "for an expensive ride." "For example, candidates looking to 'appear tough on crime' often seek endorsements from police unions, and then repay the favor at contract time. If we don't break this 'ruinously expensive collaboration between elected officials and unionized state and local workers', we will never get out from under our massive public pension burdens. Quite simply, they will crush us."

And the **CEO's** of automotive, financial, and other big industries continue to be paid obscenely large million dollar salaries (with additional annual bonuses and stock shares) for their nodding approval to union collective bargaining agreements. But take no steps to actually fund what they agree to. Just kicking the problem on down the road, until they are replaced or take early retirement with 'golden parachutes'. How is it they are permitted to escape with their loot into retirement? How about some 'claw-back' from their now private fortunes? And how is it that the tax-payer is then on the hook for the shortages suffered on their watch?

"**Private wealth at the expense of public debt.**" Are the members of their board of directors mere figureheads?

Can the unemployed and indebted man living upon the streets suddenly convey a donation of large sums of money to some persons or charity towards which he has suddenly conjured up some charitable feelings?

How is it that the federal government can continue to come up with funds from the American Treasury **for charity** to Haiti, Indonesia, Chili, Turkish disaster relief funds etc., when this nation is broke and owing. And what was the source of Obama's 'private stash' that he was distributing to the citizens of Detroit, so that they would 'love him', a couple years ago. So what are these private stashes? From what governmental source and on whose authority do they suddenly appear? The recent two billion dollars to Haiti, for example--as well as the previous and ongoing string of billion dollar benisons to each and every disaster around the globe.

How is it that the USA, the most indebted nation in the world, continues to bestow billions **on foreign aid** to Israel, Egypt, Pakistan, Palestine, and additional millions to fighting AIDS, Malaria, and other diseases around the world. How is it that the American treasury pours billions of dollars **into million-dollar privately owned** American Banking, Industrial, and Insurance companies whose greedy schemes and overcharges have impoverished the private citizen and landed themselves into financial straits of their own makings. Companies and corporations that are, themselves, deemed to be citizens. But, they are treated as privileged citizens; endowed by government with very special status and advantage over and far above the lowly wage-earner citizens that comprise the huge body politic. Governmental largess to big business interests that the IRS expects to subsidize by extractions from the private 'fortunes' of its middle class which is already economically pinched to make ends meet.

How is it that the **public "servants"** (including legislators, bureaucrats, and administration employees) have come to have acquired far better incomes and perks than the impoverished 'citizens' by whom they are employed, and to whom they seem never required to make answer. How is it that congressional delegates so inevitably become wealthy within just a few years of being elected?

"In general, (we of) the country class includes all those in stations high and low who are aghast at how relatively little honest work yields, by comparison with what just a little connection with the right bureaucracy can get you." (says Angelo Codevilla's article on <u>America's Ruling Class</u>)

In another article, ("The Illusion of Representation", by Robert Ringer), he tells us that philosopher Lysander Spooner once argued that the United States Constitution was not binding on future generations since they neither agreed to it nor signed it.

We Americans are wont to believe that the Constitution was needed to protect 'the people' by placing limits on the government. Which sounds fine, except that the Constitution has *not* protected U.S. citizens from government aggression. On the contrary, such aggression has become worse with each passing year--and alarmingly expanded under the Obama-Pelosi-Reid Regime.

Alvin Toffler's, book, *The Third Wave* pointing out the realities of so-called representative government, (while conceding that representative government was a 'humanizing breakthrough in human history'), went on to explain:

"Yet from the very beginning" this representative government "fell far short of its promise. By no stretch of the imagination was it ever controlled by the people, however defined. Nowhere did it actually change the underlying structure of power in industrial nations--the structure of sub-elites, elites, and super-elites. Indeed, far from weakening control by the managerial elites, the formal machinery of representation became one of the key means by which they maintained themselves in power."

"Thus elections, quite apart from who won them, performed a powerful cultural function for the elites. To the degree that everyone had a right to vote, <u>elections fostered the illusion of equality</u>." "Elections symbolically assured citizens that they could, in theory at least, dis-elect as well as elect leaders." "Ritual assurances often proved more important than the actual outcomes of many elections."

Ringer seconds Winston Churchill as being correct in saying that "democracy is a lousy form of government, but it's the best anyone has been able to come up with thus far." Purist libertarians would argue that people don't need government at all, but that's an impossible sell in these declining days of the American Empire. Ringer says that "through gradualism and addiction to living beyond their means, most people feel they need government to act as an enforcer to protect their lifestyle--and/ or give them an even better lifestyle."

Ringer goes on to tell us how, in a moment of morbid curiosity, he clicked on Celeb-worshipping Larry King recently presenting a panel of four 'financial experts' opining on the economy. "All of their comments were equally stupid, so I don't want to play favorites here. But one 'expert' woman did an exceptional job of unwittingly summing up why representative government doesn't work very well for those who believe in liberty." Said this paragon of financial wisdom, "If the government would just step up to the plate and help people, the economy would be fine." As idiotic as the woman's words were, the sad reality is that most politicians see such tripe as a winning message. Which is precisely why we are ever in danger of getting the whacky aspects of government we deserve.

When someone like a Barry Goldwater comes along and says something like "A government strong enough to give you what you want, is strong enough to take it all away," people shout him down as a fascist, heartless, or right-wing extremist.

Having said all this, Ringer cited Churchill. "That until a better form of government is invented (preferably one that makes it impossible to get elected to public office by promising to redistribute wealth and by granting favors to special interests), I (he would) opt to support the Constitution" "The problem, however, is that elected officials, government bureaucrats, and judges *don't* support the Constitution. At best, they ignore it; at worst, they pervert its meaning. And, without question, they hate it."

Would that our founding federalists "could return and explain to the populace what they had in mind when they started their unique experiment in representative government. Had they known what it would evolve into, I believe they might have taken a pass on the revolution and stuck with King George III. Which, in the long run, wouldn't have mattered anyway, because the Brits ultimately opted to follow America down the tyranny-of-the-majority path."

"So, until we figure out a better system, <u>your job and mine is to keep pushing back against tyranny</u>. And from this day on into the foreseeable future, it's going to take a bigger and bigger push just to hold the power mongers to a standoff. Make that a *lot* bigger push."

But there is yet cause for optimism in the political direction this nation may yet choose to follow. For in the past several years, Fox news and Limbaugh's already previously active EIB have now provided the voting public with 24/7 access to news; and to the detail of what is going on in legislative, executive, and judicial halls of government. And the public at large has begun to take notice of the self-serving aspects of legislators. And is beginning to be concerned about the bumbling of government which is, at long last, being exposed to the light of day. An interest that is being fanned as 'the American dream' is being seen to be ever less realistic in our fading economy. The voting public at large has long been fairly well educated and capable of understanding politics, but always previously excluded from access to valid sources of information which have not been readily available to the public. That is to say, a failure on the part of 'the main stream media' to live up to their responsibility to keep that public informed. And with our newly acquired access to news, comes also the <u>news commentary</u> of Limbaugh, O'Reilly, Beck, Hannidy, Ingram, Styne, Larson, Ingram, etc. to suggest some of what might actually be read--in between the lines--of 'news releases' so always slickly crafted and much hedged in double-speak and Orwellian "newspeak". The recent dramatic and stunning election changes of November 2010 have demonstrated that 'the grass-roots' electorate has now--finally--been getting access to the darker aspects of political details; and that they **are** interested, and that "The Tea Party Movement" may well be a genuine harbinger of a 'we the people' political force to be reckoned with.

One cannot fail to notice that a deep chasm of animosity between 'the main-stream media' and what are called 'conservative news media' (namely FOX News TV programs, the Limbaugh EIB program, Lars Larson, Laura Ingram etc.). A thing that I first began to perceive several years ago, and which seems to have been rapidly accelerating in the past three or four years. It is more than just difference of opinion; rather more like something approaching open warfare. At the same time, it also appears that the main steam media has been suffering economically as their ratings are greatly diminishing, and newspapers and radio and TV-station are suffering economically. A sizable portion of that may also have to do with rise of internet's open and free blogging.

One must suppose that the explanation as to why the main-stream media is become so vociferously opposed to the conservative media is that they have had to recognize that their long history of preeminent dominance in the news media has been shattered, and that their very existence is economically threatened. Why has this come to pass? I am want to suppose--as has been suggested--that they have progressively failed in their obligation to provide anything more than vague snippets of ambiguous new reports and word-for-word 'press releases' from office holders and administrative bureaucrats. Have more and more come to collude with government in keeping the citizenry **un**informed even as the chicanery of government has become ever more vicious and nefarious. Along with government and administration, they of the liberal left news media have come to consider themselves as an intellectually elite enclave; talking down to 'we the people'--the 'great unwashed masses' of we boobs who constitute the general citizenry.

But now, with the rise of the conservative news media, the main stream media (instead of reforming itself) seems to be launched upon a **campaign to silence and constraint** of the free flow of actual news and investigative journalism--of their own, and governmental misbehavior. Progressively overburdening our common language with a political correctness that encumbers political dialog, public discourse and even private communications. Orwellian 'newspeak'. Conspiring with the 'progressive socialists' whom they have helped to shoehorn into governmental congressional, administrative, and judicial offices. Conspiring to constrain and prohibit the free speech of public media of what has at last come to be a wonderfully informative and educational (though now threatened) process to the common citizen of United States of America. A mainstream media now in demise but desperately conspiring to retain their individual sinecure and obviate the will of the public.

And I was taken with Spooner's argument as to how the United States Constitution was not binding on future generations since they neither agreed to it nor signed it. I had nowhere ever seen or heard that idea previously iterated, and yet through the years, that unformulated notion had occurred to me from time to time as I, personally, or we as a group or as a nation were involuntarily being taken advantage of, on the basis of such agreements to which we (the living) had not been a party, either signatory or verbal. The Constitution of the USA seems to have served this nation well in its beginnings, but yet on rare occasions has seemingly had to be modified in the face of newly evolving political economic circumstances on several occasions by way of Constitutional Amendments--some of which themselves have had to be amended and some currently probably in need of amendment. It might be well, on general principles, to reconsider the entire document, Constitution, Bill of Rights, and Amendments for ratification, say every fifty or hundred years, or so. So that we citizens (so commonly at odds with our 'elected representatives'--who seem so commonly tempted to arrogate unto themselves an elite status with special prerogatives, as well as private personal agendas) might renegotiate for our selves the purposes, objectives, goals, rules, and mechanisms of our governing processes. And specifically keeping these to a minimum.

Contracts seem not generally well suited to stand forever and often fall into default from a progressive impossibility of fulfillment from some unforeseen or evolving cause. These needs must be, and continue to be equitability resolved in ongoing contractual agreements of 're-negotiations'. Timely such renegotiations may have real prospects of smoother functional relationships and with less rancor and hostility between the parties to an agreement.

There appears to be considerable variability in how groups of people about the world choose to govern themselves, as families, clans, tribes, and nations. Variations that are historical and deeply ingrained among themselves. Historically, individual groups have and must work these matters out among themselves with as much mutual compatibility as their situations permit. As to the lands and territories that each group and nation currently holds to be their own, these have come into being historically by chance, by 'right of conquest', and by long past negotiations.

There would seem to be no reasonable expectation that some committee, or the fiat of the United Nations is apt amiably to ever significantly alter current borders. The most that we might even hope or aim to achieve through those bogus arrangements is to limit further acquisitions of territory by brutally aggressive warfare. Meanwhile, we might also seek some amiable way as nations and peoples to permit of some limited immigration and emigrations of such individuals as might wish to make themselves more compatibly situated to the patterns of life of some one or another of foreign nations.

Back to the previous concept (as to how the United States Constitution was not binding on future generations since they neither agreed to it nor signed it). There are factions within these United States of America that cling to their grudges of some two or three generations past, when the lands and peoples were yet being settled mainly by 'right of conquest' and enforced treaties. That is the history of the human race of all past times. Enough of this whining demand and bogus claim for the divisive owing of 'reparations' and 'reverse discrimination' being owed by we modern day citizens who have not, nor could not ever have injured their ancestors. We-the-living, in our times, can see and understand how it is that they still harbor prejudice and animosities for the brutality and injustices suffered by their ancestors. But all would be better served to 'get over' 'the sins of the past', for it does nothing to facilitate the rational course of political conversation, nor ongoing smooth relationships between we, of the present. Nor are there any groups from among us whose ancestors have not also suffered their own brutalities and injustices in the course of history. Those of my own peoples have not only 'gotten over', but have even almost forgotten the injuries and insults suffered by their ancestors. But from what I can see, many among the Hispanics, the Native American Indians, and to a larger extent, those of the American Negro Slave tradition have still a tendency to cling to the past injuries of their peoples. Their wrath is misdirected. For as a matter of current fairness to we-the-living, neither I, nor any of my ancestors owned or mistreated negroes--at any time. Nor slaughtered nor mistreated any Native American Indians or Hispanic Mexicans. For that matter, many among our ancestral Anglos, had a great deal to do with the freeing of enslaved peoples in this country, though in fact, slavery is still widely practiced in this wide world. And I do not accede to the notion that the sins of my father nor of any preceding generation are my responsibility.

I do not regard the election of President Obama as being beneficial to the best interests of this nation. His background as a community organizer would seem to me to have made him better suited to demagoguery in his orations. His 'wisdom' something akin to that of the Sophists of ancient Greece.

In the past year I have already written two or three little missives to express my concerns about the Chicago mob in the white house, and the socialist-Marxist thugs who are the advisors and 'czars' to this imperial community organizer who sits in the oval office. And the arrogant self-serving professional political racketeers who occupy many of the legislative chairs and administrative posts.

I cite here some commentary about the person of President Obama, which seems to me also, to ring true. Observations concerning his origins, his person, and his credentials according to an article by Dr. Jack Wheeler Friday, 23 July 2010:

"The O-man, Barack Hussein Obama, is an eloquently tailored empty suit. No résumé, no accomplishments, no experience, no original ideas, no understanding of how the economy works, no understanding of how the world works, no balls, nothing but abstract empty rhetoric devoid of real substance." "He has no real identity. He is half-white, which he rejects. The rest of him is mostly Arab, which he hides but is disclosed by his non-African Arabic surname and his Arabic first and middle names as a way to triply proclaim his Arabic parentage to people in Kenya. Only a small part of him is African Black from his Luo grandmother, which he pretends he is exclusively." "What he isn't, not a genetic drop of, is "African-American," the descendant of enslaved Africans brought to America chained in slave ships. He hasn't a single ancestor who was a slave. Instead, his Arab ancestors were slave owners. Slave-trading was the main Arab business in East Africa for centuries until the British ended it (see the Autobiography of Henry Stanley). Let that sink in: *Obamba is not the descendant of slaves, he is the descendant of slave owners.* Thus he makes the perfect Liberal Messiah."

From "*The Week*" Dec 10, 2010 page 8 we learn some of what *"WikiLeaks"* has exposed to the eyes of the public, concerning some of the private but covert views of various high level functionary of the American Government. Their private thoughts, as it were, which once made known, could be a hindrance to ongoing intergovernmental discourse and negotiations.

We have long known of course that there has existed rather much of a tension between the Arab and non-Arab peoples of the middle east, based largely on ethnicity and aggravated by the ages-old schism between Sunni and Shiite versions of Mohammedanism. WikiLeaks now clearly informs us that officially (yet covertly), "Arab leaders have always played to public sentiment by stressing hostility toward Israel, while privately expressing greater fears about Saddam Hussein, Ahmadinejad, and radical Palestinian leaders." As that part of 'the-rest-of-the-story' comes clearly again to the fore, we may regard it as good news. It makes perfect sense that such a tension between Muslim factions surely must long have existed.

It certainly helps to explain the overall chaos within 'the middle east' in the past century or more.

WikiLeaks does us a favor in emphasizing that for us. That "the Arab World's fear of the ayatollahs, and that the entire middle east region hopes 'to see the US bomb Iran'". Informing us also, that Jordan, Bahrain, and Egypt have described Iran as 'evil' and an 'existential threat' and pleaded with the US to attack Iran. But we must of course suspect that there may well be a certain duplicity when we hear of them having made any such comments. What are they telling our antagonists? Thinking to themselves, probably, "lets you and him fight--and we will be around to pick up useful remnants". Even so, the Saudis must be taking the Iranian threat seriously, as they seem to be in the process of negotiating with America for a fleet of modern fighter jets of their own.

In light of all of America's ongoing conflict with and concerning the multiple 'hot spots' of the middle east, and more recently with Venezuela, our nation might be well advised now to be thinking more seriously that if we can get ourselves entirely **free from dependence on these foreign reserves of oil**, we might cease to be involved in their endless infighting and domestic chaos. Let them fight it out amongst themselves, China, and the several "chaos-stans".

We know that the Iranian State is waging war across the whole of the middle east, as well as around the world. A proxy war, whereby they churn up Jihadism and supply the materials and financial backing to groups such a Hezbollah (in Lebanon, Syria, Iraq, and Palestine). Obvious as that is, it would seem that our American policy is as though blind to that reality of Iran's proxy subversions.

The USA is decidedly dependent on oil to the functions of its economy. But is dependent for much of its oil supply upon the middle eastern nations centered about the Persian Gulf. It is certain that with the rise of competing economies of Asia, and India, there is competitive bidding for the limited middle east oil reserves; competition that shall inevitably raise the price of oil. And OPEC is ever inclined to raise the price of oil even apart from the fact of competitive bidding.

The United States imports 10 million barrels of oil per day--365 billions per year (two thirds of what we consume). How much of our gross national income (of about 14 trillion dollars?) is yearly spent out to the cost of oil importations? I guess it would be equal to that 365 billion (barrels per year of imports) times the price of a barrel of oil (say, $75.00 per barrel). Having never had cause to do any calculations with sums of money above about

$20,000.00 I am a little unsure of what that comes to. Could it really be as much as 27 trillion dollars per year? That sort of money being gradually diverted from foreign, into our own national economy as we gradually decrease our dependence on imported oil, could surely go a long way to the revival of our American economy.

Playing into this tug-of-war for our access to middle eastern oil, is the fact of the ever evolving animosity between the Sunny and Shiite factions of Mohammedanism. The current reigning elite of Iran is hell-bent on regaining its previous ancient dominance across the entire middle-east and becoming an Atomic Bomb toting superpower. And in doing whatsoever it might, to obstruct, weaken, and injure the economy of the USA which it deems to be 'the great Satan'. They need first to fully subdue their Sunni cousins in the middle east and gain complete control of all middle east oil reserves. They have long already been engaged in that effort, as they supply the ideology, funds, and military materials to the Hezbollah factions in Iraq, Syria, Lebanon, Palestine, and Egypt. Their proxy wars.

More recently, they now are concentrating their subversive efforts in Yemen. Once they establish their influence there, they will have surrounded the oil reserves of Saudi Arabia. AND, they would then be in a position to constrict the flow of Arabia's oil both at the straits of Hormuz (from The Persian Gulf) and (with control of Yemen) cut off access from through the Red Sea at "The Gate of Tears". And the cozy relationship Iran is cultivating with Venezuela would also seem to have some potential for restricting that flow of oil to the USA. The USA currently imports about twenty percent of its foreign oil from each of Saudi Arabia and from Venezuela.

The Iranian Jihad's animosity to our nation is far more than political in nature. In fact is, at its core, a religious-theological contempt for 'the infidel' throughout the world, of which our USA is the primary representative-- and the primary obstruction to their Jihad's agenda and mission of world conquest. Yes, aiming at a very big bite indeed. But however outrageous so radical a hope and intent would seem, yet, their current ruling elite is indeed a radical faction--comparable in their fanaticism to the Jim Jones "People's Temple" colony in Guyana of South America. That is to say, an ideology at once monomaniacal, radical, and recklessly lethal. Enabled and emboldened by their oil income to use the impoverished 'faithful of Islam' from the entire middle east as 'cannon fodder' to their misguided cause--made possible simply by the ginning up of religious fervor among their Muslim masses.

All of these things relating to the necessity of American access to oil ought certainly make our government fully cognizant of the need for a full blown effort to become self-sufficient in our oil requirements.

"*THE WEEK*" of Dec 17, 2010 has a one page article (p.15) which indicates that the icy artic ocean beds may hold up to one fourth of the world's retrievable oil. Says that the current largest land deposits of oil are first, Saudi Arabia (but there seems recently some cause to doubt that). And that the second largest available deposits are in the Canadian tar sands of Alberta, but that those (in common with shale rock deposits), are overly expensive to extract. The article also mentions again, the considerable oil deposits in the shale rock of Western United States (esp. Colorado) as well as the significant deposits in the sea beds of the Gulf Coast and off the coast of the Atlantic (again, ignoring more recent reports of oil wealth within our own borders).

But 'the anointed one' and the environmentalists continue to obstruct access to sea bed drilling off this nation's shores. And (we must suppose) these astonishing deposits in the Western States of the USA.

But now, how does the above "*THE WEEK*" article square with the Stansberry Report Online of 4/20/2006, (and reported in The Denver Post) which indicates that "hidden 1,000 feet beneath the surface of the Rocky Mountains lies the largest untapped oil reserve in the world. It is said to hold more than Two TRILLION barrels"--the Largest Reserve in the World??

Before the Stansberry report, (4/20/2006) there was the report from The Pittsburgh Post Gazette (2005), that "The Bakken" was the largest domestic oil discovery since Alaska's Prudhoe Bay. U. S. Geological Service is said to have issued an update on that report in April 2008. 'The Bakken' is a formation located geographically in the Williston Basin, though more commonly referred to technically as the Bakken Formation. It stretches from Northern Montana, through the western 2/3 of North Dakota and into Canada and has the potential to eliminate all American dependence on foreign oil. The Energy Information Administration (EIA) estimates it at *503 billion* barrels.

And immediately beneath the 'Bakken Formation' they have more recently encountered the separate 'Three Rivers Formation' which promises to be even more productive than The Bakkan.

These two reports, Concerning "The Bakken", and the other (The Stansberry Report) appear to be reporting on two different oil fields in the Western USA. One, under the mountains of Wyoming, Colorado, and

Utah; and the other, mostly in the Western two-thirds of North Dakota, northeastern Montana and on into Saskatchewan.

Yes, that is the problem. As to the Bakken and the Rocky Mtn. deposits, how does one know which of these diverse views concerning USA oil reserves to believe? These occasional few optimistic reports of vast reserves in the USA, and then no further mention whatever of the matter. As though--if true--as though it were an inconsequential matter. Whereas, if valid, that should ought to be an almost immediate game changer on the stage of current events of this nation, and in the world.

Thus, we have report of this stunning news: that **"We have more oil inside our borders, than all the other proven reserves on earth"**. Which deposits do not even include the more recent reports (of 2010) which suggest that furthermore, the icy artic ocean beds at the North Pole (to which we have access) may yet hold up to one fourth of the world's retrievable oil.

Here are the official estimates concerning just "The Bakken" formation and the larger reserve located beneath the Rockie Mts.:

8-times as much oil as Saudi Arabia
18-times as much oil as Iraq
21-times as much oil as Kuwait
22-times as much oil as Iran
500-times as much oil as Yemen
and it's all right here in the Western United States.

"HOW can this BE? HOW can we NOT BE extracting this? Because the environmentalists and others have blocked all efforts to help America become independent of foreign oil! Again, we are letting a small group of people dictate our lives and our economy. ....WHY?" If even any one of the above three mentioned reports of extensive oil field reserves is valid, we have enough oil available for drilling to free up this nation entirely of dependence from any outside source whatsoever! ("let my people go") Enough natural resource to provide income producing jobs to a significant portion of the currently unemployed and willing of this nation; in addition to the large potential for earnings from funds invested right here in our own nation.

There is an article (page 56-63 of Scientific American; October 2009); by Leonard Maugeri which I have here abstracted. Yet another optimistic detail on which to ponder:

The article says that currently one is able to extract only 35% of oil field content, but advancing technology suggests that by 2030 it may be possible to extract 50% or even 65%. Note also that "estimate reserve of a field is difficult to discern. For example, the Kern River oil field (Bakersfield, CA) was brought in in 1899, and its reserves were estimated then to be 70 million barrels. But by 1942, it had produced 280 million. And its reserves then estimated at yet 60 million.

But by 2007, it had produced 2000 million barrels; and reserves then estimated at still 270 million. Maugeri estimates that there are enough known global reserves to last the remainder of the century. Though this nation's 'proven' oil reserves are currently 29 billion barrels, yet the National Petroleum Council estimates that there are 1,124 billion barrels, of which 374 billion barrels are recoverable even at only the current 35% yield limit. (35% recoverability?) Strangely, this article does not even make mention of the Bakken and the Rocky Mtn. deposits of TWO TRILLION barrels. (I note as an aside, that reports concerning the Bakken suggests a recoverability of only 1%? Apparently harder to get at, account of being widely layered between geological strata, rather than concentrated into a convenient globular pool.)

Moreover, the USGS survey does not include the unconventional oil sources such as ultra heavy oils, tar sands, oil shales, and bituminous shists, which together are at least as abundant as conventional oil sources--although technologically much more difficult to extract.

Abstract by RGB 7/12/2010

The only other thing I know about the alleged Williston Basin Area Oil Field (the Bakken) is that my brother just happened to be in that area in the summer of 2010. He says that while there is modest activity on the USA side of the border, that activity on the Canadian side seems to be booming. Also, my brother-in-law lives just southwest of Williston, and works in the oil fields there; and he says that that things seem to be coming alive in the Williston area. Oil goings-on! Says Williston is growing. They can't build houses fast enough. They are moving in old unused houses from smaller nearby communities. So . . . <u>the evidence</u> of the reality of the oil boom <u>does not square with the dearth</u> of any much news thereof. And I myself drove through Williston and the Williston basin in October of 2010, and I can personally assure you that the area is indeed booming. As I drove at dusk from Williston to Stanly, I counted 52 drilling rigs at work including the flares of some that were a bit further afield which were beginning to illuminate the evening sky. What are we to make of these things?

We are told that fully one-third of all domestic oil and 45% of natural gas in the US comes from the Gulf of Mexico and most all of that from off the coast of Louisiana.

But just recently I have abstracted the following information from <u>Scientific American; July 2010</u>:

> We are told of a vast shale deposit--The Marcellus Formation, stretching from Tennessee into New York. Enough natural gas there to supply the USA for 40 years, we are told. In the past 2 years these shale gasses are being heavily utilized and piped into the Northeast. There is already a backlog and a large demand for certified welders to bring the supply to the users in the Northeast. There are 107,000 jobs in Pennsylvania for drilling and pipe welders. A vertical shaft goes down 3000 to 8000 feet. 12 horizontal shafts radiate outward horizontally for up to a mile. Large quantities of water, sand, along with 0.5% Chemicals including HCL, ethylene glycol, and glutaraldehyde. The drilling is taking place in Pennsylvania but not in New York--ecological concerns related to possibility of water table degradation from the above said chemicals.

> And there are similar such deposits also in Texas and Oklahoma, as well as in Colorado.

Natural gas emits 40% less carbon dioxide than does the burning of coal.

As Jack wheeler puts it "the Great New Cause of the Left, its substitute for Marxism as a rationale for control of everyone's life, Warmism." An ancillary pretext to bolster the Marxism which has demonstrated its failure in Russia. But no reasonable person believes "climate theology's high priests" any more, especially since they made clear that salvation can be obtained only by strangling struggling economies, imposing new taxes on energy, and surrendering national sovereignty to global overlords.

A senior member of the U.N.'s Intergovernmental Panel on climate change let slip the perpetrators' real motive last week when he said the goal of any international treaty should be **"redistributing the world's wealth" from richer countries to poorer ones.** Developed nations, the UN official said, "have basically expropriated the atmosphere of the world community," and must do penance by paying a minimum of one hundred billion annually to poorer nations. P. 23 of *THE WEEK*

But we are badly mistaken if we suppose that this business of 'climate control' is gone for good. For its powerful and fundamental purpose is that of emplacing a mechanism to require prosperous and civilized nations to subsidize the third world nations which are unable or unwilling to shape their own countries into prosperity and civil deportment among themselves. And the greed factor of private interests within our own nation--though for now frustrated--are still dreaming and drooling over their personal plans for raking in billions and trillions of dollars in profits from their plans (which they have already formulated) to serve as Wall Street intermediaries for the nefarious buying and selling of "carbon credits". They have in fact already once set up the mechanism for the Carbon Credits Exchange (CCX) which has already once made its way to the securities exchange board. The so called "carbon credits" are conceived of as being past debts owing by the wealthier nations of the world, to the third world countries for our nations' (i.e. the wealthy nations) having polluted the world's atmosphere through our industrial processes by which we supply our civilized nations with energy and products for our consumption. They produce little or nothing, and sell to us their unexercised right to production. For this unexercised right, we are to pay them cash with which they can buy arms and munitions to continue to raise havoc among their own peoples and threaten ours. When I buy a tank of gas, I am expected then to pay for a second tank of gas--the price of which belongs to the underdeveloped nations abroad. The more we produce to sell and donate to their impoverished peoples, the more we then owe them. Cute little game. Fortunately, however, Al Gore's CCX has crashed and failed. But we can be assured that Al Gore and his powerful private interest associates will push again for some form of 'climate control', such as will once again enable them to corner the world market on Carbon Credit sales.

And our nation would be well advised to wrench itself free from this bumbling committeeism called The United Nations. For it's main but covert purpose is that of getting into the pockets of the more prosperous of nations, to the benefit of the desperately poor and chaotic nations that they represent--while their representatives, of course, enrich and empower themselves personally--and with little or no actual hope nor intent of actually being of much benefit to the peoples they are intended to represent. Here again we note the reality of 'agendas'; and a co-mingling of agendas, some of which are at cross-purposes to one another. To the degree that any two or more agendas make common cause and purpose with one another, we might well call that by the name of "conspiracy". Even though "conspiracy" is a word implying disreputability, and none is wont to own the label nor be accused of such. No, who would wish to have 'the tail of the donkey' pinned upon themselves?

Will the chronically chaotic and misgoverned nations of the third world ever be willing or able to bring stable representative government 'for, of, and by the people' to their own individual nations? It seems about as likely as the remote hope for any lasting peace and stable government in Palestine. My impression of history is that tribalism does not readily transform into any stable form of nationalism. Something inherently improbable and

217

unlikely in any such 'great leap forward'. Brother Vic loaned me his copy of a fascinating book (The Autobiography of Henry Stanley), which well describes the primitive tribalism of 'Dark Africa' (as he discovered in his several armed expeditions into the interior) in the last half of the 1800's. A fractured 'barbaric' tribalism that seems yet to grip a large portion of Africa, whose mineral wealth seems probably yet largely untapped--apart from that of diamonds and gold.

Glenn Beck (of FOX News TV) has provided us with considerable detail concerning the long term goals of the euphemistic 'one-worlders' whose vague objective is to 'create a level playing field' for all persons across the globe. So far as I have heard, the current leading vocal advocate and economic force behind this agenda is George Soros, an 80 year old agnostic of Jewish heritage who originated out of Hungary. He is said to be a self-made multi-millionaire whose main <u>pass-time and hobby</u> has become the planning and devising of schemes for the manipulation of political-economic affairs of governments. Seemingly, with plans for a one-world government. I am of the impression that he has no family other than a brother. Soros is said to have brought about the collapse of the Hungarian, Romanian, and the Czechoslovakia Communist regimes. And is said to have been primarily responsible for the collapse of the British Pound. Beck says that Soros is under indictment for currency manipulation in France, but that he currently resides here in the United States. But Soros is said to be one of most wealthy individuals in the world, so that he is effectively protected from legal charges so long as he doesn't kill, assassinate, or overtly precipitate chaos.

Yes, it is this same George Soros who we now discover (courtesy of Glenn Beck research team) to be deeply involved in the current political goings on in this country. I haven't yet figured out for how long he has been at this in this country, but one must presume that he has been reaching his tentacles into the mix of our nation's politics already for many years, judging from the host of social and political organizations to which he is a hefty contributor of money. Beck has had two scrolls compiled (each scroll 20 feet long) listing each of these separate organizations that are economically (and, presumably ideologically) beholden to him. The people who run each of these many separate organizations, are--as it were--his minions. So, apparently, Soros does not have his hand directly into this infamy, but would seem to have a personal 'understanding' with each of these minions as to what it is they are to be perpetrating upon this nation--under the guise of euphemistically named subversive political organizations.

But what is in it for Soros, that he plays his game with such patient determination? And at so much personal expense? It would appear that money is no object to him, as he so wealthy that he is inapt ever to manage to get it all spent. And, in fact the financial chaos he is able to precipitate, seems to bring him continuously additional wealth as he is able to predict and facilitate the economic ruination with his intentional market manipulations, so that he profits by being able always to win on betting short on the basis of his inside information and economic influence in each issue at hand.

Is he into economic chaos and ruination because he a perverse and evil person? In fact he has enjoyed so much economic success and acquired so much wealth, that he has come literally to regard himself as a god, and regards his political intrusions as a benison to mankind. And besides gaining personal success in the playing of his games of manipulations of the powers that be, he has yet an even more all encompassing objective. He would appear to be a true ideologue, and truly believes and intends on the creation of a world order of true equality for all persons. In common with the radical leftists and 'progressive socialists' currently involved in the ruination of the social-economic condition of this country, it is his (stated) belief that American <u>Capitalization</u> is <u>the primary obstruction to his new world order</u> plans, and that he is dedicated to the death of capitalism. Of course we do not know what is his end stage goal, but for the time being, he is able at least to make common cause with the Obama/Chicago political machine, the American Communists, and the Progressive Socialists of this land. Soros is an 80 year old man, and he will not be around forever, but we can be fairly confident that he has his handful of primary confidantes who will press forth his agenda beyond the hour of his demise.

We might list some of the euphemistically named organizations to which Soros has ties. So many, that it is difficult for one even to name them all, let alone be aware of what are their supposed objective, as opposed to the covert agendas to which they play. A short list of some of these Soros organizations would include: SDS, the new SDS, NPR, OSI, Tides Foundation, Apollo Alliance, Center for American Progress, Acorn, SOS, One America Votes, One Nation Rally, National Welfare Rights Organization, Weather Underground Revolution, Midwest Education Association, Socialism Scholar Conferences. Among the Soros minions we would include such as Van Jones, Mark Lloyd, Jeff Jones, Ehers, Bernadine

Dorn, Cass Sunsteen, John Podesta of Center for American Progress, and Andy Stern of the Service Employees Union.

A Summary of Life

GREAT TRUTHS THAT LITTLE CHILDREN HAVE LEARNED:
1) No matter how hard you try, you can't baptize cats..
2) When your Mom is mad at your Dad, don't let her brush your hair.
3) If your sister hits you, don't hit her back. They always catch the second person.
4) Never ask your 3-year old brother to hold a tomato.
5) You can't trust dogs to watch your food..
6) Don't sneeze when someone is cutting your hair..
7) Never hold a Dust-Buster and a cat at the same time.
8) You can't hide a piece of broccoli in a glass of milk.
9) Don't wear polka-dot underwear under white shorts.
10) The best place to be when you're sad is Grandpa's lap.

GREAT TRUTHS THAT ADULTS HAVE LEARNED:
1) Raising teenagers is like nailing jelly to a tree.
2) Wrinkles don't hurt.
3) Families are like fudge...mostly sweet, with a few nuts
4) Today's mighty oak is just yesterday's nut that held its ground...
5) Laughing is good exercise. It's like jogging on the inside.
6) Middle age is when you choose your cereal for the fiber, not the toy.

GREAT TRUTHS ABOUT GROWING OLD
1) Growing old is mandatory; growing up is optional...
2) Forget the health food. I need all the preservatives I can get.
3) When you fall down, you wonder what else you can do while you're down there.
4) You're getting old when you get the same sensation from a rocking chair that you once got from a roller coaster.
5) It's frustrating when you know all the answers but nobody bothers to ask you the questions...
6) Time may be a great healer, but it's a lousy beautician

7) Wisdom comes with age, but sometimes age comes alone.

I am astonished that this rogue government continues in their headlong pursuit towards the routine of customary depredations one must eventually expect from tyrants and totalitarianism. Yes, and astonished at myself for having actually--for the first time in my life--become personally cognitive of; and then concerned to the point of alarm; at what I perceive to be the looming possibility for disaster upon the near horizon of this nation. How is it possible even for the dimmest among we citizens to fail to notice the omens; nor recall the many mass political purges about the world that have come to pass even only in our own lifetimes.

History is prophesy. <u>One must not forget "the killing fields" of even just the past 70 plus years</u> of my own life. Six million Jews and additional millions of Poles and other undesirables eliminated by Hitler, 66 million deaths at the hands of Stalin; even more millions than that in the rise of Mao's regime, and Pol Pot's mass murder of 1.7 million in the much smaller nation of Cambodia. Others in Franco's Spain, and under Pinochet in Chili, under Castro in Cuba, and yet again in Argentina. More recently, the genocides in the Balkans, in Uganda, the Congo, in Darfur. I haven't yet heard the final estimate of victims under Saddam Hussein.

"On rare occasions, a unique figure bursts onto the national stage and has a dramatic impact on politics, culture, or both. Glenn Beck is one of those figures. He is surely the biggest, fastest, most controversial star in the political commentary business in my lifetime" says Robert Ringer. "He's real, and he has succeeded in enlightening his audience." "If you have not heard the Glenn Beck programs on Fox News you have missed the most honest, factual documentation of the criminal corruption of what is happening in Washington". Beck is knowledgeable, factual, rational, and focused on the key issue: America's loss of liberty. Though I do not agree with his personal religious views, there certainly does seem to a problem of moral decadence that is a part of a core problem of individual misbehavior and civil indecency that contributes to the ongoing decline of our institutions.

I was having my similar concerns as to "Glenn Beck's Departure from Fox News", as those iterated by Robert Ringer as he asks, "how might his departure come about?"; and suggests four possible avenues of exit. "As I watch him strip BHO and other members of 'Crime Inc.' down to their dirty underwear every day at 5:00 pm, I ponder what the Obamaviks will do to try to stop him from destroying their full-speed-ahead efforts to transform the U.S. into a collectivist paradise."

RINGER PONDERS THE POSSIBILITIES FOR BECK'S EXIT FROM FOX NEWS:

1) "Assassination. On more than one occasion, Beck has alluded to cement boots and his ending up at the bottom of the East River. He has also assured his audience that he has no inclination to jump off a tall building, and if something like that were to ever happen to him, it would not be accidental. Even more ominous is that Beck continually tells his audience that this isn't about him, that each and every one of them must stand up and carry on the fight. When he says this, it sparks memories of Martin Luther King Jr.'s famous words at a rally in Memphis the night before he was murdered: 'We've got some difficult days ahead. But it really doesn't matter with me now. Because I've been to the mountaintop ... and I've looked over, and I've seen the promised land. I may not get there with you, but I want you to know tonight that we as a people will get to the promised land.' Anyone who has read even a nominal amount of political history knows that those on the far left unabashedly believe that their morally superior objectives justify the use of violence. The problem they have with Beck is that using violence to eliminate him is dangerous, given that he has already warned the public to be on the lookout for his sudden demise. Plus, a martyred Glenn Beck could be as powerful for the liberty movement as a martyred Barack Obama would be for the movement to turn America into a socialist police state."
"So, let's hope that no harm befalls Glenn Beck", (or Obama).

2) Rupert Murdoch's News Corporation is run by "Roger Ailes who has almost single-handedly propped up the free press in this country, being so good at his job that Fox News has been able to render its left-wing media competition almost irrelevant." But both Murdoch and Ailes are aging and once either is gone, there is no assurance that Fox News will continue to support the controversial Glenn Beck. "Murdoch's children and son-in-law are liberals who have long complained that Fox News is

too conservative." Once Murdoch is gone, both Ailes and Beck "would quickly be out the door". Where then will Beck find platform or voice for his political crusade?

The Godfather option. Just send 'the boys' of Czar Mark Lloyd's Diversity squad over to have a little chat with Rupert Murdoch and make him 'an offer he can't refuse'. For Cass Sunstein wants to use government power to stop 'conspiracy theories'. (Translation: Repress the truth by using whatever means necessary to silence the opposition.)

Beck has said that "even if the bad guys succeed in forcing him off radio and television, he will come back with a louder voice and larger platform than ever". "The biggest platform of all would be president of the United States." But "Beck says he would never run for president, because he wouldn't want to risk losing his soul. The implication is that a person can't run for president, and certainly can't hold the office of the presidency, and keep his honor intact." Still, says Beck, "Americans are looking for someone like George Washington". "Clearly, he has a vivid sense that he has been put in his current high-profile station in life for a purpose. Which means he may not have a choice but to throw his hat into the political ring." Like George Washington, who did not want to be president.

"Much like the Founding Fathers", Beck seems to have "committed himself to using his fame, his fortune, and his enormous talents to help defeat the poisonous progressive movement that is fundamentally transforming the United States into a destitute socialist nation."

"Would enough Americans be willing to open their minds to the truths he would expose to elect him president?"

"In any event, if the presidency is not in Beck's future, it will be interesting to see what his platform will be three to five years down the road. Right now, at Fox News, he's a ticking time bomb for the progressive movement in this country."

As to the gun control, though Beck consistently reiterates the theme of non-violence, yet he would surely be agreeable to the what Jefferson has said, to whit: no free man shall ever be debarred the use of arms. The strongest reason for the people to retain the right to keep and bear arms is, as a last resort, to protect themselves against tyranny in government.

Another year has winded down and I find myself by force of habit to reflect upon the year to recollect and evaluate my somewhat (if any) progress as to whether it may have encompassed anything of note. My 77th year is more than half completed, and I have once more been enjoying relatively good health, though it must be true that I am slowing down somewhat--a thing inevitably more obvious to those of my acquaintance than to myself. There are several writing projects upon which I have been working the past years, and will require my ongoing efforts in the coming years. I will be content if I can bring one or two of them to completion within the upcoming year. I am hopeful that the second edition of my *"Inheritors of a Few Years"* will come off the press with in a month or two so that I can get copies mailed out to members of my extended family and friends before long. And I have some other books of interest which I have read and which I expect to send out along with the book mailings to a few who seem apt perhaps to take an interest in this or that particular sort of information.

I have worked 112 days this year to supplement my income and hope to work as much or more in the coming year, for in troubled economic times it seems prudent for one to continue to bring in some little income, not knowing but what there may be some use for it, as life's calamities and setbacks stalk especially the older models of us citizens. Remembering too that the influx of paper bills and metal coinage have a substance or tangibility enough to keep an old geezer assured that he seems yet to have a least some little of use even among a younger population than that to which he has generally been accustomed.

Through the years of my travels along the DNA trail I somehow managed to come into a small stash of old family photographs. Some of them dating back as far as 1888. They turned out pretty good. So? what to do with them? I fiddled around with the photo lab equipment at Wal-Mart and managed to get a half dozen sets of the photos printed, and then passed out these sets to a few of my people who seemed to me likely to have some interest in them. Amazing, the new technology that becomes available from year to year.

One more thing off my mind as I prepare myself for the inevitable end of times. Through the years my music system has been forever getting outdated and needing to be replaced. Stated out 78 speed platters, to 331/3 platter, to 43 speed, to the crummy 8-track tapes, to cassette tapes, to CD discs. Repetitious expenses all along the way. And now all of sudden I find myself in possession of what they call an iPod, and am having to try to figure out how to comprehend its workings. But at least I do not have to buy a whole new set of albums, as I can transfer the music from my old CDs into the new system.

The past couple of years I have found myself gradually with enough less of personal or financial problems that I have been sort of swept up into an interest--actually a deep concern--about the left wing political course of events that seems to me to be threatening to sweep America into political and economic chaos. It appears that I am far from being alone with concern for the political direction towards which this nation has been headed under the direction of the Obama administration and its connection to the Chicago political machinery, and connection to an ideological socialism that appears to be leaning heavily from innocuous sounding 'progressivism', and directly approaching onto something near to an equivalence with the socialism of Mussolini and Hitler; and Communism like onto that of Stalin and Mao. The lives of some half a billion people have been sacrificed to these ideologies with no positive benefits to improvements of any society, but rather always increasing brutalization upon on increasingly desperate populations hoping and crying out for relief and a measure of peace.

Whatever the shortcomings and the injustices within the United States of America, and whatever the ignorance of the peoples of the world, there seem yet to be thousands and millions who envy the lives of our citizens and are--or would be--willing even to risk death, were there any real possibility of their being permitted to leave their native lands where they remain hopelessly desperate; in order to enable them to migrate to the USA, Canada, or England, for example. And had they any realistic hope of finding a way safely to cross unknown, barren, war-torn, landscapes and then to find passage across storm tossed, vast, and unforgiving oceans. And were they to believe they had any but the vaguest of any probabilities of being admitted and accepted among the 300 million of "our huddled masses, yearning to be free" once having arrived at American shores. If I were one from among 'the have-not' Mexicans, I would long ago have found my way into America, since access from Mexico is relatively an easy matter, even when done illegally. Yes, and I would have schemed mightily to have arrived here from no matter where among the 'third nations' of the world--if news of the existence of such a place as America had ever once come to my attention.

"Nothing in all the range of human complaints excites my sympathy so much as sleeplessness. The eternal inescapable sleepless night", (says Hertzler, in "The Horse and Buggy Doctor"). People long for sleep. The deeper the better. They do what they can from what little is available to them to facilitate sleep. They ruminate on their wearisome repetitive compulsive fears, concerns, regrets, delusions. The effort of analysis if not beyond their mental powers is unattainable in the face of their mental fatigue. Comforting hopes and wishes, stir the morass of their unresolved chaotic thought to no avail. Sleeplessness remains. Extreme physical exhaustion might bring some sleep. So might EtOH and other substance readily available. All have collateral unwanted side effects. Some substance are available through local physician--but people can become dependent and are then need of cure of dependences.

How many nights have I too, ended up with my abandonment of the attempt to sleep--lest I find myself returned to the disturbing dream from which I have escaped into wakefulness; or entangled in some repetitious ruminations of mere semi-sleep?

This little essay is now mercifully near its end. I always hate to tackle these little writing projects. For they require of me a good deal of time and energy. And as they gradually come together, they are sometimes responsible for inhibiting my journey into peaceful slumber. Why then take the trouble? Partly because it is pleasing to me to finally have done with it. And because the various topics are matters which have come to my attention during the past year, and the writing is a part of my effort to understand and come to grips with some of what I have pondered. Besides that, if I am not preoccupied with some such activity as to require of me some effort and determination, I am reduced to an aimless wandering through my declining years. Not a comfortable prospect to me. Makes me vaguely uneasy. By nature, I prefer to rage against the dimming of the light. And yet, always embrace the hope of yet another peaceful slumber.

SUSSER SCHLAF
From Goethe's Egmont Tragedy

Sweet sleep!
You come like pure bliss,
Unasked for, unprayed for,
(And hopefully) Most readily.
You loosen the knots
Of serious thoughts.
Mix up all pictures
Of joy, and of pain.

Unhindered flows the cycle
Of inner harmonies.
And wrapped
In pleasing delusions,
we sink
And cease to be.

"Peace attend thee"
R. Garner Brasseur, M.D.

Summary, Year 2011
R. Garner Brasseur, MD

nother year is gone. Time then again to summarize some of what I've done and read, some of what I have thought, and some of what has crossed my mind in 2011.

You may remember that my summary for 2010 had some information concerning our country's need to strive for oil independence, and reporting on the vast oil reserves upon which this nation sits. The text dealt with the sum total of oil reserves in North America, but more especially concerning The oil reserves in the Bakken formation of North Dakota. Here then is an update concerning the oil fields of North Dakota from Concordia Alumni Magazine fall of 2011 pp. 16-21. On oil from the Bakken and the Three Forks formations: May hold four million barrels of oil per square mile. 2,000 new wells drilled in 2011. Some wells will be producing 300,000 barrels per year for 25 years? There are at this time 200 active drilling rigs. Recoverable oil may come to 700,000 barrels per day. Currently producing 400,000 BPD.

To the detriment of our own national interests, our troublesome president is currently standing in the way of the building of a new oil pipe line from Canada through the United States to the Gulf Coast. However, there seems now perhaps a way around this obstructionism. Consideration is being given to the building of that pipeline from the Bakken, directly to the Gulf Coast. As it would not cross the international border, it will not be subject to the president's veto.

Here then is an item of irony worthy of one's attention:
Sent: Saturday, January 07, 2012 3:49 PM
Subject: Dept of Energy
"Absolutely...a joke... AND ITS ON US! Let it sink in. Quietly... we go like sheep to slaughter."

"Does anybody out there have any memory Of the reason given for the establishment Of the DEPARTMENT OF ENERGY During the Carter Administration? Anybody? ? Anything? ? No? ? Didn't think so! Bottom line ... We've spent several hundred billion dollars In support of an agency ...the reason for which not one person who reads this can remember. Ready??????? It was very simple.. And at the time everybody thought it very appropriate... The 'Department of Energy' was instituted on 8-04-1977 TO LESSEN OUR DEPENDENCE ON FOREIGN OIL."

"Hey, pretty efficient, huh????? AND NOW IT'S 2011, 34 YEARS LATER.... AND THE BUDGET FOR THIS *NECESSARY DEPARTMENT IS AT $24.2 BILLION A YEAR. IT HAS 16,000 FEDERAL EMPLOYEES* AND APPROXIMATELY *100,000 CONTRACT EMPLOYEES* AND LOOK AT THE JOB IT HAS DONE!" "THIS IS WHERE YOU SLAP YOUR FOREHEAD AND SAY '*WHAT WAS I THINKING?*' Ah, yes, good old bureaucracy... *And NOW _we are going to turn The Banking System, Health Care & The Auto Industry over to Government ALL IN THE NAME OF CHANGE?*" "*May God Help Us !!!*"

All of this 'progressive thought' is, of course facilitated by Minorities Studies: African-American; Gay-Lesbian; Women's etc. It ought to be called "Resentment Studies". The art of being able to take offence and aggressively displaying poses in resentment; facilitated by schooling in politically correct 'newspeak' and double talk.

In February I was off to Miles city for the funeral of Harold Kransky – an ex-brother-in-law and an important person to of some of us Brasseurs through the years. In attendance were his four remaining children, Mike, Jeff, Susie, and Steve – Yvonne having passed away several years ago. Susie's son, Jesse and his spouse from Colorado were also in attendance. I had opportunity to speak at length with these people, and later carried on some correspondence with them. I spoke also with brother-in-law, Ed Ban, from Terry Montana, who in now about 85 and seems to be the caretaker of the Catholic church properties there in Terry. In fact, he is living in the parish priest's home, the priest having died a couple years ago.

Near the end of February, the second edition of my book, "*Inheritors of a Few Years*" came off the press. I put copies of it into the hands of many of my extended family.

In early March my Dragon dictation program arrived, to facilitate the various writing projects which I am wont to undertake. It has been a struggle, but I am finding it to be of some use. On the seventh and eighth of March I visited with Jim Phalen, an old high school classmate, who was there in Santa Fe visiting his sister, Jackie, and her husband Paul. Jim and his wife are teaching English in a university in China.

Beginning in mid-March I became involved with some interesting communications with Wilbert Harsch, concerning the Meissle and Allmendinger family genealogies. He sent me some pictures, and the nicest little essay concerning the Meissle family, who homesteaded a property about 13 miles east of Haladay, North Dakota. Mrs. Meissle was a half sister to grandfather, George Boepple, as was Mrs. Allmendinger. I paid Wilbert a visit there in Pick City, North Dakota in late June, as I was heading west to attend the wedding of grandson, Beaux, (to Christa Krug) in southern Oregon – and en route from having attended the wedding of grandson, Mischa (to Andrea Dankert), in Milwaukee, Wisconsin. (They then relocated to Seattle, where he will continue into the fourth year of his Neurology residency training.) In the course of my trip I had opportunity to see and visit all of my 4 children, 20 grandchildren, and even my one great grandchild (Sebastion), the son of Real's son, Cauxby (married to K'la Davis).

In mid-March I received communication from Georgia, indicating that brother Duane seemed to be on the decline, in consequence of the definite onset of Alzheimer's dementia. Georgia was determined to keep Duane comfortably settled at home, for as long as possible. However, Duane was also weakening physically, and at years end, Georgia – alone – could no longer manage Duane. He has been admitted to a nearby rest-home, where she can visit him easily.

In early April, Bayloo got me set up with an iPod. I searched the recesses of my dimming recollections to find the larger part of the music which through the years I have come to love. Thus, I have ready access to music which I feared I might never again hear. It's a great addition to my quality of life in these aging years.

In late April, I received an e-mail from Mark Krahn (Ookie's second son), who lives in Austria. He has begun to take an interest in genealogy, and so I have communicated some of my genealogy information to him. About the same time, I received communication from Bethany, Brent Krahn's oldest child. She had been home for Easter, and had perused the genealogy book I had earlier sent to Brent. They, having discussed the subject during her visit home. She was now interested in learning from me something more of what I might tell her concerning especially the spouses of my various sisters – including, of course, that of her own grandmother, Ookie. And thus began another bit of e-mail communication.

--Unlocking The Universe--284 Science Channel---

Each evening while watching Fox News, I scan the schedule of programs for the coming 24 hours and select for automatic pre-recording any that appear of interest to me. At any one time, there are something perhaps like 130 such recorded programs ready for our viewing, of which only 20 or 25 being of ever any potential interest to me--mostly programs of science, history, astronomy, and natural history. Perhaps an additional 20 are old 'situational comedies'--most of which I have already seen but may someday watch again.

I am astonished at how much good and interesting information is available through these programs. My day-by-day selections for pre-recording amount to only, say, 2% of (only) 10 channels that I find to have much possibility of content.

Though I am aware that this pre-recording device has been available since at least 1985, it is something that I have come to use in only the past 6 or 7 years, since we are signed on with one of the local DSL providers. I have no basis for even estimating what percentage of households in this nation have the capacity and the custom of using this pre-recording device, though I suspect that very close to 100% of households have and are accustomed to watching TV--many for 4 to 6 hours or more each day. In my state of partial retirement, I am watching TV for something like 4 hours daily--mostly (say ¾ of that time following the news of) FOX-TV. Additionally, I am often attuned to listening to talk-radio (mostly, to Rush Limbaugh) some two or three hours each 'work day' as I preoccupy myself with various reading and writing projects. Why, would one preoccupy with all this news content? Partially, I suppose, because (we older models with not much family about to require our time with their constant day-by-day concerns and the coming and goings thereof) we many possess the time and concern for the reality of the national and international politics and strife which threatens always to ruin our domestic tranquility--and our very lives. Recollections of WW-II, WW-I; Korea, Vietnam, and our genetic memory of the harshness of circumstances of our ancestors in mother-Russia and mother-Germany before finding some little peace and tranquility among 'the huddled masses' of America. And remember also the more recent happenings such as the Cuban Missile Crisis, Ruby

Ridge, Waco, the Oklahoma City bombing, and 9-11, to say nothing of now the common awareness that the Chicago Regime is spending us (nationally and individually) into oblivion and fomenting class and economic strife within the nation. All of which informs us that such hazard has the potential for descending upon us--individually--from 'out of the blue', as it were. We have long been only vaguely aware and suspicious of the chicanery and pettiness of what goes on in politics at local, state, and even at national and international levels. But now in recent few years, we have (rather than snippets and fragments) an ongoing and comprehensive stream of political opinion, information, and detail available from the web, from FOX-TV, and talk radio. Detailed information from various sources which now enables one to read-between-the-lines, to get some realistic insight as to what is going on in 'smoke-filled rooms' behind closed doors etc.; and permitting one to doubt the superficialities of the biased news sources of 'the main-stream media'.

But I digress. A few days ago (mid-year) I viewed the first of three programs listed under 'Unlocking The Universe'--from the 284 Science Channel. A program informing us of the beginnings of the science of Chemistry as it very slowly evolved from the superstitions and ancient surmises of Alchemy, beginning in the 1700's. Primitive notions (of 'phlogiston', earth, air, fire, and water) were only finally put aside by the meticulous isolation, one-by-one of the actual primal elementary constituents of our world and universe. The program proceeds with narrative and demonstrations of the methods by which several elements were discovered, one by one--Phosphorus, Hydrogen, Oxygen, Potassium, as well as a compound gas--Carbon dioxide. The demonstrations of each of these experiments makes it wonderfully vivid to we of the audience. And once begun upon this winding trail of discovery (in about the 1700's), there were only baby steps in advancement, from one generation to the next. I have always found Chemistry to be a difficult subject--even in our enlightened age--and I am quite in awe of the persistence and incisive genius displayed by these pioneers in the field of Chemistry. Many of these earlier discoveries seem almost as though 'stumbled upon'. But really astonishing was the highly systematic approach by the Frenchman, Lavoisier who is credited with the recognition of Oxygen, even though Priestly was the first to discover it. His elaborately furnished lab had so much equipment that his must have been the best equipped laboratory in the world at that time. Measuring and weighing even the invisible gases whose very existence was nothing more than surmise to be demonstrated by experimentation and collection of data. I am now interested to find some biographical works concerning Lavoisier, for he needs must have had an immediate predecessor from whom he acquired his determined interest and equipment.

And finally then, this fellow Melendeev working from data collected by such as Lavoisier, was able to systematize the information into the earliest version of what we now call the periodic table of elements. A tale of slow enlightenment from 'the dark ages'. Dare I mention the insights of Darwin and Einstein? What a tribute to the potential of the minds of mere mortals is all of this!

After work one evening in late July I tuned in to FOX-TV, but there was no news. Only just this disappointingly endless ongoing wrangling in Washington, D.C. about whether this county is going to continue to borrow itself into oblivion: or, hopefully, become responsible enough to bite the bullet and back off from this notion of 'distributive justice'. A weary dream.

Along with Andy Rooney, "I'm lucky that things annoy me, cause if they didn't, I'd have hardly anything at all to write or talk about." Or to supply me with concerns enough to power the unpleasant dreams which not infrequently disturb my sleep.

And then in the subsequent early morning I had this peculiar dream of being caught up in community that had come to the conclusion that it was necessary to form a local government from scratch, having not until then had one. A strangely detailed dream of step by step progression from a shoestring operation, two-man ruling authority to bring about some work projects and setting some few simple regulations; and progressing to rules and regulations that became rapidly ever more ridiculously expensive with unanticipated expenses and expansive controls that were useless and counterproductive of any much benefit. It was humorous to me in a pathetic sense, and I was at times laughing in my sleep as it continued.

And when I fully awakened I set out upon my two mile hike before the day's temperature became too excessive. As I walked, my ipod list opened up to a song by the White Girls from the movie, _Oh Brother Where Art Thou_. "There's a dark and a troubled side of life; but there's a bright and a sunny side too. Though you meet with the darkness and strife, the sunny side you also may view, Keep on the sunny side, always on the sunny side. Keep on the sunny side of life. It will help us every day. It will brighten all the way if we'll keep on the sunny side of life"

Perchance, I came upon an article in the UND Alumni magazine about a rustic rural lad (Schlenker) from Ashley, ND who attended the UND Medical School. He was the founder and overworked self-employee of a reproductive fertility lab in Colorado. But he had a passion for music composition, and he devoted his free time to that interest. Thus he has had two main passions. One, the medical vocation at which he was able to earn his living. Music, the other passion, had seemed to him unlikely to sustain him economically. But it was always his hope and vague intent to arrive into enough economic security so as to enable him to devote more time and energy towards his avocation. And he was eventually able to accomplish just that.

The principle of his accomplishment is quite the same as that which has progressively consumed also much of my own free time through the years. When not preoccupied with the details **of** a profession for the earning of a livelihood, I have gradually become ever more preoccupied with things such as (including) genealogy, and then into an interest in writing--which was enforced upon me by my occupation; and in my efforts to keep in touch with my rather large extended family. It begins to seem to me that a life perhaps ought (ideally) to follow such a course of a diversity of interests. Find oneself a trade or profession to assure oneself of a livelihood. And then pursue in one's leisure hours, other evolving passions of interest that are creative or artistic, though never having any necessary intent of earning any significant income there-from. Done merely with an intent of making a contribution of perhaps some value to one's posterity.

RGB 3/14/11

Lew and Carla (Bayloo's sister) Schrober visited us a few days from Kansas City, in early December. A nice change of pace from my usual routine, and a little diversion into the playing of whist. We don't often get much company here on the frontier in New Mexico.

At years end, Bayloo and I traveled out to visit the family of her oldest daughter, Kim and Wes Mikes for the holidays. Their son, Jordan, and his recently acquired wife, Maria also came by for a couple of days. They, both now entered into the legal profession within the past couple of years, are now living up near the Hollywood area.

On the second to the last day of the year, my granddaughter, Tristan picked me up. She and I drove over to Palm Springs where we spent an hour and a half visiting with grandson, Jonah and his girlfriend. Tristan recently finished her master's degree in Architecture, and is in the process of closing out her affairs here and moving to Beijing to start a new job. She tells me she was the valedictorian of her of her graduating class. She and I had a nice visit that afternoon as we rushed along the crowded freeways. Jonah, now about 23 and graduated a couple of years past from Portland State College, has a nice job doing computer work there in Portland, and still lives at home.

As I was telling Tristan, oh yes, there are distinctions between 'the lower class', 'the middle class', 'the rich', and the 'super-rich'. Still, I am not sure in this nation as to which represents the largest body of the voting public. Is it the lower class, or the middle class? It seems to me as though both the lower and the middle classes are generally quite supportive of governmental socialistic handout programs. It bodes ill.

There is a difference between "the rich" and "the superrich". They play different games. "The rich" play then at games like unto that of chess--in a temporal world, intermittently and in "the public eye" while "the superrich" behind the scenes <u>play at what appear to be games</u> with a much broader goal and world-wide scope such as three-dimensional-chess or "stratageium" (See Star-Trek episode of game between Data and __??__) of actual consequences. Playing for money. We of the bourgeoisie (middle class) play more at games (i.e. monopoly) with an imitation of fiat paper money. The 'specie' backed paper--silver certificate--having been replaced about 1965 by the worthless "bank note", is something akin to that of the game of "monopoly" which has been created for us by the superrich, who don't want us (of the bourgeoisie and lower classes) to contaminate the metals of intrinsic value (gold and silver) which have been secreted away to their own enjoyment and personal economic stability, for their world shaking behind-the-scenes manipulations; with esoteric long-term goals, (one-world government and 'social justice' among we of the have-nots) spanning generations of their families--who constitute an egalitarian society (see Swift's "*Gulliver's Travels*"--an elite class of much privileged 'citizens' of a society that lives on an island floating in the sky while ordinary citizens are constrained to work-animal status and live upon the land (by the sweat of their brows).

Even so, in the real world, the daily labors of the bourgeoisie and lower classes continues to produce the necessities of daily bread from the fields, laboriously mine out the ores of earths mantle, construct the physical structures of the necessary habitations, haul and redistribute the fruits of their labor, and produce the sequential generations of 'canon fodder' for the manipulations of the superrich who (through the Federal Reserve System) cycle the economy between 'boom' and 'bust' cycles, to defraud the ordinary citizens of their possessions and savings. Profit, they call it – but in actuality it is excessive profit, which makes it more akin to something the nature of fraud. Especially since their methods appeared to be somewhat devious.

"In general, the country class includes all those in stations high and low who are aghast at how relatively little honest work yields, by comparison with what just a little connection with the right bureaucracy can get you." "The appetite of the ruling class for deference, power, and perks grows. The country class has come to disrespect its 'rulers', and wants to curtail their power and reduce their perks. The ruling class wears on its sleeve the view that the rest of Americans are racist, greedy, and above all stupid. The country class is ever more convinced that our rulers are corrupt, malevolent, and inept. The rulers want the ruled to shut-up and obey. The ruled want self-governance. The clash between the two is about which side's vision of itself and of the other is right and which is wrong... One side or the other will prevail. The clash is as sure and momentous as its outcome is unpredictable."

What Angelo does not say is that liberals (as animals of the pack) are cowards. The legislators and their bureaucratic minions hate us because they are afraid of us, afraid of anyone standing up to them, calling them what they are - fascists - and not apologizing for their principles or country.

All but the bare essentials of the requirements of the bourgeoisie (middle class) and lower classes (proletariat) are confiscated by progressive taxation, continuous monetary devaluations (the unseen taxation), and wars generated by manipulation of whole nations, races, and peoples. Those born into the bourgeoisie and lower classes are 'permitted' to struggle and compete with one another in the ever elusive 'upward mobility', limited to the confines of their solitary lives and continuous mind-numbing daily labors. And what little they might have squirreled away in the course of lifetime is then confiscated at their demise by inheritance taxes and recycled into 'the commonwealth'.

The dollar is diminished by the printing of fiat (unbacked) money at one end. At the other end, it is diminished by our losses at IRA and Roth retirement stock accounts. And then again through income taxation. The progressive income tax alone is a major obstruction to the possibility of ordinary folks in getting themselves involved into the beginnings of the capitalization process (by which they might strive to escape their personal poverty) since they are thus prevented from accumulating savings from their already meager earnings.

But all legislation and each policy have consequences. Though we mere mortals may make our feeble efforts to anticipate and visualize those consequences, experience informs us that our performance in that effort is poor. For consequences are much of the nature of the 'Gordian Knot', seemingly impossible to undo. Even one's brazen intellectual attempt to slash to the core of the knot is unapt fully to suffice. That which is so easily proposed is not infrequently counterproductive; and there always remains the remote consequences--seemingly far beyond our poor powers of comprehension. Nor is the impulsive character of the mass of the voting public generally attuned to anything more than the immediate possibilities--to the benefit of their brief mortal existence. A great much of wishful thinking in that. Which makes it the easier for them to be misled by the glib promises of political demigods.

The point is, that the weight of voter support for socialism is such that it hardly seems likely that there is apt to be any drawback from welfare-ism unless and until the (legislative and administrative) credit card has been nullified by a healthy dose of economic reality that (we would like to believe) will show up in the voting booth once the regime of Obama's 'hope and change' rhetoric is seen to have demonstrated its fraudulence.

Early in the history of this nation our government resorted to the printing of paper money to finance the war of independence. But such paper (fiat money) without the backing of 'specie' (gold or silver) rapidly depreciated into worthlessness in the minds and eyes of the ordinary man. Their misplaced confidence was soon seen to have been the only backing of the ever fresh greenbacks. Hope and faith in it soon withered. "Not worth a continental (paper dollar)", was the expression. And eventually it was necessary to revert to 'specie'--or at least to the "gold certificate" or a "silver certificate" . . . which could actually be 'redeemed' for 'specie'. Now . . . over the course a few generations, the American public has again--as though forgotten--the lessons of past generations concerning the need for a valid 'medium of exchange'. Because the 'bank note' and the 'silver certificate' had much the same appearance, and were in circulation together for a time, folks began to accept (or at least tentatively to accept) the one for the other--as though they were the equivalent. But again, I recall a period of time in which I again (belatedly) began to sort through those 'greenbacks' that passed through my hands--to save the silver certificate, and spend myself free of the 'federal reserve note'. And . . . ('The Fed', in cahoots with our government) having succeeded in foisting that deceit upon us; finally, in the mid 1960's, began to physically extract the very silver content of our coinage! "Bad money dives out good money". Those who could afford to save anything at all, saved onto themselves the remaining coins that still contained the silver; and spent the 'slugs'. I still remember those years when we belatedly began regularly to go through our pocket change--to put aside "the good stuff". Even as a school-boy, it always seemed to me that those occasional silver dollars that passed through my hands were well worth hoarding away--if only one could accumulate some little excess from out of one's desperate economic circumstances.

One fourth of the world's wealth at the beginning of the 20th century was said to have been possessed by The Rothchilds, Warburg's, Rockefellers, and J.P. Morgan.

In 1500, The total volume of gold possessed by all of mankind was said to constitute a 2 square meter cube. I read that during Spain's civil war (1936-1939) the Russians transported 552.3 tons of Spanish gold to deposit in Russia. (See "*Iron Cavalry*" by Zumbro, p. 258) Nothing is said as to whether is was ever returned to Spain. One might suppose that it might have been considered to have been payment for Russian war materials that were shipped to Spain to waste in the Spanish Civil War.

The total volume of gold possessed by all of mankind is said currently to constitute a total volume of still only ten cubic yards--a weight of about 250,000 tons (said to have been only 125,000 tons in 1908). Thus having doubled in about a hundred years? As far as I know, South Africa remains the primary ongoing source of new supply, but I would not be surprised to hear that Russian supply might be something near its equal, for it is a vast territory with large mountain chains of probable mineral wealth. 500 ton/year are said yet to be produced from South Africa's mines. Other ongoing sources include Russia

Having been slowly weaned from the touch of gold and silver in one's hands, there seemed not much alternative to the ordinary citizen. Since the whole populace continued to believe (or pretended to believe) in the ongoing utility of the paper 'bank note' as a medium of exchange, what alternative do we have? Why not continue to earn them (and get them spent rapidly on something of value to oneself, before anyone was the wiser)? I mean – on a practical basis – what other 'medium of exchange' can we collectively use between us? And eventually, the public began to suspect (and then become aware) that the printing press monopoly continued churning out the 'greenbacks'. Ever more 'money', chasing the always limited things of actual value. If total non-monetary assets are thus limited, and the volume of paper bills represent its equivalent value, that implies that each additional dollar bill pushed into circulation becomes worth progressively less and less--as the printing presses continue to puke them forth.

Finally, gold no longer being used to back up our dollars, where then has our gold gone? I recently read that about 30% of the world's gold coin and bullion is in the USA. We are given to believe that our government has put it into storage--as though to vaguely suggest that, perhaps, that it still had some sort of connection to our currency. Somewhere in the mid-1930's? the government built a gigantic vault at Ft. Knox, in Tennessee, to store the gold which was to be securely placed there. A symbol--at least--of the value of the dollars we still strive to acquire. Yet another source suggests that there is more gold stored 5 stories underground and beneath the bedrock of a building in New York City? Fort Knox is closely guarded and protected by a certain regiment of our military force. No one is permitted to tour the facility to view--or be tempted by--that mountain of gold. The vault is set apart with several surrounding fences and barricades and each patrolled by well-armed guards. Ft Knox, you know, must certainly be guarded and protected, because all of that inert gold is there. Or, is it because there is no gold there--and nothing else of value, either?

What specifically do I now discover about the CFR (Council of Foreign Relations) which brother Gene often rhetorically indicted. But he never got around to enlightening me with the details of its potential dangers to the state. It is indeed more than a figment of the imagination of the paranoid. And as an organization it does have (and long has had) an agenda which is being advanced in a stealthy creep--a world agenda.

According to Griffin's book, *"The Creature from Jekyll Island"*, the CFR was originated in 1921 by 'Colonel' Edward House, a wealthy and highly influential person with strong <u>English</u> Family <u>connections and loyalties</u> whose family deviously accumulated its influence and personal wealth out of America's south during the end of and subsequent to The Civil War. It was 'the colonel's' strong economic and political connections that nominated and elected Calvin Coolidge into The White House. And the colonel's influence over Coolidge was so heavy that he might almost have been said to have been co-president. Indeed, he was housed in the White House. House was the driving force behind the creation of The Fed. Coolidge admitted that he relied upon the experience and advice of House.

The New York based CFR has a membership of only a few thousand members--a small minority of whom constitute its core of ever advancing agenda for 'One World Government'. From among the CFR membership since 1921 there have been 21 secretaries of Defense or War, 19 secretaries of the Treasury, 17 secretaries of State, and 15 CIA Directors. Ten of Obama's fourteen cabinet members are CFR members. And many of 84 prominent mainstream media have directors or senior executives who are also members of the CFR.

Seven reasons to abolish the Federal Reserve System

From J. Edward Griffin's book "*The Creature From Jekyll Island*"
- Incapable of accomplishing its stated objectives.
- It is a cartel (which is to say, a sort of conspiracy) operating against the public interest.
- It is the supreme instrument of usury.
- It generates our most unfair tax (progressive surreptitious devaluation of the dollar).
- It encourages war.
- It destabilizes the economy.
- It is an instrument of totalitarianism.

While reading and pondering the contents of this book I was astonished at my own ignorance of the monetary and economic forces behind the (only) superficial interpretations of the history with which I had previously been acquainted. I wonder how many of our federal legislators have read or are otherwise acquainted with this history of the self-serving cabal of conspirators that manipulate the economic and social fate of our nation through the machinations of 'The Fed'. Cabal--definition states it as being a small group of powerful men united to serve their own interests and agenda, with but little concern for the best interests of their clientele--in fact, intentionally at the expense of those whom it is supposed to be serving. A cabal that has been in cahoots with our legislators from its inception in 1913. And how do our legislators benefit from their ongoing consent to 'The Fed'? It enables congress to find the funds to send 'pork' to their constituents, so as to enhance the probability of their ever always fresh re-election. From whence they enjoy their privileged status and enlarge their personal fortunes. 'The Fed' was created and enabled by congress and maintains an informal sort of covert partnership with them. A partnership which works to the advantage of both congress and The Fed. Is it possible(?) that most or many of our 535 federal legislators are so completely unread or non-comprehending as not to grasp what the machinations of 'The Fed' have done and are doing to contribute to the economic collapse of this nation and of capitalism. Why does The Fed want to collapse our national economy? Stated plainly, The Fed, which is engineering the demise of our nation is, in turn, in cahoots with their cabalist counterparts in Europe-- from which 'The Fed' of our nation has its roots; and to which they always have been (and still are) intricately intertwined as to aims and objectives. In cahoots also with the CFR. And its ends are being furthered by the IMF (International Monetary Fund--founded about 1945 or shortly thereafter) and the UN's push for a one-world-government.

Even as a hick schoolboy in rural America, an occasional elementary thought of economic and political flavor was wont to flash through my mind. Like, "why is it that we have geographical borders between nations such that prohibit me from merely walking the face of the globe? For, though it is one geologically unified world, the borders seen on our maps cannot actually be seen to exist as geological entities." But soon the thought is gone and I have not enough facts, information, or insight to suggest to me a possible answer. And as a lad with a newspaper delivery route and a bicycle to maintain, I had a great many other things to think about through each evolving day and year. And I had no plans for an extended journey abroad anyhow.

Now, 65 years later, it becomes apparent that I was not the only person to whom such riddles occurred. And I am only recently discovering that my fleeting and innocent question (and the extensive ramifications thereof) has long been upon the minds of this world's political and economic 'wizards' who churn and manipulate the world's chaos to suit their own purposes. This, at the expense of the best interests of 'our huddled masses yearning to be (and to remain) free'.

In fact, The Fed and its European cohorts, along with the CFR (Council of Foreign Relations), and through the IMF and the UN has already gotten our nation thoroughly involved in what is rapidly becoming a de facto One World Government! The question now being, is there yet any way, or any realistic hope that we citizens of the USA may yet extricate our nation, and reclaim our national sovereignty and economic independence from the clutches of "The New World Order"? Only that, seems likely to preserve to us American citizens and our offspring, the benisons which our people have enjoyed and the prosperity which has flowed to this nation from the Constitution and The Bill of Rights--secured to us from the foresight of our founding fathers some two hundred plus years ago. It may be that we are best yet advised to consider something akin to 'Fortress America' and leave the wayward world to its own nefarious devices.

Already within this nation, half of its citizens no longer pay income taxes. Are, instead, recipients of unearned governmental largess. In other words, our nation is now arrived at that point (of which our founding fathers cautioned us to avoid) where the majority is constituted of the lower class and the disabled. And now are politically enabled to vote the assets of the nation and the wealthy, to themselves. Meanwhile, the Washington politicians are ever tempted to encourage this pilfering of the national wealth in order to maintain their own elite status and privileges.

I had sent to my grandson - Real's son, Raubaux (Ribs) – a copy of my recently published genealogy book, along with my summary letter pertaining to the year 2010. Then, in early May, I received from him a nice letter. And thus began another bit of communication between us. Not long previously, Ribs had ended up in the hospital, recovering from appendectomy surgery. Having been taken aback, he seems to have become a bit more philosophical. Tells me that he is reforming from some of his bad habits and has now taken to the straight and narrow of religion. I saw him again at the time of Beaux's wedding, in June. He went with me one Sunday to the Unitarian meeting in Ashland.

I am reminded by Mark Twain's autobiography notes, that the detail of each individual life--moment by moment, through the long years--is almost entirely a private and internal thing that transpires within the head of each person. What we see and hear of even those few beings with whom we are most acquainted, is only "the thinnest of a layer of epidermis" (a veneer) of the total individual. Yes, the individual acts, behavior, mannerisms, speech, and conversation, all are merely superficial representations of the imminently more vast material of what it is that comprises the life of each individual. Says Vladimir Nabokov, "our common sense tells us that our existence is but a brief crack of light, between two eternities of darkness."

I regularly use a bandana as a head cloth to protect my sinuses by day and night, and to cover my eyes (to create darkness) when I nap. After repeated passage through the washing machine, I note that the head cloths become progressively ever more threadbare so that I must eventually recognize that they no longer serve their purpose. That is to say, they begin to lack substance--in the same way as a memory only faintly resembles an actual past experience.

It is difficult for me to conceive what an individual life would, or could be, if one had no language or words with which to organize and wrangle his moment by moment perceptions and brief insights together into thought, ideas, and concepts. The concentrated effort of writing a thoughtful letter or an essay forces one into an even greater effort.

Without the ability to organize our thoughts, we might merely possess a vague emotional tone to overlie the fundamental urges and reflexes necessary to sustain the elementary conditions for homeostasis of the ongoing life processes. The urge to breath. The urge to suck. The urge to eat. The urge to eliminate. The urge to move. The urge to sleep. The urge to protect oneself from threats to one's being and threats to the few comforts that abound in the mostly hostile world in which we are immersed. The urge to procreate. The hope to some little recreation to divert the mind from the troubles of this world.

In my infancy and childhood, I gradually accumulated a few words that became a language, but it never dawned upon me that my native tribe and family--and then, the actual formal process of 'an education' was gradually expanding the horizons and potential of my existence. It was happening without my being aware that it was occurring. Shaped (or misshapen) by the community of those about me. And the influence of those about me continued on into my early adulthood, middle years, and old age--by the customs and habits of my closer circle of friends and family.

Somewhere along through the course of my years, I even gradually found it necessary--or expedient--to move from what had been a mandatory discipline of writing, to an urge (or an aspiration) from within, to ponder and reflect on my experience and my fund of slowly acquired information (and misinformation). As no one has the luxury of having an ever attentive companion to hear and dwell upon one's fragmentary ongoing stream of disjointed thoughts and questions, one then must then resort to the regular necessity of communicating with oneself. Yet another slow and tedious process. As a part of one's cultural endowment from one generation to the next, we are treated to a cachet of commonplace adages, proverbs, maxims, and epigrams containing astonishingly sagacious and intuitive information such at to present us with something equivalent to "an **Aha**! experience".

What is an **epigram**? A dwarfish whole, its body wisdom, and wit . . . its soul.
A **Maxim**--a minimum of sound, and a maximum of sense.
Proverbs--short sentences drawn from long experience.

One such 'Aha!' moment of wisdom that recurs to me since the days of my youth was that of "know then thyself". Implying that one might--and even ought to--somehow--probe into the mysteries of one's own psychodynamics. Psychology, Psychiatry, the nature of dreams, and Psychopathology became subjects of special interest to me, and my course of formal studies and clinical experience through the years kept me continuously in touch with these things.

Yes, there is such a thing as conversation--a part of our cultural endowment. It keeps a pair or a group of people 'together', once thrown together by the fates and constraints of time, place, and mutual interests. It involves a certain minimum of recollection and reflective analysis as it moves along. It facilitates our people in functioning together for a common cause or purpose, such as that which gives to us mere mortals the mighty additional advantage of unified (as compared to individual) effort and action. Even the youngest of children can manage some of it and tend to improve with age and experience. But far the greatest proportion of our everyday 'conversation' is rather more superficial in nature, dwelling on the commonplace of one's physical and interactive matters in the act of living and working together to earn one's livelihood and 'making a life' together, within a family or a tribe.

I note in "The Week" that 50% of Americans age 85 and beyond suffer from Alzheimer's Dementia, as our brains slowly shrink in substance by some 15% from the prime years of our lives. Also, a report indicating that

10% of Americans take some form of antidepressant (Prozac, Paxil, Zoloft, etc.) on a daily basis--the most commonly prescribed medication for adults up to 59 years of age. Yet, there is said to be very little evidence that these medications are any more effective for treatment of depression than are placebos. That was certainly the way it seemed to me when I was employed in therapy sessions at the state psychiatric hospital 1991 through 1999. Our methods of titrating the drugs and dosages seemed to me all rather vague, haphazard, and speculative. Medications for anxiety states do seem to me to be more definite. The question then, is how much does anxiety contribute to what we nominally call by the name of depression.

I am reminded of that element within the nature of man that continuously dreams and prays for advancement of the circumstance and substance of their lives. Hope, they call it. We all share to some degree in that hope. Toward such hopes, we work and strive; some more, some less. Thought too, goes sometimes into that hope and striving. Wishful thinking and magical routines and incantations become something akin to that. But, I was thinking specifically about the time, the deep thought, and even the sometimes inventive effort that goes into the notion of 'the perpetual motion machine'. I am reminded of a brother who even went to the effort and expense of manufacturing one such perpetual motion machine, only to discover, to his astonishment that it didn't work. But he had enough sense of humor to recognize that stark and unexpected reality, and kept the device around as a sort of monument to delusion. Yet another brother (with more of the element of wishful thinking) wrapped layer upon layer of tinfoil about a cardboard box, supposing that it would somehow produce an endless supply of energy. In so far as I know, it didn't. But he was probably just spoofing me. I, too, independently, frittered away a few hours now and then in drawing little pictures and diagrams to aid my imagination in discovering how one might actually then construct one such device. Fortunately, I discovered each newly evolving obstacle to my plans in the drawings--sparing myself the effort of actual manufacture. Later, thinking about it more philosophically, it occurred to me that even had one been successful in creating any such perpetual motion machine, yet, (though a giant step forward) as soon as one attempted to harness its necessarily feeble motion to the required effort of work, it would prove unable to the task. So, not only could one not build any such perpetual motion machine, but even if that were possible, it would prove itself an exercise in futility.

Now, from my thoughts concerning the perpetual motion machine,

I turned my attention to a couple of programs on the evening news. One, concerning the ongoing wrangling and discussion of how to shore up the looming economic failure of the intent of our legislators to grant to every citizen of this nation 'a natural right'(?) to premium health care at governmental expense. How to do that without requiring payment for the time and effort of those who are expected to supply the methods, energy, systems, physical structures, and materials that constitute the dispensing of health care. A system that is already being 'paid for' with 1.) borrowed money, with 2.) heavy taxation, and with 3.) the even larger (but hidden) effective taxation brought about by the ongoing printing of fiat paper money--each new dollar of which inevitably diminishes the purchasing power of every citizen's every earned or saved dollar, and every asset he possesses.

The second program of the evening was like unto the first, in that it touched on the subject of how can the government guarantee to every citizen's family a right to own their own home. Something noble in that intention, too; except, of course, that the government cannot actually provide that benison, except by extracting the price from 'the forgotten man'--namely, you and I, the tax-paying citizen.

And both of these problems are like unto yet a third and all inclusive question of how can our spend-thrift government continue to function and spend what it does not have, when it is already living on borrowed money. What perpetual motion mechanism will permit this to continue? In June of 2011 we note again this tendency toward 'hubris' among our elected representatives to the Legislature. The 'obnoxious pit-bull' Anthony Wiener had fallen despite his mighty and prolonged aggressive denials of mis-behavior. But we do well to recall what Tucker, on Fox News says--that all men are creeps, but that the rich and the powerful are the creepiest. There is probably at least some element of truth in what he says, but a bit harsh as it applies to the mass of our gender.

This same day we note the otherwise blue sky is 20 percent diminished by the diffuse haze of smoke that fills the skies of New Mexico, smoke derived from the three hundred square miles of forest afire in Arizona. All that smoke clogging half a continent, and we are yet to believe that perhaps the exhausts of the engines of the automobiles of America are the primary cause of global warming? But through that haze, we see the most beautifully dark red sun in the sky at 7:15 this evening.

Somewhere about the first week in July 2011 I stopped over from my travels to spend a day or so with brother Vic in Yakima. The subject of timepieces came up when we were talking about our mutual experiences as locomotive firemen when we were young men trying to earn enough money to get our college educations. Vic tells me that his daughter, Yvette had given him a wristwatch as a gift recently. She had known that he liked a watch with large face numbers. He wasn't wearing it, but he walked back to his bedroom to fetch and show it to me. He was fumbling with the wrist band, having some trouble getting it on his wrist. When he pronated his wrist, one got the immediate impression that it was heavy, for the weight of it caused it to lurch to the ulnar side of his wrist. His wrists are not overly large and the disproportion of size of the watch to the lesser size of his wrist immediately struck me as outrageously funny. I could not constrain my spasm of laughter as the tears welled up in my eyes. Catching my breath, I looked and pondered the humor of it once more, and was once more caught up into a peal of laughter as he deadpanned to me an offer to look at the face of the thing. It did indeed have large numbers. The body of the watch must have been at least a huge two inches in diameter and must have been nearly a quarter inch thick. Another pause as I catch my breath, then another irrepressible peal of laughter. It seemed to be getting ever more humorous the more I pondered it. I finally had to retreat in laughter to the basement which he uses for his den and study room. I read a few more hours that evening in some of his manuscript he had presented to me for my perusal. But even as I read, every now and then the thought of the big face watch recurred to me and interrupted my reading for 15 or 20 seconds as I struggled to repress my laughter.

We discussed the get-together of our graduating medical school class from the year of 1960. The UND alumni thanked me for contributing my few brief lines of my progress though life; and they inquired whether I was yet going to send them an electronic e-mail copy of a personal photograph. But my want of facility with these modern gadgets and marvels disbars me from accommodating to anything so intricate as that. If I can find out about any <u>one</u> such day as our med-school classmates might gather, I would then make an effort to attend <u>that</u>. Not that I was much acquainted with any of them. So far as I know, they were generally all good and honest people, but we were all then competitively preoccupied with scholastic matters. It may be that through the years they and I may have stumbled on some matters of mutual interest that may lighten our residual estrangements from one another. And curiosity continues to be a driving force.

Later, Vic send me some books. I first went through *"The Road"*, because the print was large and the pages were sparse; and I was in a lazy mood, not wanting to overtax my lethargic synapses. Here was a strange tale to fill some empty pages. What is written is the ending of a story that has no body or beginning (even wanting a conclusion). It reminded me that some twenty or thirty years ago the thought had crossed my mind; that a person might become rich--if only one could figure some way to sell bottled tap-water to the 'huddled masses, yearning to be free'. I ought to have acted on the impulse, but I had not then yet realized what dolts we mere mortals be.

Among the books Vic send me was the Mark Twain collection – a thick pocketbook. I have over the years already read a great deal of what he has written. What an amazing original was Mark Twain. What a remarkable repertoire he owns of adjectives and synonyms; and what a prolific crafter of adjective phrases. I paged through the book and found myself somewhere the middle of *"The Mysterious Stranger"*. Of course, after reading to its end, I was obliged to finish it from the beginning. What kid would ever abandon a bowl of ice cream still half uneaten?

One evening after work I found myself in Twain's story of *"A Campaign That Failed"*. But I couldn't make much headway through it. It was so humanly funny I managed only a few pages. My concentration was repeatedly interrupted into long pauses by my efforts to stifle my spasms of laughter and the rivers of tears that clouded my vision. Perhaps my progress through that tale had best wait until I find myself in some fit of depression.

War seems to be the main business of mankind as a collective mass, says Twain. Just as sex seems to an underlying theme that runs nearly uninterruptedly through the mind of the adult individual of our species; so also the war theme seems to constitute the connecting narrative that strings together what generally passes as history. "No single piece of Real Estate on this globe remains in the hands of its original inhabitants." My 2011 summer vacation occupied me from June 16 to July 14. In those few weeks of my odyssey across the countryside, revisiting the various many neighborhoods of my life experience and having many a cause to recollect some of what I thought myself to remember as to the facts of the recollections and ideas in my memory banks, I became again aware that there was many an error harbored amongst them. Humbled, every day, by my having to recognize and reform the errors of my always too vague store of recollections--as when confronted by an obvious reality in the immediate light of very day. Sometimes even having to endure the ignominy of being corrected by on occasional acquaintance or friend. I often find my mere recollections in obvious need of correction by stark reality. Yet, it is also the case that one's perceptions of reality are--at times--in disagreement with what seems logical even to oneself, and thereby in need of a second look. One must then either ratify or refute one's own observations. Yes, perceptions of reality in need of correction by one's rational faculties. Memory, face to face (vis-à-vis) and opposed to one's powers of reason.

DOG-GONE

From my daily Journal dated Monday, June 27 2011:

Up at eight o'clock a.m. Take my meds and minerals and then depart Real's place in southern Oregon. I stopped to visit Dorothy (my third cousin) and Joe Lavallee In Central Point, Oregon. We talk genealogy. They serve me breakfast of eggs, toast, and musk-melon. After an hour I drive over to look up Larry Otis, in Grants Pass — they, not at home. Continue north on Highway 5. Stopped at Sunny Valley for gas. Then stop an hour at Aurora rest area, to nap before arriving at Jauhn's place, about 6:00 PM. Talk with Massey and Norge. An hour later Jauhn arrives. Supper of veal at seven. I then set out upon my one-mile hike at dusk. The dog, Frodo followed me. Upon return, we were affronted by two big black dogs contesting our passage. Frodo immediately sensed the threat, turned tail, and took off like a shot. Immediately the two big dogs, 30 feet in front of us, came towards us in swift and determined pursuit. I felt fortunate that they whizzed right past me in chase of Frodo. I immediately preoccupied myself in a quest for a couple of sturdy sticks in the bar pit, lest the dogs next turn their attention to me. My last estimate was that the dogs had gotten at least as far as Noah's Arc Corner as I was hurrying along toward home. I did not hear any yelp or dogfight sounds in the distance. Darkness had fallen. Jauhn was in the U-Haul truck unloading boxes. I exchanged a few words with him before I reached the porch. Massey asked me about Frodo. I told her that two big dogs were after him. She was immediately agitated, says she thought the dogs would kill Frodo. It hadn't occurred to me – she might be correct. But it was my thought that Frodo would simply have eluded the two dogs and would then circle about to return home, though he hadn't yet arrived. Massey immediately started calling for the dog and then got Norge and me to go looking for him in the car. We went as far as Noah's Arc Corner, calling the dog. Then came back with nothing to show for our efforts. We supposed that the killer dogs were with their owners at the near corner--halfway to the point of the encounter. We stopped there, and Massey walked up to the trailer. Two fellows and these two dogs came out as she made inquiry. Yes. I recognized that these were the very two dogs in question. Both now wagging their tails and putting on a show of friendliness. Back to the house we go. Now Jauhn drummed up an even larger ruckus, and we all had to get into the pickup with flashlights, to search through some supposed trails or fresh blood in the weeds and tall grass. Jauhn had just been up to the near corner to talk with the dog owners and they threatened and told him to get off the property. We four again in the pickup were now using search lights and calling Frodo. No response. No clues. Things were getting surrealistic. We were soon far out through the undergrowth, and pushed on and on with this futile search in the darkness and the thorny tangle of heavy weed and Black-Berry growth. This is nuts, thinks I. But, I can see that my voicing that sentiment is not destined to bring it to a halt. Worse, I begin to sense that I, now, may be beginning to be perceived as the culprit responsible for the evil in this grievous loss these fine folks are sorrowing over. As I walked back toward home base, halfheartedly flashing my light across the underbrush, I am thinking that this drama is far out of proportion to any logical response that I could have imagined, and I could well suppose that the high drama would continue through the evening and into the night. Fault seemed destined to fall upon me; and it began to dawn upon me that I had best steal away and out of this scene as soon, and as silently as possible. I had lost my cell phone and supposed it was most likely in the living room chair where I had earlier sat talking with Massey before supper. I found it there immediately – to my relief – and immediately, without a word to anyone, hiked out to my pickup, backed out, and headed for the highway. Jauhn had already been voicing his intent of getting this incident reported to the police. Again, rather out of proportion, thinks I. Even though by now – as the dog had not returned, nor responded to our calls - even I was now supposing that the dog may well have been killed; as unlikely as I had originally thought that to be. I now began to see it as probably having been done; and nothing about combing acres of tall grass and thorny underbrush with flashlights, was apt to produce the dog either dead or alive in the dark of night. And I wasn't about to waste further time or energy in what was already an 'overkill', of futile flailing effort. As I drove on out of that dead end street I was forced to pass by the pickup Jauhn had parked on the edge of the road as he and Norge were still plunging about with flashlight, in the darkness. Jauhn could not have missed seeing me making my getaway. And he, and Norge were quickly right behind me, as I noted through my rear-view mirror. Suspicious of my motive, and sudden getaway, presumably. A couple of phone calls to my cell phone – which I did not answer. To my surprise, even 3 miles from the scene, I became aware that he was directly behind me – as I could hear him honking the horn. I pulled into a driveway and stopped, and he pulled up beside me. "Where you going", says he. "I'm heading North to continue my trip", says I. I note Jauhn's thinly veiled anger at his father (because I am at fault in the loss of the dog? Or because he expects to me to be a witness when he presents his case to the cops?). I cannot conceive that the police are going to take an official view of any such 'crime' as a missing Frodo dog. Who would they charge? Where is even the evidence of a dead dog? So far as I am aware, the owners of the two big dogs are not going to admit that their dogs had injured any person or other dog. Though I saw part of the chase, I hadn't seen or heard the commotion of any actual dogfight. And the owners of the two big dogs, would have had much less chance than I, of either seeing or hearing what may have ended any dogfight.

Jauhn wanted me to give my testimony (to the police) of what little I did see. He was in a heat of passion about it. And in a heat of passion about my intending to make my escape of involvement in--what seems to me--an exercise in futility. As he wanted my testimony, I recited it to him and Norge. At that point, and as I would not return to 'face the music' of it, he called me a name. And he firmly exclaimed that I would henceforth no longer be welcome at his home. And so it ended.

As I continued east on Highway 26 and North on Highway 5 towards Seattle, there were a few ringings of my cell-phone which I did not answer.

Having myself been a newspaper delivery boy; and having had other unpleasant confrontations with dogs in the course of my life; and having had two of my relatives die of rabies in consequence of being bitten by rabid dogs, I have never developed any close personal relationships with dogs--or cats either. I have not failed however to notice that a lot of people seem to me to be astonishingly much attached emotionally to their dog and cats, and I can thus comprehend how very much they tend to be affected by the loss of their pet. Although I don't get closely attached to dogs, I will say (as I told Jauhn) that the dog here under discussion was absolutely the finest dog of my life's experience; and I am sorry about the loss of the dog. If I could restore the dog to the family, I certainly would have made every effort to do so. But, I can't.

I would have found myself very uncomfortable among those folks that night – as well, perhaps, for some good long while yet to come. It was raining heavily that night in Washington State, but I located a Wal-Mart store at the southern edge of Longview. There, in the parking lot, I read a while in the pickup cab, before passing the night in the solitary comfort of my sleeping bag with the gentle patter of rain upon the camper-shell roof.

"Everyone you know is going to hurt you at some time of another. The main question then is: Is this person worth the trouble?" Sometimes the answer is yes.

Here is a related and interesting addendum: Having twisted my knee while dancing at Michah's wedding, I was still limping a bit when I stopped to visit brother Phil several days later. He gave me a putting-iron to use as a walking stick when we took our daily hike together. Back home a few weeks later, I took to taking the putting-iron with me on my daily hike--as a sort possible defense, lest I again encounter some threat from stray dogs. And then, one day it happened. There were two big and unattended dogs standing on the corner directly where I must pass to get home. As with the two dogs encountered by Frodo and I, they were at full attention, focused, poised, and aimed directly at Bayloo and I as we approached. As I lifted the putting-iron from my belt loop I wondered if these dogs might have had some experience with guns. I lifted the putting-iron and aimed it at one of the dogs, as though it were a rifle. His demeanor instantly changed; his ears drooped, his tail dropped, and he slinked away like Wiley Coyote. I then aimed it at the other, with the same result.

And yet, another curious piece of information which I acquired six months later. I am given to understand that – in fact – the dog was recovered uninjured several hours after I departed Portland. Just as nephew Andre had suggested when I told him of the incident the following day. Well, life is an adventure; and "all's well that ends well".

After many years of finding myself lost out upon the highways--and having then to extricate myself from each such difficulty--I find myself being finally able to traverse, especially the western part of the country, having but rarely to have to refer to a map. What mostly guides me in such a feat is that I have acquired 'rough' and 'vague' information and familiarity about the roads and landscape. The specifics tend to remain uncertain. And so it is with much of the information within my head. Vague and rough information nevertheless serves often adequately to enable one to bumble and feel one's way along through many an uncertainty.

After my ill-fated visit to the home of Jauhn and Massy, I continued northward, where I visited and spent the night at the home of nephew, Andre and Gretchen. Only the three youngest daughters are yet at home – Anna, Claire, and Emma. The following morning I **drove** to Sedro Wolley to visit sister Ookie in the nursing home. I wouldn't say that she seemed terribly pleased to see me, but after she had lunch she seemed more cordial. Brent soon came by. We talked a bit, and I showed them my little cachet of photographs, which I had recently obtained from Phil. We three went through them for the next 20 or 30 min. She has long been chronically ill and tired, so I left her to her nap and departed shortly after 3 PM.

After stopping over a couple of days in Yakima with Vic and Marg, I stopped by the farm July 2 to spend a few days with brother Duane and Georgia. I stayed out from underfoot, in the bunk house, where I caught up on some of my reading, and visited intermittently with them, before and after meals. I tried to draw Duane out and test the limits of his mental status. His immediate memory seemed good enough that he could carry out a conversation about ordinary everyday details of his life and career on this farm. But his remote memory seems flawed and gives evidence of some unfilled gaps. He has trouble remembering the names of persons with whom he has communication. He is quick to notice what is happening in his immediate surroundings. He hears the chickens clucking out in the yard. He sees the reflection of some faint lights on a kitchen cupboard, and wonders if someone might have driven into the farmyard. He retains his ironic sense of humor, as demonstrated by an occasional witticism. He is accustomed to being generally alone with his thoughts and has no outside conversational contacts to speak of. I asked him about his correspondence and he correctly informed me that he hadn't written a letter in years. He and Georgia, not uncommonly disagree on this or that, and he seems to have gotten out of the habit of any much discussions with her. One evening after supper we conversed until about 11:30 PM. His wit and philosophical disposition continues to be evident even through his diminished conversation. Curiously however, he has a couple of vague stories that he launches out upon repetitiously, but rather than listening to it again, I usually head them off by countering with some question, to return his thoughts to some time or another in the history of our own family. He often starts out saying he left home at age 12. I correct him, to see how he tolerates my intrusion – it was age 14. Several times he starts out upon a story of how some adult women picked him up as a youth and wanted to adopt him. I steered him away from that one, as Georgia starts to get uncomfortable with it.

On July 5, I arrive into Spokane, to spend a few days with Dot and Phil, in their new house of his own design, about 10 miles west Spokane. Dot still works, but Phil is retired. Each day Phil and I take a two-mile hike. A habit he seems to have acquired only in the past few years, as he has discovered that regular exercise is decidedly useful to the control of his diabetes. On the ninth, I stopped by to visit and spend the night at the home of Pierre and Jackie, in the foothills west of Hillsboro. The next day I stopped to spend the evening and stay the night at the home of Real and Cheri, in the foothills southwest of Jacksonville. I then head south into California, on my way home.

On the last days of my vacation, I stopped over in southernmost California to visit an old high school classmate who lives there and still works full time as a pharmacist. He never uses all of the vacation time to which he is entitled. His work seems to double as his social life, and he often contributes financially to some one or another needy person of his acquaintance. Both of his ex-wives and both siblings are deceased, and he lives alone in a large two-story apartment that is carpeted and neat as a pin, but with no furniture at all, except for a big easy chair that faces a big-screen TV. The second floor has only a narrow bed near the center of the otherwise large empty room. And there are two bedrooms; one, with tall stacks of books upon the floor. I slept on the floor in a sleeping bag, in the other bedroom. His passions at this point of his life appear to be automobiles, books, and movies. He possesses and babies five 'hot' automobiles, one of which burns a special blend of high octane gasoline, yet he doesn't much travel, except locally and often into nearby San Diego on weekends. He has but one son, whom he rarely sees, and has no grandchildren. In earlier years, he was accustomed to doing a lot of biking and played a lot of tennis, but seems now in later years largely to have given that up. I generally visit him once or twice a year, and he often sends me a book or two each year. His parents and siblings are all deceased. I had the place to myself the following day when he went off to work. I slept in, and when I woke, a few thoughts were on my mind: here was I, a healthy old man with a whole three days at my disposal. Today, by the consent of Lynn Fitz, I am alone into his large comfortably cool, apartment in El Centro, California. Lynn and I will have supper together this evening and chat a bit – probably spend some time in the swimming pool. But, until then, how shall I occupy myself this day? I have just finished having a bowl of cold cereal, standing before the kitchen sink, as there was no table nor chair. I could listen to music. I could read a good book, I might exercise an hour, and I could watch one of about 2000 movies he has on video or CDC. Instead though, I might just sit me down right there, comfortably ensconced and unmolested by neither phone nor insect interruptions to reflect and cogitate. Just sit, as did Buddha, beneath the Banyan tree, to discover what thoughts might come to me. Me, an ordinary fellow with no connection (of which I am aware) to the gods, as I have come to be an agnostic. If there be a God, perhaps He might seize upon this moment to manifest himself to me this day. Just as Einstein once opined, "God does not play dice', so also am I wont to opine that He does not play favorites. Might inspire me with some all-consuming mission. Might make me aware of some great cause for which to pine and burn. Might give me a vision of the true nature of time, space, the nature of reality; and the interrelatedness of all these things. Might give me the power accurately to see into the upcoming future and provide me sufficient insight, will, and wherewithal, such as to facilitate the hopes of the yearning masses of depressed and needy peoples about the world in their quest for opportunity of employment in this world, so as to enable them to earn a wage to support their needs; and thus provide them enough of personal dignity to calm their anxieties and live their always separate lives together in some measure **of** mutual trust and harmony. But then, why need I to be an intermediary in this? Let the divine miracle make its way directly to those in need of it--while I continue my leisure in comfort.

I awoke on a Sunday morning in mid-November 2011 from a fairly restful night of slumber, but in the past final hour of more (? who can say how long it actually takes for even what seems a lengthy dream to unfold itself the subconscious state of sleep?). I was caught up into rather an interesting and unusual dream. One particularly interesting feature was it's remarkable continuity. It was as though I were moving from page to page in a book, and the subject matter shifted logically from subject to subject, each having been dealt with in some little detail or scenario, and continuing on to the end of the book. The subject matter was the laying out of (my own or someone else's) living through a life of obvious excessive opulence and privilege. No voice actually communicated to me, but there was within my consciousness an unspoken commentary of criticism, pointing out to me the injustice of these goings-on at government expense. I can't say whether it was yet while in that dream-state, or in transiting into a state of wakefulness that it occurred me. Occurred to me the thought that all of the information in this 'book' (in my dream) has been 'lived' and brought to my attention from fragmentary sources that are already lodged somewhere in the my own memory banks. I pondered there, in my rousing state, that I might set myself to the task of now arising to write out in manuscript form this very detail of what my subconscious mind had already just 'revealed' to me. Why not(?), since the organized detail of that script needs must be somewhere within my mind. But immediately next, I came to understand that the mirage was destined to recede even as I make the effort. I have traveled that route before. Very limited communication between the conscious and the subconscious mind. Wisdom is understood to be a fusion of the intellectual and moral, spiritual and practical dimensions. The state of one's mental being, is a fusion of the conscious and the subconscious minds.

In the past year I have been assigned to an ever lessening number of work shifts from month to month, until at the end of October I had no work whatsoever. Being uncomfortable without work or income, I found myself again in that most discouraging of all jobs – hunting anew for employment. At my age – near to retirement – it makes no sense even to consider the expense and trouble of setting up my own office. I found a temporary piece of work, one day a week, on the south edge of Albuquerque, 60 miles from home--nothing much else being immediately available to me locally. Then, in mid December, there arose the possibility of taking a job in far-off Fargo, North Dakota. Here was yet another opportunity for adventure, a job, and an income. It caught my fancy, and I began to make my arrangements to begin the new job in mid January of 2012. There is no telling as to how long the job shall last. The young optometrist who is hiring me, is hopeful that an increase in the flow of patients will sustain his intended expansion. I hope so too. Whether or not that hope will be fulfilled, remains yet to be seen. This much is certain, an older fellow can generally expect to find it ever more difficult to find employment. And I shall inevitably be put to pasture; and then to meta-pasture.

"May the menace of the years yet find us unafraid."

R. Garner Brasseur, MD
Completed early February
2012